THE CIVILIZATION OF THE AMERICAN INDIAN SERIES

FIVE
INDIAN
TRIBES
OF THE
UPPER
MISSOURI

EDWIN THOMPSON DENIG

FIVE

SIOUX

INDIAN

ARICKARAS

TRIBES

ASSINIBOINES

OF THE

CREES

UPPER

CROWS

MISSOURI

EDITED AND WITH AN INTRODUCTION BY

JOHN C. EWERS

UNIVERSITY OF OKLAHOMA PRESS: NORMAN

By John C. Ewers

Plains Indian Painting: A Description of Aboriginal American Art (1939; New York, 1976)
The Horse in Blackfoot Indian Culture (1955; Washington, D.C., 1980)
The Blackfeet: Raiders on the Northwestern Plains (Norman, 1958, 1983)
Indian Life on the Upper Missouri (ed.) (Norman, 1961)
Blackfeet & Gros Ventre Tribes of Indians: Appraisal of Lands in Northern Montana, 1888 (ed.) (New York, 1973)
Chippewa Cree Tribe of Rocky Boy, Montana, & the Little Band of Indians (New York, 1973)

Library of Congress Catalog Card Number: 61-9005

ISBN: 0-8061-1308-1

Five Indian Tribes of the Upper Missouri: Sioux, Arickaras, Assiniboines, Crees, Crows, is Volume 59 in *The Civilization of the American Indian Series.*

EDITOR'S ACKNOWLEDGMENTS

I AM DEEPLY GRATEFUL to Charles van Ravenswaay, director of the Missouri Historical Society, St. Louis, both for his permission to edit and to publish the Denig manuscript in the archives of that society and for his active encouragement of the project. Mrs. Frances R. Biese, formerly archivist of the Missouri Historical Society, was exceedingly helpful in locating information on Denig's career as a fur trader on the Upper Missouri, 1833–56, in the correspondence and records of the American Fur Company and its successors in the library of that society.

It was Chris Vickers, of Baldur, Manitoba, who furnished the Bureau of American Ethnology a photostatic copy of Denig's handwritten will which enabled handwriting experts of the FBI Laboratory in Washington, D.C., to identify the manuscript in the Missouri Historical Society as being written in Denig's hand. Their contribution was of crucial importance to the entire project.

Robert L. Denig, brigadier general, United States Marine Corps (retired), of Virginia Beach, Virginia, able student of Denig family genealogy, graciously lent me letters from Denig's daughters telling of the last three years of their father's life. Father Louis J. Hanlon, S. J., Missouri Province Educational Institute, St. Louis, furnished a photostatic copy of Denig's letter to Bishop Miege in the archives of that institute.

The first four chapters of this book were first published separately in the *Bulletin* of the Missouri Historical Society, St. Louis, during the period 1950–52; while the fifth chapter, "Of the Crow

Nation," was published as *Anthropological Papers, No. 33* of the Bureau of American Ethnology in 1953, and is now out of print. (See the bibliography at the end of this volume.) The unique value of this material to students of history and ethnology as well as to all those who enjoy reading authentic accounts of the Old West, has suggested the desirability of bringing these chapters together and reprinting them in book form. I am grateful to both the Missouri Historical Society, St. Louis, and the Smithsonian Institution for permission to do so. The editor's introduction has been revised and a number of the footnotes rewritten in order to incorporate information obtained by the editor since the first publication of the individual chapters of this work.

JOHN C. EWERS

Arlington, Virginia

CONTENTS

ILLUSTRATIONS

MAP

EDITOR'S INTRODUCTION

MUCH OF OUR PRESENT KNOWLEDGE of the life and customs of the buffalo-hunting Indians of the Upper Missouri before 1860 has been derived from the descriptions of their customers written by those practical businessmen—the fur traders. In order to gain a precarious foothold in the Indian country, to establish and expand their business, these men had to gain a working knowledge of the Indian languages. They also had to obtain a fund of reliable information on the locations and populations of the several tribes and of their major subdivisions, their abilities to supply furs and peltries and the kinds of goods they wanted from the white traders in exchange, their friendship or hostility toward neighboring tribes, their ways of fighting and peace making, their political organization, and the character of each of their prominent chiefs.

A few of the most intelligent traders recognized that the information they gathered and the observations they made upon Indian life and customs would be of interest to others, even to people far removed from the Indian country. Were it not for the writings of those men, we would have much less understanding of the history and ethnology of the Upper Missouri region than we now possess. The earliest historical record for this region is the fur trader Pierre La Vérendrye's account of his visit to the Mandan Indians in 1738. Six decades later Jean-Baptiste Trudeau penned the first description of the Arikaras. And in 1805, François La Rocque, a Canadian trader, traveled with the Crows and wrote the first report on the customs of that tribe. Other fur traders made valuable contributions to the history and ethnology of this region through their writings. Nevertheless, it can be said that no other trader-writer provided the wealth of detailed information on the Indian tribes of the Upper Missouri that appeared in the prolific writings of Edwin Thompson Denig, who devoted twenty-three years of his life to the Indian trade of this region.

Edwin Thompson Denig was born in Stroudsburg, Pennsylvania, March 10, 1812. He was the son of Dr. George Denig, a successful physician, and Eliza McClintock Denig. The Denig family traced its descent from Harald Ericksen, a chieftain of the Danish Island of Manoe in the North Sea. Edwin's great-grandfather, Johan Peter Denig, emigrated to America. He arrived in Philadelphia on September 15, 1748, and settled in Lancaster County, Pennsylvania. The year after Edwin's birth his family moved to McConnellsburg, Fulton County, Pennsylvania. It was there, in the rugged Alleghenies, that the boy grew to manhood. Although Denig's writings clearly indicate that he was a man of better than average education for his time, nothing is known of his schooling or of his youthful activities prior to his entrance into the fur trade at the age of twenty-one.

Probably Alexander Culbertson, a native of nearby Chambersburg, induced Denig to seek a career in the western fur trade. Culbertson, three years Denig's senior, had gained some experience in the trade on St. Peter's River when he visited his family in Pennsylvania during the summer of 1832. The following spring Denig joined Culbertson in the service of the American Fur Company. Records of that company, in the Missouri Historical Society, St. Louis, dated April 10, 1833, credit Edwin T. Denig with $400 for "Services ending 1 year from date."

Denig first traveled up the Missouri River in the second year of steamboat service to the American Fur Company's posts on that river, aboard the *Assiniboin*. That steamer and its sister ship, the *Yellowstone* reached Fort Pierre, the principal trading post in the country of the Western (Teton) Sioux, toward the end of May, 1833. Among the passengers on the *Yellowstone* were the noted German scientist-explorer Maximilian, prince of Wied-Neuwied,

xiv

and Carl Bodmer, author and illustrator respectively of *Travels in the Interior of North America,* a work which for more than a century has been regarded as a classic on the Indians of the Upper Missouri. For the German prince and his talented artist companion the trip offered an opportunity for a year's adventure and observation in a strange and exciting environment. For Denig it marked the beginning of twenty-three years' residence among the Upper Missouri tribes as a fur trader. He became one of many subordinates in the employ of the American Fur Company, the principal firm engaged in the fur trade of the Upper Missouri. Its chain of posts extended upriver to the country of the Blackfeet near the Rocky Mountains and that of the Crows on the Yellowstone.

Denig's early years in the fur trade were spent in the country of the powerful Sioux. On June 3, 1833, he wrote from Fort Pierre, "I will remain here this year." Young Denig must have learned the business rapidly, for he was in charge of a small winter trading post subordinate to Fort Pierre during the winter of 1834–35. This house was located in Sioux country on Cherry River, a tributary of the Cheyenne, some sixty or more miles northwest of Fort Pierre.

In the spring of 1837, Denig held the position of post bookkeeper at Fort Union on the Missouri near the mouth of the Yellowstone. In a letter to Jacob Halsey at Fort Pierre, dated March 25, 1837, Denig stated that he was well satisfied with his position and much preferred Union to Pierre. This letter also revealed that he had followed the custom of white traders in that region in taking an Indian wife, and that he was the father of a boy. When smallpox reached Fort Union that summer, Denig became infected but recovered "favorably." Years later he wrote two accounts of the terrible ravages of that plague among the Assiniboines who traded at Fort Union, based upon his firsthand knowledge of the circumstances.[1]

When John James Audubon, the noted artist-naturalist, visited Fort Union in the summer of 1843, Denig assisted him in collecting bird and mammal specimens and helped him to obtain the head of

[1] See Edwin T. Denig, *Indian Tribes of the Upper Missouri,* Bureau of American Ethnology *Forty-sixth Annual Report,* 399–400, and pp. 71–72 of this book.

an Indian chief from a tree burial near the fort. Denig enlivened Audubon's stay with stories of Indians and animals of the region. At the naturalist's request he wrote a description of Fort Union. Dated July 30, 1843, this is the earliest known example of Denig's descriptive writing.[2] It is also the most detailed description of the construction and use of that most important Indian trading post on the Upper Missouri ever published. Denig stated that he was then in charge of the office of the fur company at Fort Union, a position comparable to that of chief clerk. His old friend, Alexander Culbertson, was Fort Union's bourgeois at that time.

Charles Larpenteur, a fellow subordinate in the service of the company, severely criticized Denig for his love of liquor, mentioning an occasion in January, 1844, when Denig was unable to travel to Woody Mountain to trade for buffalo robes in the camps of the Crees and Chippewas because he had imbibed too freely.[3] Drinking was common among field employees of the company, forced to spend long, monotonous winters at isolated posts in the cold north country. Denig was no teetotaler. In a letter to Alexander Culbertson, dated December 1, 1849, he wrote, "I would also request as a great favor if you will bring me up a keg say 5 galls of good old Rye, to have the pleasure of drinking your health occasionally. I can hardly look upon myself as the infernal drunkard represented and presume as no accident happened to the 2 g^l keg of last spring, the 5 g^l keg will be equally safe." In the same letter Denig reported, "Next year after the post has been thoroughly purged of all superfluities In a trade of 400 packs, I shall clear 6000$ if 500 packs are traded 9000$ will be the profit. . . . you can assure yourself of my showing a neat balance to our credit." This was the kind of report on Denig's activities that the company preferred to take seriously.

At that time Denig had risen to the position of bourgeois in charge of Fort Union. Fort Union was not only the "principal and handsomest trading post on the Missouri River," as Denig himself

---

[2] *Audubon and his Journals,* (ed. by Maria R. Audubon and Elliott Coues), II, 180–88.

[3] *Forty Years a Fur Trader on the Upper Missouri: The Personal Narrative of Charles Larpenteur* (ed. by Elliott Coues), I, 162, 184–86.

termed it; it was also the company's key point in its control of the Indian trade of the Upper Missouri. There the Assiniboines, Plains Crees, River Crows, and some Chippewa Indians traded. From Fort Union trade goods and supplies were dispatched to the upriver Blackfoot and Crow posts, and to it came the spring returns of furs and skins for reshipment downriver to St. Louis. No field employee of the company then held a more responsible position than did Denig, except for his old friend, Alexander Culbertson, who had been promoted to general supervisor of all the company's posts on the Missouri.

During the winter of 1849–50, Denig again rendered valuable services to naturalists. At the request of Alexander Culbertson, and with the assistance of Ferdinand Culbertson, Denig prepared skins and skulls of birds and mammals of the Upper Missouri for use in scientific study. On December 1, 1849, he wrote A. Culbertson: "I am progressing with my specimens of animals for you as I have said I would & have already prepared the White Wolf, the Beavers, the War Eagle, the Caputi Argali or Antelopes head, and sundry other smaller matters which will be in order to put into every museum you think propper." The following June, Alexander Culbertson's brother, Thaddeus, visited Fort Union. His *Journal,* under date of June 17, commented: "We were received very kindly by the gentlemen of the post, Mr. E. T. Denig and Ferdinand Culberston. They showed me quite a good collection of stuffed skins made by them for Professor Baird, at the request of my brother. This must have cost them a great deal of labor and considerable expense, and they deserve many thanks from the students of natural history for whose benefit this collection was made."[4] Thaddeus Culbertson brought back many, if not all, of these specimens for the collections of the Smithsonian Institution, which was then only in the fourth year of its existence. The earliest accession book of the Division of Mammals of the United States National Museum records specimens from Fort Union received from "E. T. Denig

---

[4] Thaddeus A. Culbertson, "Journal of an Expedition to the Mauvaises Terres and the Upper Missouri in 1850" (ed. by John Francis McDermott), Bureau of American Ethnology *Bulletin 147,* 105.

and A. Culbertson." A few of them are specifically noted as "Prepared by Denig." Several other specimens, listed as collected by Thaddeus Culbertson at Fort Union, also may have been prepared by Denig. In toto these specimens include skins of the wolverine, plains wolf, lynx, beaver, mountain sheep, antelope, white-tailed jackrabbit, and grizzly bear; the head of a bison; and skulls of elk, mule deer, and bison. Thus in 1850 the Smithsonian Institution acquired an extensive representation of the mammals of the Upper Missouri as a direct result of the interest and labors of Denig and the Culbertsons.

In the summer of 1851, Father Pierre Jean De Smet, the well-known missionary to the Indians of the Northwest, spent more than two weeks at Fort Union. He found in Denig a man who knew the Upper Missouri tribes well and who was sympathetic toward them. Between the famous Catholic priest and Denig, who was Swedenborgian in his beliefs, a firm friendship developed that endured for the remainder of Denig's life. De Smet encouraged Denig to write for him a number of sketches of the manners and customs of the Assiniboines and neighboring tribes. Denig lost little time in initiating this project, for in September of that year Rudolph Kurz observed that Denig was recording "stories" of "Indian legends and usages" for "Père De Smet."[5]

We may never know the full extent of Denig's writings for Father De Smet. However, we can trace some of them with precision through the published correspondence of the priest. De Smet expressed his "gratitude for the manuscript you have had the kindness to prepare for me, and which I shall be most glad to receive and peruse," in a letter to Denig written in May, 1852. By the next fall the priest had received the manuscript. On September 30 he wrote thanking Denig profusely for "your very interesting series of narratives. . . . I have read the present series with absorbing attention and growing interest. My imagination has often carried me back to scenes long familiar to my experience and to others of a general and kindred nature which your pen has so well portrayed,

[5] *Journal of Rudolph Friedrich Kurz* (ed. by J. N. B. Hewitt), Bureau of American Ethnology *Bulletin 115*, 133.

in your valuable descriptions of their religious opinion, of their great buffalo hunt, their war expeditions, and in the history of old Gauche and of the family of Gros François."[6]

Father De Smet incorporated much of Denig's information in a series of letters to Father Terwecoren, editor of the *Précis Historiques*, Brussels, Belgium. These letters were reprinted in English in the book *Western Missions and Missionaries: A Series of Letters by Rev. P. J. De Smet*, published in New York City in 1863. Letters X through XIII, comprising more than seventy pages of that volume, deal in turn with "Religious Opinions of the Assiniboins," "Indian Hunts," "Indian Warfare," and "Tchatka" (a biographical sketch of the Assiniboine chief, old Gauche). In the thirteenth letter, Father De Smet gratefully acknowledged his debt to Denig. "I cite the authority of Mr. Denig, an intimate friend, and a man of high probity, from whom I have received all the information that I have offered you concerning the Assiniboins, and who resided among them during twenty-two years." Denig's account of the family of Le Gros François was not published until after De Smet's death.[7]

Rudolph Friedrich Kurz, a young Swiss artist, possessed of a burning desire to sketch wild Indians in their home environment, spent seven months at Fort Union, from September 4, 1851, to April 19, 1852. His *Journal* contains a vivid account of life at Fort Union during that period. Frequent references to Denig in this journal provide an insight into his character that cannot be found in Denig's own, very impersonal writings.

Before his arrival at Fort Union, Denig had been represented to Kurz by a former, dissatisfied employee as a "hard man, liked by nobody . . . keeps two Indian wives . . . squanders all he has on them; begrudges anything paid to employees, oppresses the engagees with too much work, is never satisfied, etc."[8]

On first meeting Denig, Kurz described him as "a small hard featured man wearing a straw hat, the brim of which was turned

---

[6] *Life, Letters, and Travels of Father Pierre Jean De Smet* (ed. by H. M. Chittenden and A. T. Richardson), IV, 1215–16.

[7] *Ibid.*, III, 118–24.

[8] Kurz, *Journal*, 101.

back. . . . He impressed me as a very prosy fellow. He stopped Bel-lange [Kurz's traveling companion from Fort Berthold to Fort Union] short, just as the latter was beginning a long story he wished to tell; on the other hand, he ordered supper delayed on our account that we might have a better and more plentiful meal. A bell summoned me to the first table with Mr. Denig and the clerks. My eyes almost ran over with tears! There was chocolate, milk, butter, omelet, fresh meat, hot bread—what a magnificent spread! I changed my opinion at once concerning this new chief; a hard, niggardly person could not have reconciled himself to such a hospitable reception in behalf of a subordinate who was a total stranger to him."[9]

It is apparent, however, from Kurz's later observations that Denig exercised an authority over his men that would have been the admiration of his seafaring Danish ancestors. Denig's crew of some fifty men included workmen of a score of nationalities, many of whom lacked both skill and ambition. He kept them "strictly under his thumb." When they worked satisfactorily, he offered some diversion for them. Denig himself even played the fiddle for the dances held at the fort. But if they shirked, he limited their victuals. He expected his clerks, as good petty officers, to give him moral and, if need be, physical support in handling his men. He insisted on economy and efficiency on the part of his clerks to keep the overhead at a minimum.

Kurz observed that Denig had risen to his position of command as a result of "his commercial knowledge, his shrewdness, and his courage at the posts where he was earlier employed."[10] As a successful trader he also had to gain and hold the friendship of the Indians. Denig's marriage to the sister of First to Fly, a prominent Assiniboine chief, had aided him in his trade relations with that tribe. Kurz also learned that Denig had "made a thorough study of Indian life—a distinct advantage to him in trade."[11]

But it was not enough for Denig to know the Indians' languages

[9] *Ibid.*, 120.
[10] *Ibid.*, 123.
[11] *Ibid.*, 126.

and their manners and customs. He must conduct himself in such a way as to win their respect. Denig believed most Indians esteemed white men for those talents they did not possess themselves; that though he had a keen eye and was a sure shot, the Indians would never admire him for his hunting ability. He thought that white men who adopted Indian dress and tried to follow Indian customs only succeeded in degrading themselves in the eyes of the Indians. Although Denig had two Indian wives, he encouraged them to live as much like white women as was possible in the Indian country. Records of Denig's purchases from the company (preserved in the archives of the Missouri Historical Society in St. Louis) tell of his importation of fine clothes for his wives and children, fancy foods for his table, and toys for his children. He kept up with the news and thought of the times by reading newspapers and books on philosophy and religion brought upriver from St. Louis. Edwin T. Denig was far removed from the crude hunter-trapper-trader stereotype of western fiction. Undoubtedly his way of life helped him to maintain the high degree of objectivity toward Indian cultures evidenced in his writings.

In his long conversations with Kurz, Denig revealed a very limited appreciation of art, but a lively interest in religion and morals, about which he expressed very definite opinions. One evening Denig came round to the subject of love. "Love—damn the word!—is a madness in the brain; a contagious disease, like small-pox or measles. I would rather have a dose of epsom salts than to recall the folly of first love—pure love. If it is not stopped, that lunacy makes one ridiculous, childish, ashamed of himself." Kurz, a confirmed romanticist, probably swallowed hard before he added the following sentence to his diary. "There is always something true and worth while in what he says, only he expresses himself in strong language."[12]

Denig stoutly defended his right to have two wives on the grounds that his first wife was sickly. Yet she was the mother of his first child, and she afforded companionship to his younger wife, so he would not abandon her.

12 *Ibid.*, 180.

Much of Denig's conversation with Kurz concerned the Indians in whom both were interested. Denig enjoyed telling the young artist stories of his experiences among the Indians, of Indian customs and outstanding Indian personalities. Denig also read to Kurz the manuscript he was preparing for Father De Smet, and he told him of his concern for the future of the Indians. He went out of his way to give Kurz opportunities to meet Indian chiefs and prominent warriors who visited the fort, to attend councils he held with these Indian leaders, to obtain Indian artifacts and animal specimens for his collections, and to hunt and to study the wildlife of the plains in the field. Denig seemed to have been as eager to help this unknown Swiss artist as he had been to aid the famous Audubon and Father De Smet.

In the middle of the century, Henry R. Schoolcraft, of the office of Indian Affairs in Washington, was busy collecting information on the Indians of the United States for historical, anthropological, and administrative purposes. To students of the Indians who had traveled extensively or lived in the Indian country he sent copies of a printed circular of "Inquiries Respecting the History, Present Condition, and Future Prospects of the Indian Tribes of the United States." One of these circulars reached Denig at Fort Union. Cooperative, as he had always been in furnishing information about the Indian tribes he knew well to earnest inquirers, Denig systematically set about assembling data for Schoolcraft. He prepared an Assiniboine vocabulary of more than four hundred words which Schoolcraft published in the fourth volume of his imposing six-volume compilation, *Historical and Statistical Information Respecting the History, Condition and Prospects of the Indian Tribes of the United States* in 1854. Eight years later F. V. Hayden referred to this as "the most important vocabulary of the language" of the Assiniboine "prepared by Mr. E. T. Denig, an intelligent trader."[13]

Denig also painstakingly prepared answers to the 348 questions

[13] Ferdinand V. Hayden, *Contributions to the Ethnography and Philology of the Indian Tribes of the Missouri Valley*, American Philosophical Society *Transactions*, Vol. XII, Pt. 2, p. 381.

regarding Indian cultures asked in Schoolcraft's circular. His reply was made in the form of a "Report to Hon. Isaac I. Stevens, Governor of Washington Territory, on the Indian Tribes of the Upper Missouri, by Edwin Thompson Denig." This was a manuscript of 451 pages. In his letter of transmittal, Denig revealed his scholarly research methods. He had not been content merely to draw upon his knowledge of Indian life obtained through long association with and observation of Indians. He had pursued "the different subjects . . . in company with the Indians for an entire year, until satisfactory answers have been obtained and their motives of speech or action well understood before placing the same as a guide and instruction for others." Internal evidence in the manuscript itself and a statement in the letter of transmittal to Governor Stevens referring to the author's "constant residence of 21 years among the prairie tribes" attest that the manuscript was completed in 1854. This report remained in manuscript for seventy-six years. It was published in the *Forty-sixth Annual Report* of the Bureau of American Ethnology in 1930. Although, as its published title *(Indian Tribes of the Upper Missouri)* implies, this work was intended to cover all the tribes of the region from the Dakotas to the Crows and Blackfeet, the wealth of detailed information presented refers primarily to the Assiniboines. Much of the material on the other tribes takes the form of brief comparative statements. As it stands, this work may be regarded as the most complete and authentic description of Assiniboine Indian culture in the mid-nineteenth century known to ethnology.

By 1854, Denig had resided continuously in the Indian country for twenty-one years, except for one brief visit to his relatives in the States in the summer of 1845. His diligence and his ability had brought him success as a fur trader. He held partnership in the company, receiving one twenty-fourth of its profits from the trade. Yet in a letter to Bishop Miege of St. Louis, written September 1, 1854, he revealed his intention "to leave this country in a year or two."[14] This decision was based primarily on his consideration for the welfare of his children. There were no schools in the Indian

14 Letter in the Archives of the Missouri Province Educational Institute, St. Louis.

country of the Upper Missouri. Denig had sent his eldest son, Robert, to Chicago to be educated. But now he had three other children to be considered—Sarah (born August 10, 1844), Alexander (born May 17, 1852), and Ida (born August 22, 1854).

Nevertheless, as long as he remained in the Indian country, Denig continued to write about the Indians. As a doctor's son he had acquired at least a smattering of knowledge of medicine. At Fort Union he had served as an amateur doctor and surgeon in the absence of any trained physician, tending the sick and the wounded victims of accidents and gunfights. Even after he became bourgeois, he continued to perform these services for his employees and for Indian visitors to the fort. It was natural that he should have had a particular interest in Indian medicinal practices. It is not surprising, therefore, that *The Medical and Surgical Journal* of St. Louis, in 1855, should have published a seven-page article by Denig bearing the quaint title, *"An Account of Medicine and Surgery as it exists among the Cree Indians. By a non-professional observer, who has resided for a number of years among them and is familiar with their language, habits and customs."*[15]

In the summer of 1855, Denig took his Assiniboine wife, Deer Little Woman, and his mixed-blood children to visit his brother, Augustus, in Columbus, Ohio. In St. Louis en route Denig and Deer Little Woman were formally married by Father Daemen. Their children were baptized while in that city. Denig's daughter recalled that the family found the climate in Columbus too warm for them. Otherwise they might have settled there. Instead they returned to Fort Union by a roundabout route, traveling from St. Louis to St. Paul and the Red River Settlement of present Manitoba by horse and wagon. Throughout this journey Denig was searching for a suitable future home for his family. The Denigs reached Fort Union on November 28, 1855, after a wagon trip of nearly three months' duration, much of it through unsettled Indian country.

The Denigs spent the winter at Fort Union, during which the father continued his writing. But in the middle of the following

[15] *Medical and Surgical Journal* (St. Louis, Mo.), Vol. XIII (1855), 312–18.

summer the family moved to the Red River Settlement in Canada. Denig received a payment from P. Chouteau, Jr. and Company at Fort Union on July 13, 1856. His will, dated September 12, 1856, at Red River Settlement, Red River of the North, must have been drawn up shortly after the family's arrival there. Very little is known of Denig's life in Canada during the next two years. He placed Sarah and Alexander in Catholic schools. He "established himself as a private trader on the White Horse Plains west of the present city of Winnipeg."[16] His friend, Father De Smet, wrote him on January 13, 1858: "I rejoice greatly at your success and in the welfare of your children."[17]

Late in the summer of 1858, Edwin T. Denig was stricken with an inflammation. His daughter, Sarah, believed it was appendicitis. Denig died on the White Horse Plains, September 4, 1858, and was buried in the Anglican cemetery near the present village of Headingly, Manitoba.[18] He was only forty-six years of age at the time of his death.

Denig's FIVE INDIAN TRIBES OF THE UPPER MISSOURI.

Edwin T. Denig's close friend and long-time colleague in the fur trade of the Upper Missouri, Alexander Culbertson, survived Denig by twenty-one years. Prior to 1936, the Missouri Historical Society of St. Louis purchased from A. C. Roberts, of Spokane, Washington, a collection of manuscript materials comprising accounts of five Indian tribes of the Upper Missouri. Mr. Roberts stated that this collection had been in the possession of his recently deceased mother, Julia Culbertson Roberts, who in turn received it from her father, Alexander Culbertson. The writings bore internal evidence of composition in 1855 and 1856, but their authorship was not known. In the archives of the Missouri Historical Society this material became known as the Culbertson manuscript.

16 Chris Vickers, "Denig of Fort Union," *North Dakota History,* Vol. XV, No. 2 (1948), 136.
17 De Smet, *Life, Letters, and Travels,* IV, 1499.
18 Vickers, "Denig of Fort Union," 136.

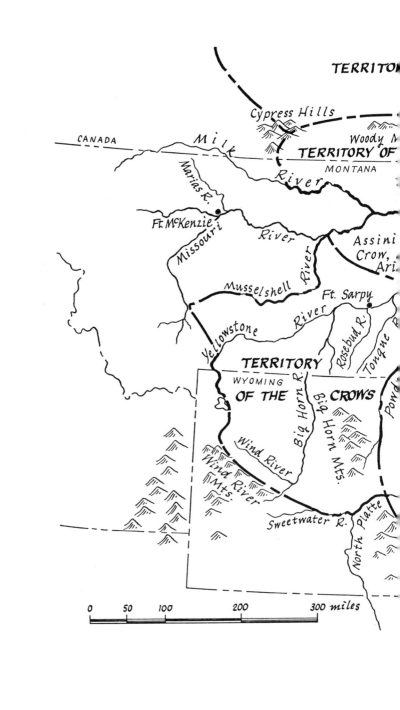

TERRITOR

Cypress Hills

Woody M

CANADA

Milk

TERRITORY OF

MONTANA

Marias R.

River

Ft. McKenzie

Missouri

River

River

Assini

Crow,

Ari

Musselshell

River

Ft. Sarpy

Yellowstone

River

Rosebud R.

Tongue R

TERRITORY

WYOMING

OF THE

CROWS

Big Horn R.

Big Horn Mts.

Powd

Wind River

Big Horn R.

Wind River Mts.

Sweetwater R.

North Platte

0   50   100   200   300 miles

OF THE CREES

Assiniboine River

Pembina R.

NIBOINES

Souris

Turtle Mtn.

White Earth

nion

Souris R.

Devil's Lake

Red River

ssouri

Mandan &
Hidatsa Village

Knife R.

Arikara Village

Heart R.

Missouri

James

tory
en over
Sioux

Cannonball R.

NORTH
DAKOTA

SOUTH
DAKOTA

Grand River

River

Lac qui Parle

Moreau River

Cheyenne R.

Ft. Pierre

Big Sioux R.

ck Hills

Teton R.

Y

White R.

OF THE SIOUX

River

Niobrara River

Missouri

Laramie

Platte River

River

South Platte R.

NDIAN TRIBES OF THE UPPER MISSOURI IN 1855

Early in February, 1949, this editor saw and read portions of the Culbertson manuscript in the Missouri Historical Society. He was impressed with its historical and ethnological value. It appeared to him that the author's style, as well as some of the specific information in the manuscript, resembled closely that of Edwin T. Denig's published work, *Indian Tribes of the Upper Missouri.* Upon request, the Bureau of American Ethnology kindly furnished this editor an example of Denig's known handwriting in the form of photographs of his handwritten will, executed September 12, 1856, which he was able to compare with the writing in the Missouri Historical Society manuscript in March of the same year. Similarities between the handwriting of the two documents appeared so marked as to justify obtaining the opinion of handwriting experts. Accordingly, photostats of pages of the manuscript together with photographs of Denig's will were submitted to the Federal Bureau of Investigation. On April 15, 1949, handwriting experts of the FBI Laboratory, Washington, D. C., reported their conclusion that the handwriting of the two documents was by the same individual. Thus, nearly a century after it was written, an important Denig manuscript was discovered.

This manuscript, here published under the title *Five Indian Tribes of the Upper Missouri,* actually comprises portions of a book which Denig had carefully planned but doubtless was unable to complete before his death. His letter of transmittal accompanying the manuscript *Indian Tribes of the Upper Missouri* expressed Denig's dissatisfaction with the organization of that report, because of the limitations imposed upon it by the nature of the questions asked by Schoolcraft which he attempted to answer.[19] In the introductory chapter for his new book Denig carefully explained his plan for the organization of the work:

"The plan intended to be pursued in these pages, that the reader may understand the different traits of Indian character without difficulty or confusion, is, first to give a short history of each tribe, its geographical position and other peculiarities; after which an inquiry will be instituted into their government, condition, man-

[19] Denig, *Indian Tribes of the Upper Missouri,* 393.

ners, and customs as a body. Most customs and opinions are common to all tribes, but wherever any great difference is observable, or marked traits to be noticed, they will be found in the compendiums of their separate histories. This is necessary to avoid the constant repetition that would follow if detailed accounts of each tribe were presented.

"The Indians of the Upper Missouri territory may be divided into two classes, the roving and the stationary tribes—the former comprising the Sioux, Crows, Assiniboines, Crees, and Blackfeet, the latter, the Gros Ventres, Mandans, and Arikaras. My object is to show the state of these Indians in former times, what their present condition is and what circumstances have tended toward their general advancement or decline; and after a general and minute research into all their motives, acts, religion, government, and ceremonies, conclude with a history of the American fur trade embodying many statements of various matters incident to the lives of trappers and traders."

Just how much of this ambitious writing program Denig was able to complete before his death is not known. Certainly the manuscript in the Missouri Historical Society contains no tribal accounts of the Blackfeet, Gros Ventres (Hidatsa), and Mandans; no general description of the common factors in the cultures of the Upper Missouri tribes; and no history of the fur trade such as Denig promised in his introduction. If Denig wrote chapters dealing with any or all of these topics, those portions of his manuscript either have been destroyed or their present whereabouts are unknown.

The Denig manuscript in the Missouri Historical Society comprises his complete tribal descriptions of four tribes and the nearly complete description of a fifth tribe. This manuscript is in two parts. Although the pages of one part are numbered from 1 to 153 in pencil, pages 60 through 92 are missing. Present are chapter 1 (pp. 1–10) comprising the author's introduction; chapters 2 and 3 (pp. 11–44) entitled "Of the Sioux"; chapter 4 (pp. 45–59) entitled "Of the Arickaras"; the latter and undoubtedly the greater part of chapter 6 (pp. 93–120), comprising a description of the Assiniboines; and chapters 7 and 8 (pp. 121–53) entitled "Of the

Crees or Knisteneau." Because it appears to have been the author's plan to consider these tribes in geographical sequence from south to north following the course of the Missouri River, it is most probable that the missing chapter 5 described the Mandans and Hidatsas who resided between the Arikaras and the Assiniboines. The second part, entitled "Of the Crow Nation," is separately paged (pp. 1–75). But there can be little doubt that it was intended as a later chapter in the same book.

In his opening chapter Denig took pains to state the major purpose of his book: "It would be well for the public if everyone who undertook to write a book was thoroughly acquainted with the subject of which he treats, but unfortunately this is not the case— authors spring up everywhere, and the community is saddled with an immense effusion of literature, the greater part of which when divested of the writer's own fancies and feelings, and submitted to the test of truth and experience, amounts to nothing. This is particularly the case in most of the works purporting to describe the actual life and intellectual capacity of the Indians of North America; much evil has been the consequence of error thus introduced, bad feelings engendered, and unwise legislation enforced, which will continue until our rulers are enlightened as to the real state of their Government, character, organization, manner and customs, and social position. Most information extant on these heads has been published by transient visitors amongst the tribes, travelers through a portion of their country, or collected from rude and half-civilized interpreters whose knowledge is but a degree in advance of their savage parents, and also impose upon their credulous hearers tales of fiction mingled with some ceremonies; which with a hastily collected and ill-digested mass of information form the basis of works by which the public are deceived as to the real state of the Indians. Even foreigners who have possibly passed a winter at some of the trading posts in the country, seen an Indian dance or two or a buffalo chase, return home, enlighten Europe if not America with regard to Indian character; which is only the product of their own brains and takes its color from the peculiar nature of that organ. Hence we find two sets of writers both equally wrong, one setting forth the Indians as a noble, generous, and chivalrous race far above the standard of Europeans, the other representing them below the level of the brute creation. People cannot form an opinion in this way—a correct knowledge of any nation, and more particularly of a savage one, must be and only is attained by being as it were raised in their camps, entering into their feelings and occupations, understanding their language, studying their minds and motives, and being thoroughly acquainted with their government, customs, and capacities.

"Of the few traders who reside in the Upper Missouri territory, but a small portion have had the advantage of education, and these are so variously and constantly occupied as not to be disposed to apply their talents to writing histories, indeed it has been their policy to keep people in ignorance as to the trade and real disposition of the Indians, thereby preventing competition and discouraging visitors, both of which militate against their interests. Neither do the gentlemen at the head of the Indian trade desire on all occasions to advance their opinions to persons who cannot, or will not, appreciate them.—Truth, though mighty will not at all times prevail, although stranger than fiction, cannot be realized. The strange sights and occurrences incident to the country, be they ever so truthfully described, are rejected by previously formed opinion, and the narrator stigmatized, even in the mildest language he could expect, as a teller of strange stories. The author of these pages feels this in the commencement but cares little about it, having set out with the determination to present facts in as true a light as his powers admit, and with the experience of 22 years amongst the Indians, speaking their language, and having been placed in every possible position that men can be amongst them, presumes his opinions are entitled to respect."

Denig's first concern seems to have been with setting the record straight regarding not only the history and ethnology of the Upper Missouri tribes, but with respect to the character of these Indians as well. He did not name those individuals who were the objects of his caustic jibes in the first of the two paragraphs quoted above. However, there can be little doubt that he was thinking primarily of George Catlin and Prince Maximilian, whose books, published a decade earlier, had gained wide circulation. Doubtless Denig was familiar with them. Indian-loving Catlin had spent eighty-six feverishly active days on the Upper Missouri from Fort Pierre northward as far as Fort Union in the summer of 1832. It was patently impossible for him to gain more than a superficial familiarity with the several Indian tribes of this region in so short a time. He was dependent upon the information he could obtain from experienced fur traders for much of the data presented in his book. Catlin's thinking was colored by his romantic concept of the Indian as nature's nobleman. Maximilian, however, passed the greater part of a year on the Upper Missouri in 1833–34, wintering among the Mandans. He was a trained scientific observer, and he also relied heavily upon the information the fur traders supplied him. In his criticism of these writers Denig revealed the common disdain of the old hand for the greenhorn. However, in the case of Maximilian, certainly, Denig's strong criticism does not appear to be justified.

There can be no question that Edwin T. Denig was better qualified than any other man of his generation to write on the history and ethnology of the Indian tribes of the Upper Missouri. His broad experience among these Indians spanned the years between Catlin's and Maximilian's travels on the Missouri in the early 1830's to the beginning of Sioux hostilities along the Oregon Trail in the middle 1850's. He knew intimately many of the Indian leaders whom Catlin and Maximilian barely met and whom Catlin and Bodmer pictured in their colorful portraits. Indeed, one of Catlin's heroes, The Light (incorrectly named "The Pigeon's Egg Head" by Catlin), whose travels to Washington to visit the Great White Father and subsequent murder by his own people was one of the classic tragedies of the Upper Missouri, was the brother of one of Denig's wives. Even though this man was killed before Denig's marriage to his sister, Denig had the unique opportunity to learn the story of The Light's travels and their tragic aftermath directly from the lips of his relatives.

Denig was an objective observer of the Indian tribes of his acquaintance. He knew Indians well enough to view them as human beings rather than as noble redskins or as dastardly savages. His long experience among the Upper Missouri tribes enabled him to distinguish significant differences as well as basic similarities among neighboring tribes of the same culture area. He knew the warlike character and fighting tactics of the mighty Sioux before either Sitting Bull or Crazy Horse was born. And his knowledge of these Indians enabled him to predict with uncanny accuracy the nature of Sioux warfare with the United States before it commenced. Writing in 1855, when Sioux resentment of white men's destruction of game along the Oregon Trail was ripening into open hostility, Denig calmly stated: "Although in the end the Sioux will be conquered yet they will give the troops some trouble. They can by retiring into fastnesses in the Black Hills, by crossing and recrossing rivers, and by their swift mode of travel avoid a general battle and harass the troops wherever small detachments are to be found. If united among themselves they can keep up the war for several years, or when too sorely pressed can make peace with the view of getting supplies, and on the withdrawal of military force commence a new desultory warfare on small parties of travelers. Unless a line of military posts are established along the Missouri as high up as the mouth of the Yellowstone, and these well garrisoned, the Government cannot expect to subdue this fierce and powerful nation."[20] Two decades of costly, intermittent warfare with the Sioux proved both the truth of Denig's prophecy and the wisdom of his recommendation.

Although Denig's firsthand knowledge of the Arikaras may have been limited, he was well acquainted with the prominent chiefs and the people of the Assiniboines, Crees, and Crows, for the hunting bands of these tribes came to Fort Union to trade during the two decades Denig was stationed at that important post. In addition, Denig probably learned much about the history of the Upper Missouri tribes from his colleagues in the employ of the American Fur Company. They included not only his old friend Alexander Culbertson, who played an important role in the Blackfoot trade

[20] E. T. Denig, "Of the Sioux" (ed. by John C. Ewers), Missouri Historical Society *Bulletin,* Vol. VII, No. 2)1951), 185–86.

from the middle 1830's, but such old hands as Robert Meldrum, who had traded with the Crows since 1827, and James Kipp, who had known the horticultural tribes farther down the Missouri since 1822.

Nevertheless, Denig was not infallible. His frequent errors in dating events suggest that he wrote from memory without the aid of a journal or diary maintained over the years, and that he had a rather poor memory for exact dates. Some of the events he described may have become somewhat distorted through years of verbal retelling prior to the time Denig recorded them on paper. The editor has been able to check a considerable number of these dates and events in the scattered literature on the Indians of the Upper Missouri and has commented upon them in his footnotes. However, so rich is Denig's material in stories and descriptions mentioned by no other writer that we must rely upon Denig alone for our knowledge of many of them.

The history of the Denig manuscript from the time it was written at Fort Union in the years 1855–56 until it came into the possession of the Missouri Historical Society some eighty years later is of itself an intriguing problem. That it should have been handed down in the family of Alexander Culbertson is not surprising, for Culbertson was Denig's long-time friend and colleague in the fur trade of the Upper Missouri. He undoubtedly encouraged Denig's writing and took a great interest in it. And Culbertson survived Denig by many years. More difficult to determine is the relationship of this manuscript to the published writings on the Indians of the Upper Missouri of the noted geologist, Ferdinand V. Hayden, who traveled extensively in the Dakotas and on the Missouri and Yellowstone in the years following 1853, and whose interest in Indians was only secondary to his research in geology.

On January 9, 1856, Hayden wrote to his friend Professor Spencer F. Baird of the Smithsonian Institution in Washington: "Mr. Denig is now collecting and preparing material for a great work on the Indians of Upper Mo. for Mr. Culbertson. Mr. C. has with him manuscript for one volume, which I have requested him to show you at W. I think you will find more reliable information in it than in a score of other works on Indians. Mr. C. has agreed with me to write a physical description of the country, essays on Indian languages, etc., and revise the whole and see it through the press as joint author. It will be published a year from this winter, in two large octavo vols, well illustrated & under the auspices of Mr. Culbertson."[21]

This project failed to develop as planned. Probably Denig needed much more time to complete his manuscript than Hayden had estimated. It is unlikely that Denig finished the ambitious task he had set for himself before his death in 1858. Furthermore, Alexander Culbertson had had no experience either as an author or an editor. However, four years after Denig's death the American Philosophical Society in Philadelphia published a monograph entitled *Contributions to the Ethnography and Philology of the Indian Tribes of the Missouri Valley* bearing F. V. Hayden's name as author. In the introduction to this work Hayden wrote:

"In all my researches in the Northwest, most important aid has been rendered to me by different members of the American Fur Company. All of their stores of knowledge of Indian life, language, and character, which they had acquired by years of intercourse with the different tribes, were freely imparted to me, only a small portion of which is given in the following pages. I am especially indebted to Mr. Alexander Culbertson, the well-known agent of the American Fur Company, who has spent thirty years of his life among the wild tribes of the Northwest, and speaks several of their languages with great ease. To Mr. Andrew Dawson, Superintendent at Fort Union, Mr. Charles E. Galpin, of Fort Pierre, and E. T. Denig of Fort Union, I am under great obligations for assistance freely granted at all times."[22]

The mere mention of Denig's name in this list of acknowledgments is no true measure of Hayden's debt to Edwin Thompson Denig. Why did not Hayden mention Denig's "great work on the Indians of the Upper Mo." which he had praised so highly in his letter to Professor Baird of January 9, 1856? We may never know

[21] Letter in Archives of the Smithsonian Institution, Washington, D. C.
[22] Hayden, *Contributions,* 234.

why the great geologist failed to give adequate credit to Denig. But the fact is clear that page after page of Hayden's descriptions of the Sioux, Arikaras, Assiniboines, and Plains Crees are nearly verbatim renderings of selected portions of the Denig manuscript in the Missouri Historical Society. Hayden's entire brief description of the Crow Indians, comprising pages 391–94 of his 1862 work, is but a slightly edited version of the early pages of Denig's "Of the Crow Nation." At the conclusion of that description Hayden wrote: "I have before me the materials for an extended sketch of the manners and customs, together with biographical sketches of the principal chiefs of this tribe, but as they will doubtless appear in a future work in course of preparation, I shall close with a brief notice of the different vocabularies of the Crow language which have been published from time to time."[23]

Even though Hayden failed to name the author of these "materials" he had before him, there can be little doubt that he referred to Denig's long chapter, "Of the Crow Nation," which Denig wrote at Fort Union during the winter of 1855–56. This may have been the last as well as one of the best of Denig's writings on the Indians of the Upper Missouri. Hayden did not publish it. But it appears in full as the last chapter in this book.

Whether the Denig manuscript in the Missouri Historical Society is the one actually handled by Hayden in the preparation of his 1862 work, or whether it is an incomplete draft or copy which was retained by Alexander Culbertson, is questionable. I am inclined to believe that the Missouri Historical Society manuscript lacks many pages which were available to Hayden, including the entire chapter 5, describing the Hidatsas and/or Mandans. Possibly these pages were lost during the years the manuscript was in the possession of the Culbertson family. Neither the original manuscript of F. V. Hayden's *Contributions to the Ethnography and Philology of the Indian Tribes of the Missouri Valley* nor the papers with which Hayden worked in preparing this manuscript are preserved in the archives of the American Philosophical So-

23 *Ibid.*, 394.

ciety. If another and more complete copy of this Denig manuscript is preserved, its whereabouts is unknown to me.

In belated justice to Denig we should now recognize that he was the real author of a very large portion of the ethnographic material published in Hayden's monograph nearly one hundred years ago. Yet in his role as editor Hayden omitted more than half of the historical and ethnological materials appearing in the Denig manuscript in the Missouri Historical Society, and which appears in the pages of this book.

Surely the time has come for Edwin Thompson Denig to receive the recognition he so richly deserved. In his own time this scholarly fur trader's knowledge of the Indian tribes of the Upper Missouri was recognized by those able men who knew him. Among them were the artist-naturalist, John James Audubon; the missionary, Father Pierre Jean De Smet; the compiler of information on American Indians, Henry Rowe Schoolcraft; and the pioneer geologist of the West, Ferdinand V. Hayden. Yet during his lifetime, and for many years thereafter, Denig's Indian writings were buried in the works of other men. We know now that Denig was both the most prolific and the most knowledgeable writer on the Indian tribes of the Upper Missouri in the mid-nineteenth century.

FIVE
INDIAN
TRIBES
OF THE
UPPER
MISSOURI

I : OF THE

SIOUX

THE COUNTRY CLAIMED by the Great Sioux or Dacotah nation is very extensive. Commencing on the North Eastern limit at Lac qui Parle an imaginary line would run in a N.W. direction taking in Lac du Diable; thence inclining south by west including Turtle Mountain and the head of Pembinar River it would strike the Missouri River at the mouth of Apple River below the Gros Ventre village. Crossing the Missouri it would proceed up the Grand River of the Arickaras (or even some distance west of this river) bearing west by south until reaching near the head of Powder River. From this point it would continue along the range of mountains called the Black Hills in a southern direction until reaching Fort Laramie on the Platte, thence down that river for some distance, afterwards east to the junction of L'eau qui Court with the Missouri River, thence down that stream to the mouth of the Big Sioux River, this being the boundary line to which their claims have been extinguished by the United States. Proceeding along the Big Sioux River inclining northeast, taking in the Vermilion and Rivière aux Jacques, their lands would terminate by a junction with the starting point at Lac qui Parle. This is the general outline of their country, although the Government has bought some portions of it along the St. Peters extending some distance into the interior.[1]

[1] Alfred Vaughan, Indian agent for the Upper Missouri tribes, described the boundaries of the Sioux Country in almost these same words in his report of September 10, 1856 (*Annual Report* of the Commissioner of Indian Affairs, 1856, p. 84).

That part of their land east and north of the Missouri is the most sterile and with the exception of some coulees and hills caused by the rivers and creeks, presents an ocean prairie many hundred miles in length and breadth, very level and devoid of trees or even shrubs. The soil is loose and sandy; grass is sparse and in no great variety. That known as the short curly buffalo grass is the most abundant. This used to be the great range for the buffalo, but of late years they are found in greater numbers west of the Missouri. The soil is entirely too dry for agricultural purposes except along the banks of streams where it is very rich. In some parts where vegetation is luxuriant, the grass is very nutritious and would, in common with most of the N.W. territory, afford good grazing for horses, horned cattle and sheep. Small lakes are to be met with in this region from which the Indians get their supply of water when traveling, which they only attempt in the summer and fall when the buffalo chips answer the purpose of fuel. The terrible snowstorms that sweep over these plains in the winter compel them to place their camps along the rivers where timber is to be found. Along the Coteau de Prairie, or dividing ridge between the waters of the Ioway and Missouri, near the head of La Rivière aux Jacques is found the celebrated red stone to make their pipes. This kind of stone is not found in any other part of their country and is of course valuable.[2]

The face of the country west and south of the Missouri is more rolling and diversified on account of the large streams by which it is intersected. The principal rivers on this side are L'eau qui

---

Lac qui Parle forms part of the boundary between present Lac qui Parle and Chippewa counties in southwestern Minnesota. Apple River, designated Apple Creek on Lieutenant G. K. Warren's map of 1855, enters the Missouri from the northeast below modern Bismarck, N. D. L'Eau qui Court (Rapid River) is the Niobrara River, a western tributary of the Missouri, entering the latter in Knox County, Nebraska. Rivière aux Jacques (James River) flows into the Missouri from the north below present Yankton, N. D.

[2] The red stone from this quarry was named catlinite in honor of the American artist, George Catlin, who visited the site and popularized it through his writings and exhibitions of paintings. His original painting of the quarry, as it appeared to him in 1836, is in the collections of the Smithsonian Institution. The quarry is now included in Pipestone National Monument, Pipestone County, southwestern Minnesota.

Court, White River, Medicine Creek, Teton River, the Cheyenne, Moreau, Cannon Ball River, Heart River and Grand River. Most of these are navigable with skin boats during spring thaws, and are well timbered along their banks. The trees grow in large groves or points, frequently reaching from one bluff to the other the whole width of a valley. The largest and most common trees are the cottonwood, elm and ash, although others of smaller growth are found. Though there are many tributaries to the rivers named running through the interior these are short and only convey the water caused by rain and snow to the parent stream. They are termed coulees, seldom extending more than from one to three miles, and are usually covered with various bushes, small trees, grass and weeds. Between rivers and beyond the heads of the coulees are large tracts of table land from ten to fifty miles in breadth on which no timber is seen, but where the spontaneous grasses are very thick and of fine quality. It is in such spots as these the buffalo delight to roam undisturbed, quietly cropping the choice blades in happy ignorance of the murderous intentions of the hordes of hunters roving through the country. Springs impregnated with saline substance are often met with, and the water drunk with avidity by these animals. The most fertile region, however, and the one approaching nearest to a habitable district is on the headwaters of the Cheyenne and Moreau rivers, commencing at the eastern base of the Black Hills and running northeast for the distance of sixty or eighty miles. The prairies here are undulating, well wooded and watered and present much varied, beautiful and enlivening scenery to the eye of the traveler. Indeed with but the exception of that part of Sioux lands situated west of the Mauvaises Terres on the head of White River, the rest can by no means be set down as an arid or barren district, though to what extent grain could be produced has not been determined.

The Black Hills are the most eastern spurs of the Rocky Mountain range, several thousand feet high, well covered with timber, of which pine is the principal. The Hills or Mountains thus called commence near the head of Powder River running nearly a northeastern direction to within about 50 miles of White River, the intermediate space to that stream being occupied by the Bad Lands. The Sioux seldom camp for any length of time in the Black Hills. But little game is found there and it consists of panthers, bears and bighorn which are difficult to find or kill. Not much grass is found on the sides of the mountains, at least not enough to support the horses of a large camp for any length of time. They frequently visit the place, however, in search of lodge poles which they make from the tall, straight young pines. At these times the camps are usually placed at the base of the mountains where grass is plenty, and when buffalo are not to be seen, they subsist on elk, blacktail deer and bighorn sheep. Much superstition is attached to the Black Hills by the Indians. The principal peak, called the Hill of Thunder, is volcanic, and in 1833 was in almost constant action. In almost any clear day large volumes of smoke could be seen, which the Indians took to be the breathing of the Big White Man said to be buried beneath. Unnatural noises are said to be heard, which, whether originating in their fancy or caused by wild beasts, are thought to be the moans of the Great White Giant, when pressed upon by rocks as a punishment for being the first aggressor in their territory. They say that he issues forth on occasions and his tracks seen in the snow are twenty feet in length. He is condemned to perpetual incarceration under the mountain as an example to all whites to leave the Indians in quiet possession of their hunting grounds. All this, the fabulous, exhibits their ancient and intuitive repugnance to the approximation of other and distant races.

At the lower extremity of the Black Hills commences the Mauvaises Terres or Bad Lands, which extend from thence to White River. This appears once to have been a continuation of the Black Hills range, but having undergone volcanic action or some other revolution, has been washed into its present grotesque appearance by the rain.[3] It is impossible to describe this singular section of the country. For the distance of sixty or eighty miles in length and

[3] Although the noted geologist Ferdinand V. Hayden made extensive explorations in that portion of the Sioux country west of the Missouri prior to 1860, he reproduced parts of Denig's description of the geography of that region almost word for word in his chapter on the Sioux in his *Contributions*, 365–67. However, Hayden corrected some of Denig's naïve geological interpretations.

from three to fifteen in breadth, the country presents the appearance of a large city, and but little imagination is necessary to descry immense public edifices, churches, towers and parapets with people on their summits. What tends to make it more so is that mountain sheep (bighorn) sometimes alone and sometimes in small bands are seen on the tops of the towers several hundred feet high and entirely inaccessible to the feet of men. Here they remain in security, rolling their large horns from side to side and casting suspicious glances at the travelers below. It is somewhat strange that these animals should prefer the most barren and rugged district as their residence. Not a spire of grass, not the smallest shrub except here and there a stunted and isolated bunch of wild sage can be found through the whole section under consideration. But though the absence of vegetation would induce the belief they fared badly, yet they are invariably fat and sleek, very active, timid and difficult to kill.

Before this part of the country had been thoroughly explored by the traders there were but two roads by which it could be passed. One of these, the most direct and shortest was from the head of the Little Missouri or Teton River to White River, a distance of fifteen miles. The other was by going around the extreme end of the Bad Lands lower down on White River. The last route is the best, though some thirty or forty miles farther than the other to reach a given point on White River beyond. The writer has passed both ways several times. He has also traversed it through its entire length from White River to the Cheyenne. On one occasion, descending the almost perpendicular path by the route first named, one of the party had to be blindfolded and led to prevent his falling into the abyss below through giddiness. The path down this precipice winds round several towers, is about two feet wide, and full two thousand feet from top to bottom. By this time, we understand, several better places have been discovered by the Indians down which horses can pass in single file with comparative security. No springs nor creeks are found through the whole extent of the Mauvaises Terres. The hills are composed of clay and earths of different colors in strata running parallel through it lengthwise.

It is in this part of the Sioux country the immense petrified turtles are found, some of which are estimated to weigh two thousand pounds. Many other petrifications of fish, worms, and shells are also seen, most of which are said to have been submarine. Gigantic fossil remains of animals now extinct have also been discovered here by naturalists and traders. The pumice, scoria, rocks in a state of fusion, calcined earths, etc., tend to confirm us in the belief of the whole being the work of volcanic agency.

For some distance up White River the country is fine and well stocked with herbage. But as we near its head commences the sandy desert which continues for two or three days' march in the direction of the Platte. Traveling in wet weather through this part is next to impossible. Both men and horses sink to the knees and progress slowly. Along L'eau qui Court lower down, and between it and White River, the prairie assumes its ordinary character and is not remarkable in anything except the numerous villages of prairie dogs scattered along the whole extent of this and White River and frequently met with in other parts of the Sioux country. . . .[4]

Crossing the Sioux Country in the middle of the portion south and west of the Missouri, say in a direction from the mid-length of L'eau qui Court to Grand River, the prairies, although occasionally from 20 to 50 miles in breadth, cannot come under the head of plains such as the district on the opposite side. The distance is not great between the rivers on the west side. Although their junctions with the Missouri are widely separated, their heads all come near each other as they take their rise at and along the Black Hills. In traveling through in transverse direction a man on foot seldom is obliged to camp without water, the heads of coulees of one river extending to within 30 or 40 miles of the tributaries of the other. The intervening prairie is frequently furnished with springs and small groves of trees. Comfortable camps can usually be found by anyone a little acquainted with the geography of the country through the entire length and breadth of the interior.

[4] I have omitted Denig's lengthy description of prairie dog villages which is published almost verbatim in Hayden's *Contributions,* 367–68.

In the winter, however, accidents do happen. People are frozen to death in crossing these prairies. In these storms it is impossible to travel. The sun is invisible and even other objects are hidden at a distance of from 50 to 100 paces by the particles of snow being whirled through the air by the wind. This is called pouderie, which, when occurring in extreme cold weather leaves but two alternatives to the traveler—to ramble on at hazard in hopes of keeping himself warm by walking and stumbling on timber, or to lie down and let the snow blow over him, remaining in this temporary grave until the atmosphere becomes clear and his direction can be determined by the sun or stars. Both these methods are often resorted to by the Indians and traders when caught in snow storms in places where timber is not to be had. Both sometimes fail, sometimes succeed.

In the winter of 1835, three men started from Cherry River on the Cheyenne to go to Fort Pierre on the Missouri. They were Canadians in the service of the Fur Company and were furnished with an Indian guide. The distance is about 60 miles over a prairie void of timber. Some snow had fallen, but the day on which they set out was clear and moderately warm for the month of January. Their expedition consisted of two carts containing some meat and grease for the fort. About the middle of this crossing the road touches one of the tributary coulees of the Teton River. Here the Indian, judging from the threatening appearance of the sky, proposed stopping, stating his reasons that a storm was coming and that wood could be found by following the coulee down towards its mouth. This being a round about way, and the men being new hands in the country not knowing the consequences, they would not agree to his proposition and proceeded on their journey. In a short time the storm came in all its fury. The weather suddenly turned very cold. The wind whirled from various points. The men, now frightened and benumbed, begged the guide to endeavor to reach the coulee spoken of. This he tried but failed to do. He could see nothing five yards before him and finding himself at a loss proposed to the men to cut up the carts, make a fire and try to weather out the storm. To this they would not accede but left their carts and animals. All now began to freeze, first the face, then the hands and feet. The Indian now made his last proposition, which was that they should all lie down together and cover with what bedding they had, let the snow cover them and wait a better time to travel. To this they also objected. The guide then left them to save himself, dug a hole in the snow, laid down and remained there about 12 hours. When the storm subsided and the sky became clear he made his way to the fort. In the meantime the men rambled on in different directions. Search was made from the fort as soon as news came by the Indian. After two days the men were found and brought to the fort. One was frozen to the top of the thigh. He died in a few days. Another lost his two legs below the knee. They were sawed off with a wood saw at the fort. The third lost his feet, his ears and some fingers. The last two recovered. The Indian only lost a portion of his ears and nose, although his feet were badly frozen.

The three streams, Cheyenne, Moreau and Grand River, approach more nearly to each other than the rest. Therefore there is not much stretch of open prairie between them. In these parts, and as we proceed west, the country becomes more hilly and intersected by coulees, and is covered with good grass. In most of the small streams forming these rivers beaver used to be found in great abundance. Lately they have become very rare, having been trapped and dug out by the Indians and free trappers residing with them. Of all the rivers Grand River is the largest, best wooded and best stocked with game. Buffalo are found along this river when the rest of the country has none. Elk rove through the large points in droves of several hundred. Antelopes in large bands cover the hills. The fertile coulees are the home of blacktail deer and the woods that of red deer. About 60 miles above the mouth of Grand River is a remarkable rock situated about a quarter of a mile from the south bank. This rock is several hundred feet long, about fifty feet high and composed entirely of shells, worms and other reptiles in a state of petrification.

The fruits and esculent roots indigenous to this section are few and only suited to the uncultivated taste of the Indians, although

EDWIN THOMPSON DENIG and his Assiniboine Indian wife, DEER LITTLE WOMAN.

Fort Union at the mouth of the Yellowstone. From a pencil sketch by Rudolph F. Kurz, 1852.

they form a considerable item in their bill of fare in times of great scarcity. The prairie turnip, called by the Sioux *teep se nah,* or by the French *pomme blanche,* is found everywhere on the high prairies. It is either eaten raw or boiled and is collected and dried in large quantities by the Indians for winter use. When dried and pulverized a tolerable substitute for flour can be made of it. In any state it will support life for several months without the assistance of animal food. This root is much sought after and devoured by grizzly bears.[5]

Wild artichokes, called *panghai* (Sioux), grow in abundance along marshy spots of the river banks. They are eaten raw, roasted or boiled, but are not dried and preserved.[6]

Wild peas, *oma ne' chah* (Sioux), grow in rich places in the banks of several rivers. These are collected and stored in holes by the field mice *(pies pies a na,* Sioux), whose nests are in turn robbed by the Indians, often getting half a bushel of peas from a nest. They are boiled with fat meat, make good soup, and are perhaps the most palatable vegetable met with in their wild country.[7]

Red plumbs, *cauntah* (Sioux), grow on small bushes in many places on the borders of most of the rivers mentioned, but are found in great abundance high up on White River and L'eau qui Court. They are best eaten ripe, but are dried and laid up by the natives, and when wanted are rendered eatable by boiling. The process of drying, however, extracts most of the fruit taste and leaves nothing but the rind.[8]

Choke cherries, *cham pah'* (Sioux), and grain de beouf, *mush tim' poo tah* (Sioux), grow on low bushes in great quantities along

[5] This is *Psoralea esculenta.* The root provides "a desirable food with a palatable taste characteristic of the bean family" (Melvin R. Gilmore, *Uses of Plants by the Indians of the Missouri River Region,* Bureau of American Ethnology *Thirty-third Annual Report,* 92–93, plates 15–16).

[6] Although this plant, *Helianthus tuberosus,* was cultivated by some of the Eastern Indians seen by Champlain in 1605–1606, the Plains Indians used only the wild plant (Gilmore, *Uses of Plants,* 131).

[7] This is the ground bean, *Falcata comosa,* used as a winter food by the Indians (Gilmore, *Uses of Plants,* 95–99, plate 18).

[8] The wild plum, *Prunus Americana,* was highly valued by the Missouri River tribes (Gilmore, *Uses of Plants,* 87).

the coulees. These with the plumbs form the principal food for bears and wolves. Both the fruits last named are dried. The former is pounded with the seeds, and cooked in various ways, occasionally made into soup, but more often mixed with dried buffalo meat bruised and marrow grease added. This is what is known among the voyagers as pemican.[9] It is convenient to carry, nutritious and rather more desirable than most of their dishes. The grain de beouf is a small, red berry with an acid taste. When dried it is made into soup by boiling or enters as a component into pemican instead of the cherries.[10]

A few service berries are found,[11] and very rarely a patch of wild strawberries is seen,[12] but neither in quantity sufficient to be ranked among their means of support. The Indians are very fond of fruit of any kind and seem to prefer that grown and preserved in their own country to the dried fruit from the United States introduced by traders. Few can have any idea, without actual observation, of the immense quantities of cherries and berries eaten by them in season. The former are masticated stones and all, making a noise with their incomparable grinders not unlike and fully as loud as horses eating corn. These fruits and roots together with some others of minor note are a great resource to a people who depend entirely upon the chase for subsistence. They can be easily cured, packed, and carried, and are of much service, particularly to their children, when meat is not to be had.

The buds of the wild rose which are very plentiful, and remain on the stock all winter, are also eaten both raw and boiled.[13] But

9 The chokecherry, *Padus nana,* supplied the name for one of the Dakota months, "black-cherry-moon," the month when chokecherries were ripe (Gilmore, *Uses of Plants,* 88, plate 13b).

10 The buffalo berry, *Lepargyrea argentea,* rivaled the chokecherry as the most popular Teton Dakota plant food. (Gilmore, *Uses of Plants,* 106, plate 20b).

11 The service berry is also popularly known as sarvisberry, june berry, or saskatoon, *Amelanchier alnifolia.* Indians used the wood of this plant for arrow-shafts (Gilmore, *Uses of Plants,* 87).

12 *Frageria virginiana,* forma *Americana.* The fruit was too juicy to be preserved for winter use. The Dakota "moon when the strawberries are ripe" corresponds to our month of June (Gilmore, *Uses of Plants,* 84).

13 *Rosa pratincola* was the most common of the several species of Rosa in the

they are an indigestible and miserable article of food, as is also the red thorn berry, *tas pan* (Sioux), known as red haws.[14] Some of the dishes prepared by the Indians in their yet uncultivated state of cooks and cookery present a mess not very enticing to the eye of the hungry traveler, and are by no means adapted to delicate stomachs and fastidious appetites. In this class may be placed a favorite one (of theirs) made of blood boiled with brains, rosebuds, and the scrapings of raw hide until it becomes the consistency of warm glue. Pounded cherries boiled, with meat and sugar and grease added, is considered a dainty and eaten with great relish. The prairie turnip sliced, dried, and boiled with the dried paunch of the buffalo, or the peas extracted from the mice's nests cooked with dried beaver's tail or good fat dog is also much admired and considered fit for soldiers, chiefs and distinguished visitors.

A great variety of roots, leaves, barks and plants are used by these Indians in common with other natives of the Upper Missouri for medical purposes, the principal of which, together with their manner of application, will be more particularly referred to elsewhere.

The animals inhabiting the Sioux districts and hunted more or less by them for clothing, food, or the purposes of barter are buffalo, elk, black and white tail deer, big horn, antelope, wolves of several kinds, red and grey foxes, a few beaver and otter, grizzly bear, badger, skunk, porcupine, hare, rabbit, muskrat, and a few panthers in the mountainous parts. Of all these the buffalo is the principal, being the most numerous and valuable for everything necessary for their support. Every part of this animal is eaten by the Indians except the horns, hoofs and hair. Even the hide is made to sustain life on trying occasions. The skin is used to make their lodges and clothes, the sinews for bow strings, the horns to contain their powder and the bones wrought into dressing tools,

Sioux Country. The fruits were eaten at times when other foods were scarce (Gilmore, *Uses of Plants*, 85–86).

[14] The fruit of the red haw, *Crataegus chrysocarpa*, was "commonly resorted to only as a famine food" (Gilmore, *Uses of Plants*, 87).

or pounded up and the grease extracted. When the hair becomes seasonable, from the beginning of October to the 1st of March, the skins are dressed with the hair on, and either worn by themselves or exchanged with the traders for various necessaries.

In the year 1833 that part of the Sioux nation residing on the Missouri and its tributaries and trading there, or roving through the country the outline of which has been laid down, were divided as follows:

TETON SIOUX[15]

Se chong hhos or Brulees	500 Lodges
Ogallalahs	300 Lodges
Min ne con zus	260 Lodges
Se ah sap pas or Blackfeet	220 Lodges

[15] Although the Tetons were known to Father Hennepin in 1680 as living twenty or thirty leagues above the Falls of St. Anthony in present Minnesota, their seven major divisions, listed above by Denig and recognized by modern ethnologists, were not differentiated by white observers until long after these Indians' migration westward to the valley of the Missouri in the eighteenth century. (See F. W. Hodge, *Handbook of American Indians North of Mexico*, 736.) In 1795, the French trader, Jean-Baptiste Trudeau, stated that the Tetons "are divided into four wandering tribes" hunting on both sides of the Missouri. ("Description of the Upper Missouri," *Mississippi Valley Historical Review*, Vol. VIII, Nos. 1–2, p. 176.) Nine years later the trader Pierre Antoine Tabeau named four major divisions of the "Titon" as the "Sitchanrhou" (Brûlés), "Okondanas" (Oglalas), "Minican-Hiniyojou" (Miniconjous) and the "Saones-Titons." (*Narrative of Loisel's Expedition to the Upper Missouri*, 104.) The Oglalas and Brûlés formerly referred to the other Teton divisions, who were later migrants westward from Minnesota, by the collective nickname, "Saone." (George E. Hyde, *Red Cloud's Folk*, 12–19.) White traders and explorers who approached the Sioux country via the Missouri from St. Louis first met the Brûlés and Oglalas and seem to have adopted their nickname for the other divisions. Differentiation of the several divisions of the Saone group progressed as the whites gained familiarity with them. In 1804, Tabeau considered the Miniconjous apart from the Saones. He also listed the "'Hitasiptchone" (Without Bows) and "Hontpapas" (Hunkpapas), as well as the "Tatchindi-chidja" (unidentified), as Saone divisions. As late as 1833–34, Prince Maximilian stated that the Teton Dakotas "are divided into five branches." (Prince Maximilian, *Travels in the Interior of North America*, [Vol. XXII of Thwaites' *Early Western Travels*], 236.) Yet Denig lists above the seven divisions of the Tetons and estimates their population in 1833, the year in which he entered the fur trade of the Upper Missouri. Denig's superior knowledge of the Saone divisions stemmed from the fact that he traded with them in the years 1833–36.

Wo hai noom pah or Two Kettles	100 Lodges	
Honc pap pas	150 Lodges	
Etas epe cho or Without Bows	100 Lodges	
	———————	1630 Lodges

YANCTON SIOUX[16]

Lower Yancton	300 Lodges	
Pah Baxah (Tête Coupees)	250 Lodges	
Wahzecootai (Gens des Pin)	100 Lodges	
Gens des Perches	50 Lodges	
Esan tees	30 Lodges	
	———————	730 Lodges

2360 Lodges

These 2360 lodges, averaging 5 souls to a lodge, would make a total of 11,800 souls. This estimate, it is believed, is as nearly accurate as can be without taking a census, although at the present time, 1855, this nation would not average more than four persons to a lodge. These bands at that time occupied separate districts, though they could if they chose hunt unmolested by each other in any place through the entire country. But being generally inter-married and connected by societies of dances and clans they usually preferred locating at a distance from each other that their hunts could be better pursued and domestic arrangements and tribal government conducted by the chiefs and soldiers raised to these offices by the general consent of each band. Where two camps are joined, each having its own head, their opinions and interests clash, quarrel follows and separation follows with bad feelings towards each other as the result, often extending to the stealing of each other's horses. But each band confining its hunting operations as nearly as practicable to a certain tract of country

[16] The grouping of these tribes under the head of "Yancton Sioux" is erroneous. The Yanktons, and the Yanktonais (comprising Denig's second, third, and fourth divisions) were traditionally and linguistically closely related. However, his "Esan-tees" were a small division of the Wahpekutes, a division of the Eastern Dakotas (see footnote 46 below).

15

accustomed to the rule of its own chief, and domestic association with their friends and acquaintances, prevents differences that arise when several bands comparatively strangers are thrown together. Partly with this view and partly to occupy their entire country where game is found, but chiefly on account of hunting advantages, the following sections were considered the residences of the different bands named. This arrangement has been continued with but little deviation to the present time. For the better understanding of these locations an outline of the Sioux Country is herein presented in the form of a map though not made out with regard to latitude, longitude or relative distances, the intention being only to show in what part of the country each band was to be found, although each of the sections named is an extensive district to the verge of which and often beyond, as well as through their interior, the bands roved and encamped wherever food, water and game were to be procured.[17]

The tract inhabited by the *Se chong hhos* is on the headwaters of the White River and L'eau qui Court, reaching down those rivers to their middle and touching the Mauvaises Terres and the Little Missouri or Teton River on the west and north.[18] For many years they were headed by a chief named *Mau Káu tó jan joh* or the Clear Blue Earth, who governed them wisely and well. This

[17] This map was not with the Denig manuscript in the Missouri Historical Society. In lieu of it we have included one redrawn from the map prepared by Lieutenant G. K. Warren to accompany his report, *Explorations in the Dacota Country in the Year 1855.*

[18] Hyde was of the opinion that the name Brûlé was not applied to this division until after it reached the Missouri in its westward migration, about the middle of the eighteenth century. (*Red Cloud's Folk,* 9–12.) In 1804, Lewis and Clark found these Indians on both sides of the Missouri, at a point near the White and Teton rivers. (Elliott Coues, ed., *History of the Lewis and Clark Expedition,* Vol. I, 217.) In 1853, Indian Agent Vaughan located them in "the country from the mouth of South-fork White River, south down L'eau qui Cour, say 100 miles from its mouth, thence to its headwaters, taking in all the country lying between North-fork White and L'eau qui Cour." (*Annual Report* of the Commisioner of Indian Affairs, 1853, p. 353). Two years later Lieutenant Warren learned that the "Brules claim the country along White River and contiguous to it." (*Explorations in the Dacota Country,* 104.) The Brûlés now reside on Rosebud, Crow Creek, and Lower Brûlé reservations in South Dakota.

man was a great friend of the whites and on all occasions protected and entertained any traders who visited his camp. Few Indians possess the power, influence and dignity this man held in his hand. Although some have been more feared, others more brave, yet by his constant equal good management and just government he kept his people in order, regulated their hunts and generally avoided placing them in the starving situations incident to other bands led by less wise and moderate rulers.[19]

This band were good hunters, usually well clothed and supplied with meat, had comfortable lodges and a large number of horses. They varied their occupations by hunting buffalo, catching wild horses, and war expeditions against the Arickaras then stationed on the Platte or the Pawnees lower down that river.

Every summer excursions were made by the young men into the Platte and Arkansas country in quest of wild horses, which were then found in large numbers. Their manner of catching them was by surrounding them and running them down on their own horses. Taking their distances at different points the wild animals were pursued from one to the other until so fatigued as to be lassoed, after which they were thrown down, bridled and either packed or ridden by the fearless cavaliers. Frequently 40 to 60 head of horses were brought home as the fruits of a single expedition.[20]

In their wars with the Pawnees and Arickaras the Bruleés generally got the better. Seldom a summer passed but many scalps of these enemies were brought to camp. Indeed, the periods of time at all seasons were short that the scalp dance was not going on and

[19] The name of this chief does not appear among the signatures to any of the treaties made by the Brûlés.

[20] In a letter to the editor, September 21, 1943, Eugene Barrett, forester, Rosebud Reservation, stated that elderly Brûlé informants told him their best wild-horse hunting grounds were a series of narrow, boxlike canyons near present Alliance, Nebraska, and a long, narrow canyon near present Cheyenne, Wyoming. They chased the wild horses in relays, reserving their best mounts for the last lap. The last group of riders carried ropes. The noose of each rope was placed over a crotched stick about four feet long to hold it open. When a wild horse was overtaken, the noose was slipped over his head with the aid of the forked stick. The rider slid off his horse to throw and tie the wild one. In breaking wild horses for riding, the Brûlés mounted bareback, securing a hold in back of the horse's front legs with their toes.

the monotonous war song heard through the village accompanied by the lamentations of the friends of those who had fallen in battle. Their foes, however, did not remain idle. Every few nights some of the Sioux horses were stolen or some lonely wanderer without the camp was killed. In 1835 some Pawnees and Arickaras stole 40 or 50 of the Bruleés horses from the camp on L'eau qui Court. The latter pursued, overtook, and defeated them within a short distance of the village. Twenty-two enemies were killed, their horses recovered, and the successful warriors returned bringing the head, hands, feet and other parts of the enemies' bodies into camp. The hands and feet were stuck on sticks and paraded through the village by old women. The scalpless heads were dragged about with cords attached, followed by small boys shooting them with arrows, with guns loaded with powder, pounding them with rocks and tomahawks, encouraged by old hags who followed heaping abuse on the now helpless and haggard remains of their once feared enemies.

This is the only band who throw antelope over precipices into pens made for the purpose, thus enclosing and killing several hundred at a time. A part of their country on White River, being broken somewhat in the same way as that described as the Bad Lands, is favorable for this purpose. The animals being surrounded by several hundred people are driven through some gap in the hills beyond which is a perpendicular descent of many feet enclosed at and around the base with logs and brush built up to sufficient height to prevent their jumping over. The goats once through the gap cannot recede and the pressure of those from behind forces those in the front over, the rear being hastily followed by the people engaged in the pursuit.[21]

21 The practice of impounding antelope was much more widespread among the Northern Plains tribes than Denig indicates. Wissler described the Blackfoot antelope pound in detail and pointed out the use of antelope pounds by many other tribes of this region. ("The Material Culture of the Blackfoot Indians," American Museum of Natural History *Anthropological Papers*, Vol. V, Pt. 1, pp. 38, 51–52.) J. H. Snowden saw and described an antelope pound on the headwaters of the South Cheyenne River on November 1, 1859, which had been built by the Arapaho Indians. (W. F. Raynolds, *Report on Exploration of the Yellowstone River*, 159–60.)

Since the emigration to California and Oregon has passed through the Sioux Country, the Bruleés have suffered more from diseases thus introduced than any other portion of these Indians, they being situated nearest to the trail. Smallpox, cholera, measles, etc., have year after year thinned their ranks so that but a remnant of this once numerous band remains. These are dissatisfied and hostile towards those to whom the cause of their destruction is attributed. Their ties of relationship being severed by the deaths of their friends, their head men falling victims, and their former good order and flourishing condition deranged, they are no more the same people. Their tempers are soured and all their fierce passions raised against the authors of these evils. No man can be found to lift his voice in favor of the white people or the government, who, as they say, sends diseases to cut them off. This band of Sioux now consists of but 150 lodges.[22] These are separated through their district in small portions, badly clothed, without game, and with but few horses to enable them to hunt. Such has been the destroying effect of these maladies that their trade scarcely affords a small wintering house from which to obtain their supplies. The whites accustomed to deal with them on terms of friendship and security are now eyed with suspicion, imposed upon if not abused, and denied the hospitality of former and more prosperous times.

The *Ogallalahs* inhabit that part of the country described from Fort Laramie on the Platte, extending northeast, including the Black Hills, the heads of Teton River and reaching as low down as the forks of the Cheyenne. Continuing west they are frequently found near the head of Grand River.[23] This part is usually well

[22] Denig's estimate of Brûlé population is identical with Agent Vaughan's estimate of their number in 1853. (*Annual Report* of the Commissioner of Indian Affairs, 1853, p. 353). However, Warren reckoned 480 Brûlé lodges in 1855. (*Explorations in the Dacota Country,* 16). In 1856, Indian Agent Twiss placed their number at 250 lodges, stating that this figure was obtained "by counting the lodges when they came to receive the annuity goods due under treaty stipulations." (*Annual Report* of the Commissioner of Indian Affairs, 1856, p. 96.)

[23] The Oglalas are the best known of the Teton Dakota divisions. Hyde has identified them as the "Ojalespoitans" who wintered near Le Sueur's post on the Blue Earth River, Minnesota, in 1700. (*Red Cloud's Folk,* 8.) Trudeau mentioned them as "Oconoma," a branch of the Sioux, formerly friends and allies of the Ari-

stocked with buffalo, and if not, elk, antelope, deer and bighorn are hunted. They are met with in sufficient numbers to support the camp, although not to afford a full supply of meat. A number of this band use rifles, are good marksmen and kill small game better than the rest of the nation. As a consequence of this advantage they are better clothed than others who, not having this kind of skins, wear shirts and leggings of dressed buffalo hides. They are also remarkable for having the handsomest women in the nation, who are very neat and clean in their dress and modest in their behavior.[24]

For twenty years the head chief of this portion of Sioux was *Mah ghah ska,* The Swan. He was a man of great natural talents, a good warrior and sensible ruler. He lived to old age and died within the last few years. He was famous for his oratorical powers, some of his speeches ranking with those of Tecumseh and Pontiac.[25]

---

karas on the Missouri, who in 1795 "wandered habitually along the banks of this stream." ("Trudeau's, Description of the Upper Missouri" [ed. by Annie H. Abel], *Mississippi Valley Historical Review,* Vol. VIII, Nos. 1–2 [1921], 164.) Tabeau recognized two subdivisions, the "Okondanas and Chihauts," both of which formerly lived with the Arikaras and were agriculturalists, but during a war between the Arikaras and some other Sioux, the two Oglala divisions joined opposing sides. They were later united, but abandoned agricultural pursuits, some time prior to 1804. (Tabeau, *Narrative,* 104.) General Atkinson made a treaty with the "Augallallas," at the mouth of the Teton River, July 5, 1825. He stated that they inhabited "a district of country on the Teton River, stretching back from the Missouri to the Black Hills." (Henry Atkinson, *Expedition up the Missouri, 1825,* 19 Cong., 1 sess., *House Doc. 117,* 9.) After the establishment of Fort Laramie on the North Platte in 1834, the Oglalas moved southwestward and traded at that post. They were frequently mentioned by travelers over the Oregon Trail in subsequent years. Francis Parkman wrote a masterful description of their hunting camp, visited by him in 1846, in his classic, *The Oregon Trail.* Hyde's *Red Cloud's Folk* traces the history of the Oglalas to their settlement on Pine Ridge Reservation in present South Dakota in 1876.

[24] In the summer of 1832, George Catlin painted portraits of two "very pretty Sioux women" at Fort Pierre on the Missouri. (George Catlin, *Letters and Notes on the Manners, Customs, and Condition of the North American Indians,* I, 223–24.) These earliest known portraits of Western Sioux women are in the collections of the Smithsonian Institution. It is not known whether they are Oglalas.

[25] The name of *Mah ghah ska,* "The Swan," does not appear among the signatures to treaties signed by the Oglalas.

The Ogallalahs, before the disturbances occasioned by emigration along the Platte took place, were considered by the traders the best and most orderly Indians in the country. Seldom if ever any difficulties were experienced in their dealings with them. The chief being their friend, and he being supported by numerous and brave relations, both the persons and property of the traders were deemed as safe when in their camp as at the fort.

The enemies with whom this band contend are the Crow Indians, who, during the summer place their camps along the head of Powder River or at the base of Wind River Mountain, which is but a few days' travel from the western extremity of the Indians now under consideration. These two nations have been at war beyond the recollection of anyone now living among them. So inveterate is their mutual animosity that this indefinite period has never been varied by even a transient peace. From time to time up to the present battles have been fought between them. The Sioux chiefly being the invaders have for their object stealing the horses of the Crows, who have numerous herds and cannot at all times guard the whole. When a war party of Sioux has made off with a band of Crow horses the latter invariably follow, bring them to a stand and a skirmish takes place. In this way in 1844, twenty-six Sioux were killed and the rest of the party flogged from the field by the Crows with whips and bows, having killed as many as satisfied them for the time. This can be remembered as one instance among Indians when the lives of their enemies were saved, the usual exterminating custom giving way to a spirit of insult and disgrace. Battles and massacres of this kind are frequent between these two nations, the Crows generally killing most and the Sioux getting the most horses.

Before the influx of strangers into the Platte and Arkansas country this portion of the Sioux could procure wild horses which, with those purchased from the traders, were enough to serve their hunting purposes. But since this means of supply has been cut off they are obliged to draw upon the Crows for animals absolutely needed for their existence.

The internal government of the Ogallalahs was severe. Their

soldiers were prompt and efficient, carrying out with vigor any laws decided upon by their chief and council. On one occasion, the camp being placed at Fort Pierre in 1836, awaiting the arrival of the annual steamboat from St. Louis, one of the wives of a trapper (a Snake woman) was fired upon and slightly wounded by a Sioux belonging to a small band of Santees then there. The soldiers of the Ogallalahs turned out to flog the offender, who, being a desperate character, resisted and was killed on the spot. In all things regarding their hunting operations and traveling they preserved order, kept together and were respected and somewhat feared by neighboring bands. All this, however, is now changed. They also have been much reduced in numbers by diseases contracted along the Platte Trail from passing emigrants, and for the same reasons as those already mentioned are bitter against all whites, particularly that portion whom they blame as the cause of their misery. The band at present (1855) may number 180 lodges, averaging from three to four souls to a lodge. They are split into different factions following different leaders, and through want of game and unity of purpose are fast verging toward dissolution.[26] Their ultimate destination will no doubt be to become a set of outlaws, hanging around the emigrant road, stealing horses, killing stragglers and committing other depredations until the Government is obliged to use measures for their entire extermination. It cannot be otherwise. It is the fate of circumstances which, however to be regretted, will become unavoidable.

The *Min ne con zus* are usually found from Cherry River on the Cheyenne to the Butte de Mince on Grand River.[27] In this

[26] Lewis and Clark's estimate of the Oglala population at 150 warriors in 1804 is patently low (Coues, *History of Lewis and Clark,* I, 217.) General Atkinson reckoned 300 warriors and 1,500 souls in 1825. (*Expedition up the Missouri,* 9.) Thaddeus Culbertson estimated 400 Oglala lodges in 1850. (Culbertson, "Journal," 136.) Agent Twiss counted 450 Oglala lodges in 1856. (*Annual Report* of the Commissioner of Indian Affairs, 1856, p. 95.) Denig seemed to have grossly exaggerated the disastrous effects of white contacts and diseases on the Oglala population trend from 1833 to 1855.

[27] Tabeau listed three subdivisions of the "Minican-Hunyojou." One of these, the "Tacohiropapais," probably were the "Ta Corpa," a village of eighty lodges which paid a friendly visit to the Arikaras in June, 1795. Trudeau stated that this

section, as indeed over all the most western parts, buffalo are as yet in tolerable numbers, having abandoned altogether the eastern districts where they were formerly seen in immense herds.

The conduct of all and every band of Indians takes its nature from the chief who, if a good and reasonable man, has wise regulations and given prudent advice to his soldiers, has consequently good followers who in course of time become tractable and well disposed by the force of habit and example. What is here meant by good Indians are those well disposed toward whites and not disturbing the order of other bands by depredations or rebellion against local privileges. In this respect the body now under inquiry were formerly more sociable, friendly and quiet than they are now. But they were always more wild than other bands, principally because of their distant position, seldom visiting the forts either on the Platte or Missouri, and never seeing whites except a few fur traders during the winter season.

They were, in 1836, governed by *Hai wah ze chah,* or La Corne Seule, and during the rule of this man they behaved themselves reasonably well. He was of the right sort, brave and sensible, and communicated to his people a like disposition. All transactions between them and the traders were carried out with tolerable satisfaction on both sides. This chief, shortly after the date above mentioned, lost his favorite wife by sickness and through reckless grief sacrificed his life in a contest with a buffalo bull. After declaring his intention to die some way, he left the camp alone, wounded a bull, attacked it on foot with his knife and was gored

group, as well as the "Chahony" (Saones), "usually wander over the country North East of the Missouri, but not finding any wild oxen or cows thereabouts, are forced to the West of this river, where these animals are found in great numbers." ("Journal of Jean-Baptiste Trudeau Among the Arikara Indians in 1795" [ed. by Mrs, H. T. Beauregard], *Missouri Historical Society Collections,* Vol. IV, [1912], 47.) In 1853, Vaughan located the Miniconjous in the "country lying north of the Cheyeume [*sic*] river as far as the Moreau river, thence southwest south of the Black Hills, as far as the mouth of Beaver Creek." (*Annual Report* of the Commissioner of Indian Affairs, 1853, p. 353.) Warren placed them "on and between the forks of the Shyene and in the Black Hills." (*Explorations in the Dacota Country,* 16.) The Miniconjous are now located on the Cheyenne River Reservation, South Dakota, within the area of their occupation a century ago.

to death on the spot, his body being found a short time after by some of his people who had gone in search.[28]

Since the death of this man the band has had several rulers in succession, none remarkable for their wisdom or capacity to govern. The result is as may be expected. They have become dissatisfied, quarrelsome and predatory. Although traders can yet deal with them in their village, yet they are liable to insult and damage. The first act of a murderous character that appeared among them was their killing and robbing the trappers who remained free in their different camps in the Sioux country or others who hunted beaver along the tributaries of the Cheyenne and Grand Rivers.

Although not much blame can be attached to Indians who war against persons transgressing on their hunting grounds—yet when they are well governed and in friendly relations towards whites and each other this rarely happens. Indians do not like to kill people who can speak their language, more especially when they are partially acquainted with them. Even the Blackfeet, the most fierce and warlike tribe on the Missouri, do not at all times harm the trappers in their country who have resided some time with them, although they show no mercy to the mountain men who are as savage as themselves and who neither wish nor expect friendly intercourse.

The band now written of, though not the worst of the Sioux Nation, are far from being the best and bid fair to become the inveterate foes of white men. Up to the date 1846, they carried

[28] George Catlin painted a portrait of The One Horn at Fort Pierre in the summer of 1832. Catlin was told that this chief's name was derived from a "small shell that was hanging on his neck, which descended to him from his father." The artist described him as of middle-age, middling stature, and noble countenance. In earlier years he had been noted for his prowess in winning foot races and in running down buffalo on foot. Some years later, while in New York City, Catlin learned of the death of this chief. His account of it differs in detail from Denig's. (Catlin, *Letters and Notes,* I, 211.) So impressed was Catlin with the drama of this story that he executed three paintings of "The Death of *Hawwanjetah.*" Two are listed as Nos. 546 and 591 in the *Descriptive Catalog of Catlin's Indian Collection* (London, 1848), and the third in the *Catalogue Descriptive and Instructive of Catlin's Indian Cartoons* (New York, 1871). The caption of the last (Cartoon No. 354) states that One Horn's death occurred at the mouth of the Little Missouri in 1834.

on war against the Arickaras, Mandans, and Gros Ventres with considerable success both in scalps and horses. In one action they killed upwards of twenty Arickaras near their village with the loss of eight men on their own side. They are better fighters and risk more in battle than the Arickaras. They are also expert in way-laying their enemies around their homes. From time immemorial they have also joined the Ogallalahs in expeditions against the Crows, bringing home large bands of their horses and generally leaving some of their own scalps in exchange.

About 1846 or '47, buffalo becoming rapidly more scarce, they found it in their interest to make peace with the Arickaras from whom they can procure corn in exchange for skins and other property. This peace still continues with but little interruption to the present day. It gave them the advantage, in company with other bands about to be noticed, to locate their camp behind the Arickara Village on the heads of the Little Missouri, a point one hundred miles farther west than their former range. Here they find game, continue the war on the Crows, visit the mouth of the Yellowstone occasionally, murder straggling white men, and help themselves to whatever horses the forts in that neighborhood can furnish. In the summer season they move back on Grand River or the Cheyenne and in the fall make the corn trade before spoken of.[29]

The *Honc pa pas, Se ah sap pas* and *Etas epe chos* occupy nearly the same district. They are so often encamped near each other and conjoined in their operations as scarcely to admit of being treated separately. That part of the country under their control is along the Moreau, Cannon Ball, Heart and Grand Rivers, seldom extending very far up on Grand River but of late years reaching to the Little Missouri in company with or stationed near the band last described.[30] Although these bands are jointly mentioned and often

[29] Lewis and Clark reckoned the Miniconjou population at 250 warriors in 1805. (Coues, *History of Lewis and Clark Expedition*, I, 217.) In the middle of the nineteenth century their population was estimated at 270 lodges by Culbertson ("Journal," 136), 200 lodges by Warren (*Explorations in the Dacota Country*, 16), and 225 lodges by Vaughan (*Annual Report* of the Commissioner of Indian Affairs, 1853, p. 353).

[30] Tabeau listed the "Hont-papas" as a subdivision of the Saones in 1804. (Ta-

situated near each other, yet sometimes they are found several days' journey apart and each is headed by its own chief. Of these the Little Bear Chief of the Honcpapas is the most conspicuous.[31] He never was nor will be a good man and has so much influence over the other camps as to bring them under his jurisdiction. At least he works matters to the disadvantage if not destruction of all traders in the country. From his youth up his hatred for the white man has been manifested and his rule commenced with killing one of the principal traders of the American Fur Company, Mr. La Chapelle. This gentleman, although married into their band, con-

---

beau, *Narrative,* 104.) General Atkinson made a treaty with the "Hunkpapas" at the Arikara Villages on the Missouri, July 16, 1825. He noted that they "rove in the intermediate country between the Missouri and the headwaters of the Saint Peter's River . . . their trading ground is on the Jacques." (*Expedition up the Missouri,* 10.) Vaughan described their range in 1853, "from the mouth of Moreau River, as high up the Missouri as Cannon-ball river or Houru river, and southwest 150 to 200 miles." (*Annual Report* of the Commissioner of Indian Affairs, 1853, p. 353.) In 1855, Warren noted, "They live on the Missouri near the mouth of the Moreau, and roam from the Big Cheyenne up to the Yellowstone, and west to the Black Hills. They formerly intermarried extensively with the Shyennes." (*Explorations in the Dacota Country,* 16.)

The Blackfoot division may have been the last of the Teton groups to cross the Missouri, and probably were the "Fire Heart's band" with whom General Atkinson treated at Camp Hidden Creek on the east side of that river on July 12, 1825. (Harry Anderson, "An Investigation of the Early Bands of the Saone Group of the Teton Sioux," *Journal* of the Washington Academy of Sciences, Vol. LXVI, No. 3 [1956], 93–94.) Catlin painted a portrait of "Mah-to-een-nah-pa (the white bear that goes out), chief of the Blackfoot Sioux," at Fort Pierre in 1832. (Catlin, *Letters and Notes,* I, 223.) Vaughan located the Blackfeet in the same territory as the Hunkpapas in 1853. (*Annual Report* of the Commissioner of Indian Affairs, 1853, 353.) Warren also found their "haunts and homes" were the "same as the Unkpapas." (*Explorations in the Dacota Country,* 16.)

Tabeau (*Narrative,* 104) listed the "Hitasptchone" (a variation of *Itazipcho,* the native name of the Sans Arcs) as a subdivision of the Saone group. Vaughan defined Sans Arc territory as the same as that of the Miniconjous in 1853. (*Annual Report* of the Commissioner of Indian Affairs, 1853, 353.) Warren also noted that the Sans Arcs "claim in common with the Minikanyes." (*Explorations in the Dacota Country,* 16.)

These three tribes are now located on Cheyenne River Reservation in South Dakota and Standing Rock Reservation in North and South Dakota.

[31] The Little Bear, *Ma-to-tchi-cah,* was listed as one of the principal men of the Hunkpapas by Culbertson in 1850. ("Journal," 135.) A chief of this name signed the Treaty of Fort Sully for the Hunkpapas, October 20, 1865.

THE ONE HORN, Miniconjou Sioux head chief. From a painting by George Catlin, 1832.

THE BLACK ROCK, a Western Sioux chief. From a painting by George Catlin, 1832.

sulting their interest, and speaking their language, was murdered in his own house on Grand River by the Honcpapas.

From this time forward depredations have been committed by these bands and at the present day the traders cannot safely enter their camps. No later than 1853, a wintering house being deemed advisable near their camp, some persons were dispatched to build, but through the instigation of the chief the soldiers cut up the carts, killed the horses, flogged the traders and sent them home. Before the treaty at Laramie these people could be dealt with although not without some trouble. But somehow since that time they have become completely hostile, more so than the Tete Coupees and others who were not at the treaty.

We see no cause of complaint on the part of these three bands. They did not contract disease on the Platte Trail, have not suffered the same calamities and inconveniences as other bands mentioned, and we cannot attribute their conduct to any other cause than the bad council and example of their rulers. Being on terms of peace with the Arickaras enables them to extend their war into the Assiniboine Country, and not satisfied with the scalps of these, whom they often kill, they cut off every white man they meet and pillage or destroy all property outside the forts at the Yellowstone. They declare war to the knife with the Government of the United States and all whites in the country, threaten to burn up the forts, make no buffalo robes except what they want for their own use and wish to return to their primitive mode of life. Each year they become more troublesome and are now more dangerous and dreaded than the Blackfeet. They visited the forts near the mouth of the Yellowstone frequently within the last few years, carrying off a great many horses, killing whites and Indians and shooting arrows into the oxen belonging to the different Fur Companies.

Although these people are at peace with the Arickaras yet they are at war with the Mandans and Gros Ventres, lying around the borders of their villages waiting a favorable opportunity to pounce upon some solitary hunter or woman in quest of fuel in the adjacent woods. The number of souls in these bands, together with that of Minneconzus, has sustained no decrease within the last 20 years, although they suffered considerably by smallpox in 1838, and have lost a good many in battle with other nations. They have recovered from these difficulties and at this time are as numerous as stated at the commencement of this history.[32]

The *Two Kettle* band, known among themselves as *Wo hai noom pah,* confine themselves to the Cheyenne and Moreau Rivers, seldom going higher up on the former river than the mouth of Cherry Creek, thence moving up and down the Cheyenne, Moreau and Grand Rivers, although not often uniting with the Indians last described.[33] This small band is headed by *Mau to to pah,* or Four Bears, who is a reasonable moderate man, keeps his people together, and makes them behave as well as the ordinary run of Indians.[34] They go but little to war in any direction, hunt very

[32] The Hunkpapas were estimated at 1,500 people and 300 warriors in 1825 (Atkinson, *Expedition up the Missouri,* 10); at 320 lodges in 1850 (Culbertson, "Journal," 135); 280 lodges in 1853 (*Annual Report* of the Commissioner of Indian Affairs, 1853, p. 353); and 365 lodges in 1856 (Warren, *Explorations in the Dacota Country,* 16). All of these figures are greater than Denig's 1833 estimate of 150 lodges. It was from this troublesome group that the famous chief Sitting Bull emerged during the Plains Indian Wars of the 1860's and 1870's.

The Blackfeet were estimated as high as 450 lodges by Culbertson ("Journal," 135). However, Vaughan reckoned their population at 150 lodges (*Annual Report* of the Commissioner of Indian Affairs, 1853, p. 353), and Warren, at 150 lodges (*Explorations in the Dacota Country,* 16). These figures are less than Denig's 1833 estimate of 220 lodges.

Mid-century estimates of the Sans Arc population exceed Denig's 1833 figure of 100 lodges. Culbertson ("Journal," 136) reckoned 250 lodges; Vaughan (*Annual Report* of the Commissioner of Indian Affairs, 1853, p. 353), 160 lodges; and Warren (*Explorations in the Dacota Country,* 16), 170 lodges.

[33] The Two Kettles (the "Ohenonpa" of the Warren map) probably were the smallest tribe of the Saone group. Culbertson listed them as the "Kettle band," at only 60 lodges. ("Journal," 136). They were not so named in the early literature on the Teton Dakotas, although Harry Anderson believes they may have been the Tacoropa division of the Mineconjous on Tabeau's 1804 list. (Anderson, "Investigation of Early Bands of the Saone Group," 93.) Vaughan located them "on Teton or Little Missouri river from its mouth to its source, and north as far as the Chayeumme [*sic*] river" in 1853. (*Annual Report* of the Commissioner of Indian Affairs, 1853, p. 353.) Warren wrote that they "are now very much scattered among the other bands" in 1855. (*Explorations in the Dacota Country,* 16.) Their descendants now reside primarily on Cheyenne River Reservation in South Dakota.

[34] Culbertson listed the Four Bears, *Mato-pah,* as the principal man among the

well and are extremely fond of getting well paid for their skins. They are shrewd, politic and sensible, would do well if they kept away from the others, and are remarkable for being good beaver trappers. But few complaints are heard against this body. Traders are respected and encouraged by them and whites as a people have some strong friends among them. But they are too few to give a director to or influence much the actions of larger bands. The Crow Necklace, Black Stone, and others belonging to that body are good Indians in every respect and deserve to be ranked among the traders' friends.[35] Not many deaths have occurred by pestilential diseases nor has war greatly contributed to reduce their numbers which, it is believed, have remained nearly the same during the last 25 years.[36] It is to be hoped that they will advance in well doing. But much is to be apprehended from their position near and example of the hostile bands, more especially as their part of the country is not well provided with buffalo in late years. The want of food and absence of game may compel them to unite with the other bands mentioned.

The *Tete Coupees, Gens des Perches* and *Gens des Pins* all come under the head of Yanctonnais.[37] In 1833 the whole of these 400

Two Kettles in 1850 ("Journal," 136). A chief by that name signed the Treaty of Ft. Sully for this tribe, October 19, 1865.

[35] Catlin painted a full-length portrait of "*Ee-áh-sá-pa,* the Black Rock, chief of the *Nee-caw-wee-gee* band" of the Sioux at Fort Pierre in 1832. Although this band name has not been identified, Catlin's statement that this man "has been a constant and faithful friend of Mr. M'Kenzie and others of the Fur Traders, who held him in high esteem" coincides with Denig's characterization of "Black Stone," the Two Kettle. Catlin described this Indian as "a tall and fine looking man, of six feet or more in stature." (Catlin, *Letters and Notes,* I, 222.)

[36] Vaughan estimated the Two Kettle population at 165 lodges in 1853 (*Annual Report* of the Commissioner of Indian Affairs, 1853, p. 353) ; and Warren, at "about 100 lodges" in 1855 (*Explorations in the Dacota Country,* 16.) The last figure is the same as Denig's estimate for the Two Kettles in 1833.

[37] The Yanktonais, referred to by some early writers as the "Yanktons· of the North," lived between the Mississippi and Red Lake in present Minnesota in the middle of the seventeenth century, from whence they were driven southward by the Crees, after the latter acquired guns from traders on Hudson Bay. (Hyde, *Red Cloud's Folk,* 4–6.) Tabeau listed seven divisions of the "Yinctons of the North" in 1804. (*Narrative,* 103.) In 1823, Yanktonai hunting grounds were described as "very extensive, spreading from Red River to the Missouri," while they traded at "Lake

lodges were governed by the great chief, *Wah na tah,* but after his death in 1840 became separated into three distinct bands each having its own ruler. The whole of them, however, rove and hunt on the east side of the Missouri and very rarely are found on or beyond its western shores. Their travel in the course of their hunts extends from Apple River down to the mouth of the Little Cheyenne, north to the neighborhood of Lac du Diable, and east along the Coteau de Prairie, but never going as low down as the head of the Rivière aux Jacques. Most of this district, though formerly the favorite range of the buffalo, is now nearly abandoned by those animals which are only found in the winter on the north and west boundaries. In 1830 the above named Indians, with some others, being encamped opposite Fort Pierre on the east side of the Missouri, killed 1,500 buffalo in a single surround. This was the greatest number killed at one time ever known by the traders. The fact was determined by the trader in camp trading the tongues as the Indians returned from the hunt. Since that time buffalo have gradually retired from the eastern territory, moving west and northwest and compelling the Indians alluded to follow. From 1833 to 1844 they were yet found in considerable numbers on the heads of the Little Cheyenne and east in the direction of the Coteau de Prairie, but since the last mentioned date but few are seen so low down, which accounts for these Indians occupying their western limits and hunting north as far as the head of Pembinar River.

In their travels during the fall they sometimes come into collision with the Half Breeds from the Red River of the North, who

---

Traverse, Big Stone Lake, and Shienne River." (William H. Keating, *Narrative of an Expedition to the Source of St. Peter's River,* I, 387.) General Atkinson located them "between the Missouri and the River St. Peters, embracing the headwaters of the river Jacques," and observed that they traded on James River in 1825. (*Expedition up the Missouri,* 9.) Vaughan's description of their hunting grounds in 1853 coincides with Denig's save that he extends their territory southward to the James River. (*Annual Report* of the Commissioner of Indian Affairs, 1853, p. 353.) Warren located them "between the James River and the Missouri as high north as Devil's Lake" in 1855 (*Explorations in the Dacota Country,* 16.) The Yanktonais now reside on Standing Rock and Devil's Lake Reservations in North Dakota, and on Fort Peck Reservation in Montana.

proceed into this part of the Sioux Country to hunt buffalo in bodies of from three to six hundred men, often bringing 1,000 carts to transport their meat and skins to their settlements. Several skirmishes have happened between them and the Indians now considered and with the loss of men on both sides. It appears that the Half Breeds get the better of the Sioux.[38] At least they are not afraid to continue their annual excursions into their country, and are known to be as good if not better warriors than the Indians. The latter, not being able to gain much in these contests, retaliate by stealing the horses from the former at their villages on Pembinar in the absence of the inhabitants on their hunts. Of late their visits in this direction have become more frequent and bold. Several of the residents have been killed in the village, and a good many horses taken, although on occasion they are followed and killed by the Half Breeds. This predatory warfare having of late become serious, the Selkirkes are about to apply to the United States for permission to make war upon the Sioux on a large scale. Indeed they either must do this or leave the lands on the American side and remove to their original homes on Red River within the English possessions.

The Yanctonnais were always considered fierce and treacherous Indians. When headed by *Wah na ton* (The Animal who Rushes) they were much the same as at the present day when governed by *Wahh pai sha* (Red Leaf), and neither the persons nor property of white travelers is much respected in passing through their camp. The former of these chiefs was a great warrior, a brave, tyrannical and desperate man. He had fought on the side of the English against the Americans in the War of 1812, had their commission as Captain, is said to have commanded a considerable force of his people and to have distinguished himself in several engagements. In one of them he was severely wounded by a musket ball entering at the abdomen and passing out near the spinal vertebra. The fact of his recovering from a wound usually mortal gave him a standing

[38] While at Ft. Union, October 14, 1851, Kurz obtained from some half-bloods an account of a recent battle with the Sioux in which the half-bloods claimed to have killed eighty of the latter. (Kurz, *Journal,* 190–92.)

as a person under supernatural protection, aiding greatly to establish him in the office of the chieftainship to which he had been advanced on account of his acknowledged bravery.

When the fur trade was opened on the Missouri River by the American Fur Company on a more extensive and liberal plan than had been pursued by the itinerant French traders, the Yanctonnais, headed by *Wah na ton,* removed from the St. Peters and made their home on the Missouri, occupying the district before stated. Before this they only visited these parts occasionally, sometimes trading on the Missouri but more frequently at Lac qui Parle and other places along the eastern boundary.

As regards carrying out arbitrary measures and forcing his people to conform to whatever rules he devised for their conduct as a body, this man was decidedly the greatest Indian chief of modern times. Strongly supported by extensive family connections, decided and brave in his actions, and feared on account of his supposed supernatural protection, his word was law and his people his slaves. Dressed in officer's clothing, top boots, green spectacles, sword and pistols, his strange appearance contrasted greatly with that of his half clad followers.

His custom was to extract high pay from the trader who wintered with his band, but in the event of receiving the stipulated amount of goods exempted the trader from any other expense and supported him in his dealing with his people. This amount was sometimes very considerable but had the advantage of making a friend of this chief without whose co-operation it was impossible to proceed but by whose assistance and counsel the Indians were restrained from acts of aggression and the trade made profitable. The concluding of this contract was a serious matter not to be got through in a hurry, but deliberated upon for several days. The chief took into consideration the goods in the camp, the prospects for furs and skins, and after reviewing the several advantages on either side, made his proposition, which if not very reasonable, was impolitic to reject. By this transaction the chief felt bound to remunerate the trader for any loss occasioned by the depredations of his people either immediately with him or located elsewhere.

In 1836 this ruler was stationed with the greater part of his band near the mouth of Apple River, the rest having placed their camp some 50 or 60 miles below where a second wintering post had been built. On moving their camps in the spring the lower Indians stole six horses besides other property from Mr. Dickson, the gentleman in charge of the post. The camps having moved off to the plains the matter lay over until the succeeding fall when the whole of the Yanctonnais came to Fort Pierre with a large quantity of buffalo robes. Before the trade was opened with them *Wah na ton* requested the clerk of the fort to make out his bill for the property taken. This being estimated in robes and mentioned to him, he caused the whole of the robes to be put in a pile and took promiscuously therefrom the number required for payment, which he handed the trader. Notwithstanding the injustice of making the innocent pay in common for the acts of a few scoundrels, not a word of complaint was uttered. Each selected what remained, if any, of his own property and commenced trading as though nothing had happened. By such examples as these he brought his people to respect his orders and by killing one or two of his band, to fear his vengeance.

Another proof of this man's power was that when horses were wanted by the traders for transporting goods or furs and the Indians were unwilling either to lend or sell them, he took the number required from the first that came to hand and made them be satisfied with the compensation allowed by the trader, whether it was much or little.

Very few Indians have the power, or if so use it to this extent. Neither can such a course of conduct be long sustained. This proved to be the case with him, although his authority lasted longer than usual under the circumstances. It could not be otherwise than that enemies were made in his band, even among that portion on whom his support principally relied. In the course of time a feeling of revenge was harbored by many who dared not publicly display it. In the height of his power, and but little beyond the prime of life, he became snowblind which ended in the total loss of sight from the formation of cataracts over both eyes.

When by this action he became powerless, the chieftainship passed into other hands. His friends left his standard and followed the rising fame of another, and he, no more feared, was shot through the heart by one of his own people.[39]

Before this event, however, the Yanctonnais made a large war excursion to the Mandan and Gros Ventres villages, and on passing the trading house of Primeau in their country, demanded ammunition of him. This he refused. They departed, fought with those Indians and lost the battle for want of ammunition. This roused their vengeance against Primeau, whom they killed on their return and robbed the post of all the merchandise it contained.[40]

The present division of the Yanctonnais is the Tete Coupees, Gens des Perches and Gens des Pins—the first being generally stationed near Apple River in the winter season and the rest lower down. The *Tete Coupees* is the largest division and headed by *Wahh pai sha,* or Red Leaf, a chief variable in temper and action as regards whites but possessing great influence in his band.[41] For many years past they have waged war on the Mandans, Gros Ventres and Assiniboines, but no great massacre has been effected

[39] Denig's account contains much information about this famous chief lacking in other sources. Members of Major Long's expedition in 1823 met "Wanotan" near Lake Traverse and were greatly impressed by him. He was then twenty-eight years of age, yet was recognized as "one of the greatest men of the Dakota nation." (Keating, *Narrative,* I, 429–37.) Samuel Seymour's portrait of this chief appeared as the frontispiece in Keating's publication. James O. Lewis painted a portrait of "Waa-na-taa" at the Treaty of Prairie du Chien in 1825, which was published in Lewis' *Aboriginal Portfolio* ten years later. A copy of this portrait by the abler artist, Charles Bird King, is in the Redwood Library and Athenaeum, Newport, Rhode Island. Catlin's portrait of this chief, painted at Fort Pierre on the Missouri in 1832 (erroneously identified by the artist as Sisseton Sioux), is in the Smithsonian Institution. A biographical sketch of "Wanota" appears in Hodge's *Handbook,* Pt. 2, p. 910, in which his death is dated 1848.

[40] Accounts of the murder of Primeau, written by D. D. Mitchell and Mandan Sub-agent Fulkerson, published in François Chardon's *Journal of Fort Clark, 1834–39* (ed. by Annie Heloise Abel), 385–89, date this act early in 1836.

[41] When Indian Agent Vaughan met the Yanktonais on the Missouri about one hundred miles up river from Fort Pierre in the fall of 1854, he called a council of their chiefs and gave them presents. Red Leaf, their principal chief, proceeded to destroy these gifts in Vaughan's presence to demonstrate his scorn for the government. (*Annual Report* of the Commissioner of Indian Affairs, 1854, pp. 88–89).

on either side. Seldom more than eight or ten men were killed in a skirmish. More frequently solitary individuals were picked off around the camps and villages of their enemies. Lately, however, overtures have been made by the Tete Coupees to the Assiniboines to make a peace. But the latter have had some experience in their treacherous manners.

In 1836 some tobacco was sent from them to the Assiniboines through the hands of one of the traders, accompanied by a request to make a peace. Contrary to the advice of their white friends the Assiniboines started to the camp of the Yanctonnais. The deputation consisted of twenty-four, mostly middle-aged men and warriors of note. On arriving at the camp and presenting the pipe of peace they were smoked with and otherwise received with every appearance of friendship. But during the ceremony, and when least expecting it, they were fired upon by their false friends. All were killed except one who made out to escape in the melee that followed. It appears the whole had been arranged to decoy them into camp with the purpose of taking their lives. By this we may perceive the little dependence to be placed in the peaces or negotiations carried on between different nations, though it is very unusual, even among the wildest tribes, to attack and kill the first ambassadors.

Having this example before them, the Assiniboines are not willing to trust themselves in their camp and war continues between them with various success on both sides. It is hardly possible for the Sioux nation to preserve peaceful relations for any length of time with any of the neighboring tribes. They are too numerous, warlike, treacherous, widely separated, differently ruled and advised, and only accede to peace proposals when the advantage is all on their side and felt by every individual. Such is the result of their peace with the Arickaras. They raise great quantities of corn. The Sioux are in want of provisions, are fond of corn, and could get it in no other way from these Indians but by being on friendly terms, for the Arickaras remain at their village and could resist (owing to the peculiar construction of their cabins) any hostile demonstrations the Sioux might make upon them. Besides this the advantage is general. Every family having skins or meat can exchange them for corn, dried squashes, etc. Therefore there is no cause for quarrel and the differences with or damage done from time to time by a few on either part are amicably settled by the better disposed majority.

Of late years the Yanctonnais have become maliciously disposed toward the U. S. Government and traders in the country. They were not at the Laramie Treaty and have by some means become infected with the spirit of hostility and dissatisfaction spreading through the whole nation, originating in the sickness and famine brought about by the western emigration along the Platte Trail. At present they are dangerous to meet and appear only to be interested in predatory war excursions, depredations on traders and setting at defiance the power of the Government by insulting its agents on all occasions.

The *Lower Yanctons* or *Yanctons* as they are called to distinguish them from the YANCTONNAIS reside in that part of the territory on the east of the Missouri lying between the Vermilion and Fort Pierre, sometimes placing their camp on the head and along the Rivière aux Jacques if game is to be had, but oftener situated on the west side of the Missouri between L'eau qui Court and White River, occupying at times different places along these rivers some distance up. Occasionally they come at and around Fort Pierre and as far beyond as the Cheyenne. As it has been stated, for many years back buffalo have nearly abandoned the eastern district and are by no means numerous on the western side so low down. These Indians are never well provided with meat, small game being seldom seen.[42]

---

[42] Hyde traced the Yankton movement southward in present Minnesota following 1670, their separation from the Yanktonais and crossing of the Minnesota River to occupy the neighborhood of the red pipestone quarry in 1700, and their later movement westward in the rear of the Oglalas and Brûlés. (*Red Cloud's Folk,* 6–8.) They were doubtless the "Hinhanetons Village of the redstone quarry" mentioned by Le Sueur in 1700. Tabeau listed two subdivisions of the "Yinctons of the South" in 1804, locating them on James River (*Narrative,* 103), while Lewis and Clark gave the Yankton range as "the Sioux, Des Moines and Jacques rivers" at that time. (Coues, *History of the Lewis and Clark Expedition,* I, 97.) Keating placed

This is the band from which the Sioux lands below the Big Sioux River were purchased by the Government. It is believed they adhered to their part of that contract and relinquished entirely their right to that part of their country. During the payment of the sum agreed upon for their land, which was paid in yearly installments, they were headed by a chief called *The Ioway* from the circumstances of having been taken prisoner when a boy and partly raised by that people.[43]

Of the whole of the rulers mentioned this man had the most intelligence. He was a good financier and was much respected by his people for the interest he took in their welfare and the general satisfaction he gave by his impartial distribution of these annuities. Although entirely deficient in letters or figures he could after a few years' practice and becoming acquainted with the relative value of merchandise, calculate to within a small sum the actual amount of goods secured for the band, reckon the same into federal money and detect any gross difference. He could also make out the annual requisition for these goods with judgment, apportion the amount of each article to the number of people, omitting such things as were of little service to his people and substituting others of more importance. His whole attention was directed to their welfare, both in this and in their tribal government. By a good selection of soldiers and supporting them in their office by placing

their hunting grounds "east of and adjoining the Missouri" in 1823. (*Narrative*, I, p. 387.) General Atkinson, two years later, noted that these Indians traded on James River and hunted "in the plains north of the Missouri, from near the Great Bend, down as far as the Sioux river. (*Expedition up the Missouri*, 8–9.) In 1853, Vaughan located them "from the mouth of White River up to Fort Pierre, both east and west of the Missouri, say 125 miles in length, and as far east as James River or Cote de Prairie." (*Annual Report* of the Commissioner of Indian Affairs, 1853, p. 353.) Warren observed that "contact with whites had considerably degenerated them, and their distance from the present buffalo ranges render them comparatively poor" in 1855. (*Explorations in the Dacota Country*, 15.) Today the Yanktons are on several reservations in North and South Dakota.

43 *Ha-sas-hah*, the Ioway, signed the treaty made by the Yanktons with the United States at the mouth of the Teton River, June 22, 1825. The signature "Ha Sazza" appears on the treaty of Prairie du Chien of July 15, 1830; and "Ha-sa-za" also appears on the Yankton Treaty negotiated at Washington, D. C., in 1837, although the English translation is there given as "The Elk's Horn."

the distribution of goods in their hands, as also by wise council and moderate behavior he brought the band to a point of order and respectable condition little if any inferior to a white border population. So friendly were they with the white people in the country that on several occasions the soldiers have killed their own people for punishment of murders, robberies and insult to the traders.

The annuities have been discontinued by their limitation as per contract and the wise chief having died, the band became divided and subject to the government of several chiefs. None ranked so high as the one named, but all were more or less favorably disposed to their friends, the traders. The good words and example bestowed upon the young were not lost. To this day they are the best of the Sioux west of the St. Peters. Their distant locality from strange and hostile tribes prevents the frequency of their war excursions but once in a while they pay a visit to the Pawnees in quest of scalps or horses. They are not usually troublesome to the emigrants along the California Route. These Indians lost also a great many by diseases caught along this route but do not appear to have the same enmity towards whites on that account. At this time we do not hear of any damage done by the Yanctons, nor is there evidenced any spirit of resistance either to emigration or to the policy pursued by the general government with regard to them. They seem to be satisfied with the stipulations of the Laramie Treaty, endeavor to conform with them, listen with interest to the council of the agent, and receive with thankfulness the annual present sent them by their Great Father.

A good many of this band have visited the United States at different times,[44] from whom the rest have learned the power of the white people, which in conjunction with their being much reduced by infectious diseases has had the effect of quelling in a great

[44] The portraits of two members of the Yankton delegation to Washington in 1837 were painted by George Cooke. Lithographic reproductions along with biographical sketches of these men, *To-ka-con* (He Who Inflicts the First Wound) and *Mon-ka-ush-ka* (The Trembling Heart) were published in McKenney and Hall's *History of the Indian Tribes of North America*, II, 171–72, 205–207, and plates 69 and 77.

measure the fiery spirit exhibited by the more distant and less informed portion. Whether it is owing to these circumstances or to their long and friendly intercourse with the white traders, to their habitual good conduct, it is plain they are aware of their powerless situation in the event of coming into collision with the American troops—so much so that it is very doubtful which side they would join in case the Government carried war into their country against the rest of the nation.

The number of this band at the present date can be set at about 200 lodges, perhaps a few more, but owing to their suffering much from want of food they do not increase in the same proportion as other bands. This circumstance, together with occasional epidemics, places them in the same class as others on the decline.[45]

The *San tees* or *Esan tees,* as they pronounce it, were formerly situated at or near the Vermilion River, hunting eastward along that and La Rivière aux Jacques to their heads, at times visiting their friends on the St. Peters, a greater portion of whom reside there. These, although not numerous, are remarkable for their thieving propensities. Indeed they are but a set of outlaws even among their own people, stealing horses from the other bands or from each other fully as often as from the traders. This small body has had several head men none of whom deserves a tribute to his memory except to be ranked among the most notorious plunderers of the age. They were formerly scattered over their district in small camps of three to ten lodges, robbing whatever they could get their hands on or lounging along the borders of civilization drinking whiskey and shooting wild turkeys. Of later years some have become mingled with other bands, returning to the St. Peters from whence they came. The rest rove through the territory named,

[45] Lewis and Clark estimated the Yankton population at 80 lodges, 200 warriors and 700 souls in 1804. (Coues, *History of the Lewis and Clark Expedition,* I, p. 94.) This number is very low compared with later estimates. Keating (*Narrative,* I, p. 380) reckoned 200 lodges, 500 warriors, and 2,000 souls in 1823, Atkinson (*Expedition up the Missouri,* 8), 600 warriors and 3,000 souls in 1825; and Vaughan (*Annual Report* of the Commissioner of Indian Affairs, 1853, p. 353), 375 lodges in 1853.

living pretty much as they always did, miserable in their homes and unwelcome visitors at other places.[46]

[46] Although the Tetons applied the name Santee to all of the Eastern Dakotas collectively Mdewakantons, Wahpekutes, Wahpetons, and Sissetons, Denig here refers only to a small, detached band of the Wahpekutes who were the westernmost representatives of the Santees in his time. Prior to 1851 this predatory band, headed by *Wamdisapa* (Black Eagle), separated from the rest of the Wahpekutes and moved west to lands about the Vermilion River in present South Dakota. This straggling band, reduced to some ten or fifteen lodges, committed the massacre of Spirit Lake, under the leadership of *Inkpaduta in 1857*. (Hodge, *Handbook,* II, 890.)

II : OF THE
ARICKARAS

THE ARICKARAS or Rees as they are called by the French traders, were originally the same people as the Pawnees, their language being radically the same, though somewhat changed by association with Sioux and other neighboring tribes.[1] That they migrated up and along the Missouri from their friends below is established by the remains of their dirt villages being yet seen along that river, in the shape of small mounds now overgrown with grass. At what time they separated from the parent stock is not now correctly known, though some of their locations appear to have been of very ancient date, at least previous to the commencement of the fur trade on the Upper Missouri.[2] At the time when the old French

[1] Virtually all earlier writers on the Arikaras noted their linguistic relationship to the Pawnees. They were most closely related to the Skidi Pawnees. The trader, Pierre Antoine Tabeau, also recognized dialectal differences among the ten divisions of the Arikaras existing in 1804. (*Narrative,* 125–26.)

[2] Prior to 1795, three smallpox epidemics reduced the Arikaras from thirty-two to two villages. (Trudeau, "Journal," 28.) Nine years later, Tabeau claimed the Arikaras had numbered eighteen fairly large villages before smallpox and some hostile inroads greatly reduced their numbers. Frequent tribal and fractional movements in the historic period also added to the large number of Arikara village sites on the Missouri. George F. Will listed twenty-one sites on the Missouri from below the mouth of Bad River, S. D., northward to Fort Clark, N. D., believed or known to have been occupied by this tribe before 1855. ("Archaeology of the Missouri Valley," American Museum of Natural History *Anthropological Papers,* Vol. XX, Pt. 6 [1924].) In the summer of 1939 a Columbia University field party excavated portions of two village sites on the Missouri believed to be those of protohistoric Arikaras, in addition to the Arzberger site, about seven miles downstream from Pierre, S. D., thought to represent "a late prehistoric horizon, basically Upper Republican,

and Spanish traders began their dealings with the Indians of the upper territory the Arickara village was situated a little above the mouth of Grand River, since which time they have made several removals and are now found at Fort Clark where the village of Mandans formerly was stationed.[3]

The Arickaras have never exhibited any very friendly disposition towards white men; indeed it is said that feelings of bitter enmity and inveterate hatred against whites are inculcated in the minds of their children as soon as they can understand. This appears to be a custom descended from their ancestors, originating no doubt in some difficulties with the first settlers of the western borders, and which was the probable cause of their emigration. Whatever the cause, this system of education has been persisted in with the young hopefuls to the present time, and its consequences

but in process of development into the more specialized and later protohistoric Pawnee (to the south) and Arikara (to the north)." (W. D. Strong, *From History to Prehistory in the Northern Great Plains,* Smithsonian *Miscellaneous Collections,* Vol. C, 380–83.)

[3] In the spring of 1795, the Arikaras inhabited two villages on the west bank of the Missouri about three miles below the mouth of the Cheyenne River. They were divided by internal dissension and harassed by powerful Sioux enemies. Jealousy among their chiefs caused two bands to secede, one moving downriver to join the Skidi Pawnees, the other, upstream to reside with the Mandans. (Trudeau, "Journal," 31.) Later that year the main body moved upriver. In August, 1796, John Evans met them on the south side of the Missouri above the mouth of Cannonball River, about ten leagues below the Mandans. (A. P. Nasatir, "John Evans, Explorer and Surveyor," *Missouri Historical Review,* Vol. XXV [1931], 450–53.) For a brief period thereafter, the Arikaras occupied two villages near present Hensler, N. D., in close proximity to the Mandans. In 1799 they quarreled with the Mandans and moved downstream. In 1804 they were living in three villages above the mouth of Grand River in present South Dakota. One village was on modern Ashley Island, three and one-half miles above the mouth of Oak Creek. The other two villages were on the west bank of the Missouri about four miles upstream, separated from each other by a small creek. (Coues, *History of the Lewis and Clerk Expedition,* I, 158–61; Tabeau, *Narrative,* 124–25.) The island village was abandoned prior to 1811. Descriptions of the villages occupied by the Arikaras when visited by Brackenridge and Bradbury in 1811, and when besieged by Colonel Leavenworth in 1823, indicate that they were the two upper villages mentioned by Lewis and Clark and Tabeau. This suggests that those villages were occupied more or less continuously from the spring of 1804 to midsummer, 1823. For later movements of the Arikaras see footnotes 26 and 27.

have been severely felt through successive generatio˙ was
with great difficulty a trade could be opened with then/ hey
inhabited their old village near Grand River, and ind' ter-
prise had established posts for the Sioux and other/ ver
down. Their thieving and murdering propensities w ut
few men would undergo the risk of living among ˍ ˍ repeated attempts resulted in the deaths of those who tried ˍˍ x-
periment. Still others ventured, and in the course of time a trade
in their village was begun, though not established on a very secure
basis. These Indians at that time numbered about 800 warriors
or about 180 to 200 cabins.[5]

These huts were built and still are by planting four posts in
the ground in the form of a square, the posts being forked at
the top so as to admit of transverse beams. To the beams other
timbers are attached whose lower extremities describe a circle or
nearly so, the interstices being filled with smaller twigs, the whole
thickly overlaid with willows, rushes, and grass and plastered
over with mud laid on very thick. A hole is left in the top for the
smoke to pass out and another in the side for the door. This is the
portion of the building above ground, but within the circle an
excavation is made two to four feet deep and the earth carried
out, which makes more room and admits of persons standing upright or walking about with ease in the interior except at the extremity of the circle, where the beds of the inmates are made. The

[4] Trudeau observed that whereas the Arikaras formerly held white men in "great
veneration," "Now they consider us only in so far as we supply them with merchandise which we bring, and which is so necessary to them, particularly ammunition."
He acknowledged, "I have never seen in them any malice towards us." ("Journal,"
24–25.) In 1804, Tabeau found the Arikaras more difficult to deal with. Their first
open hostility against the whites was evidenced in their attack and defeat of the
party under command of Ensign Pryor which attempted to return the Mandan chief,
Shahaka, who had visited Washington, to his tribe in the fall of 1807. Periodic Arikara depredations in the following four decades won for them the name of "the
Horrid Tribe" among the traders.

[5] The Arikara population was estimated at 500 fighting men by Trudeau (1795),
Lewis and Clark, and Tabeau (1804). Meriwether Lewis estimated the total Arikara
population at 2,600. (Trudeau, "Journal," 29; Coues, *History of the Lewis and Clark
Expedition,* I, 144; Tabeau, *Narrative,* 124.)

door opens a few steps off from the building on the surface of the ground, from which by a gradual descent through a covered passage of about ten feet the interior of the building is reached. The door is of wood, and the aperture large enough to admit of introducing a favorite horse to the family circle, which is often done. Around the hut on the outside a small trench is dug to guide off the rain.[6]

These buildings are placed within fifteen or twenty feet of each other, without any regard to regularity;—nothing like streets are formed, and all are so much alike that a stranger is liable to lose his way in the village.

It should also have been mentioned that within their houses cellars are dug in which their corn and other produce are stored.

These Indians cultivate small patches of land on the Missouri bottom, each family working from a half to one and a half acres, which are separated from each other by brush and pole fences of rude construction. The land is wrought entirely by hoes,[7] the work done altogether by the women, and the vegetables raised are Indian corn, pumpkins, and squashes of several kinds. The corn is said to be the original kind discovered with the continent and is quite different in appearance from that grown in the States. The stalk seldom exceeds two and a half or three feet in height, and the ears form a cluster near the surface of the ground. One or two ears sometimes grow higher up the stalk, which appears to be too slender to support any more. The grain is small, hard, and covered with a

[6] Tabeau described Arikara earth lodges he saw in 1804. (*Narrative*, 146–47.) In the summer of 1932, two houses in each of the villages at the Leavenworth site were excavated under the direction of W. D. Strong. He described their appearance and illustrated the ground plan and three reconstructed views of one of these earth lodges. (*From History to Prehistory*, 366–67, figs. 24–27.) The Arikaras were more conservative than the Mandans and Hidatsas in retaining the old style, round earth lodge as a dwelling. In 1872, they occupied forty-three earth lodges at Fort Berthold. Only twenty-eight Arikara homes were then of the more modern, log cabin type. (Washington Matthews, *Ethnography and Philology of the Hidatsa Indians*, U. S. Geological and Geographical Survey *Miscellaneous Publication*, No. 7, 4.)

[7] "Shoulder blades of cow or deer serve them as pickaxes; reeds curved at the end, separated from each other by interlaced rods and bound for a handle, are their rakes." (Tabeau, *Narrative*, 149.)

thicker shell than that raised in warmer climates. It does not possess the same nutritive qualities as food for animals as the larger kind, but is more agreeable to the taste of the Indians. Upon the whole it seems to be well calculated for them, is raised with little labor, usually producing about twenty bushels to the acre.[8] When green, a portion is pulled, and slightly boiled, after which it is dried, shelled, and laid by. This is what is called sweet corn, will preserve any length of time, and by being well boiled a mess of green corn may be obtained at any season of the year differing little from that taken from the stalk.

The Indians plant in the middle of April or beginning of May according to the mildness or severity of the spring, and the ears are taken off about the beginning of August. The crops are far from being in all seasons good. They are subject to inundations from the Missouri, or to long periods of drought. But a moderately wet season always produces well, and from two to three thousand bushels of this grain is raised by this nation.

Many superstitious rites and ceremonies are attendant on their corn planting, and indeed at different stages of the crops. Some of these or perhaps all take their rise in ancient tradition, are very singular, and exhibit the original modes of thought and worship practiced by their forefathers. Others are too indelicate for insertion in a work intended for the general reader, or even if recorded, would serve only to show man in the lowest state of animal degradation. Whatever in their histories and allegories is desirable to be known, and not too gross to be made public, will find a place in these pages when these things will be alluded to, in which perhaps those in search of their remote history can find a great field for imagination.[9]

[8] A provisional list of eleven varieties of corn grown by the Arikaras has been published (G. F. Will and G. E. Hyde, *Corn Among the Indians of the Upper Missouri*, 299–300.)

[9] *"Attached in the form of a note is a description of one of the ceremonies alluded to, which is not intended for publication, but which it is necessary to mention." —Denig. This note is not with the Denig manuscript in the Missouri Historical Society. Tabeau described an Arikara ceremony for blessing the grain as it was made known to him in 1804. (*Narrative*, 216–18.)

After corn, squashes claim their agricultural attention. These appear to be the same as those raised in the States, grow on very large and strong vines, and are of various sizes and shapes. They are either boiled and eaten when green, or sliced up and dried for winter use. In the latter case they are strung and become very hard, require an age to cook, and are scarcely eatable when cooked except by the natives, who seem to swallow them with a relish unknown to our tastes, and a preference not shown to any other edible but sweet corn.

The crops named being collected are stored away in the cellars spoken of or buried on the field in different places. These caches are constructed so as to be impervious to rain, and so well covered that no one could discover the places without a knowledge of their locality. Whatever is hidden in this way is intended to remain in the ground until the succeeding spring, at which time buffalo usually being far off, it is their only resource for food. Besides the great advantage cultivation gives these Indians over the other tribes who live entirely by the chase, they have two markets for their surplus produce.[10] The first of these is the fort of the American Fur Company stationed at their village at which from five to eight hundred bushels are traded in a favorable season. This trade on the part of the Indians is carried on by their women who bring the corn by pansful or the squashes in strings, and supply themselves by the exchange with knives, hoes, combs, beads, paints, etc., also purchasing ammunition, tobacco, and other useful articles for their husbands. In this way each family is supplied with all the smaller articles necessary to their comforts and existence. It may also be observed that though the women do all the labor of tilling

[10] Rufus Saxton claimed that the Arikaras "exported five thousand bushels of corn in 1853." ("Journal" in *Reports of Explorations and Surveys to Ascertain the Most Practicable and Economical Route for a Railroad from the Mississippi River to the Pacific Ocean,* Vol. I, 265.) Agent Vaughan reported, in 1855, "They are in a prosperous condition, generally raising a superabundance of corn and vegetables, the large surplus of which they dispose of to the neighboring tribes and traders. This year, however, the continued drought, and the very severe frost early in August, will curtail their crop about two-thirds; still they have an abundance for their own consumption." (*Annual Report* of the Commissioner of Indian Affairs, 1855, 72–73.)

46

they are amply compensated by having their full share of the profits thus accruing.

The second market for their grain is with the band of Sioux who are at peace with them. These make yearly visits to the Arickaras bringing buffalo robes, skins, meat, and other commodities which they exchange for corn, and the skins etc. thus obtained enable the Rees to buy at the fort the cloth, domestic and cooking utensils wanted for their women, and the guns, horses etc. required for the men. Frequently some of these bands of Sioux pass the winter within a few miles of the Arickara village and a running trade is kept up between them all the time, each endeavoring to derive as much advantage as possible out of the other. When the Sioux have failed in their hunt, are not well provided with skins, and are suffering for provisions—and at the same time the Rees have a good crop of corn, the latter are obliged to give considerable quantities to preserve peaceful relations. It is at such times that disturbances happen. The Sioux are numerous, starving and consequently in bad humor. The others, desirous of keeping peace and fearing their powerful neighbors, do all in their power to please. Notwithstanding this damage is done, horses are stolen, women insulted etc. These outbreaks are generally compromised by the more orderly elder men of both nations.

When these nations meet, however, the one well supplied with corn and the other with robes, times are lively, feasting and dancing goes on constantly, both in the village and camp—horse racing, gambling in many many ways. Bucks and belles dressed in their best and tricked out in all the gaudy colours of cloth, paints, and porcupine quills may be seen mingled in the dance or exchanging their professions of love in more solitary places. The old men smoke and eat without intermission. The middle aged exchange horses and other property. The soldiers gamble. And the young warriors spend both day and night in attempts at seduction of the young women in both camps. Strange scenes are witnessed here, much that would be interesting to describe, and more that would be indescribable.[11]

[11] The Arikaras traded with the Teton Dakotas for more than half a century

In the commencement of winter the Rees leave their village in quest of buffalo, which seldom come near enough to admit of their being killed close to their cabins. In that case they encamp in skin lodges mostly below their village, though not often going more than from fifteen to forty miles off. Here sometimes alone and sometimes in company with the Sioux they pass the winter in hunting, and return to their residence early in the spring bringing with them their hides in their raw state, besides as much meat as they can cure by drying. The hides are dressed into robes before the season for planting comes on, and the meat with their reserves of corn enable them to live tolerably well. But these Indians are not very good hunters, and are not well provided with horses,[12] and only turn out large quantities of robes when buffalo are plenty in the immediate neighborhood of their village. They are, however, good fishermen, which they take by making pens out of willows planted in the Missouri eddies and meat thrown in. The fish entering, the door is closed upon them, and the men jump in and throw them out. In this way great numbers of fish are taken in the summer when they have but little else to occupy their time.[13] The

---

prior to 1850. The conduct of this trade in 1795 and 1804 was described by Trudeau ("Journal," 47–48), Tabeau (*Narrative,* 131–32), and Lewis and Clark (Coues, *History of the Lewis and Clark Expedition,* I, 144). Then, as in Denig's time, the Arikaras felt compelled to engage in this trade through fear of the more powerful, aggressive Sioux. However, the Arikaras had particularly friendly relations with the Okondanas (Oglalas) who, according to Tabeau, formerly were agriculturalists and lived with the Arikaras. (*Narrative,* 104.) In the 1795–1804 period the Arikaras offered corn, tobacco, beans, pumpkins from their own fields, and horses, which they obtained in trade from nomadic tribes dwelling southwest of the Missouri, in exchange for dried meat, dressed skins, and bows and arrows prepared by the Sioux, and objects of European manufacture, especially guns and ammunition, which the Tetons obtained in their annual spring trade with their Yankton and Eastern Dakota allies of the Minnesota and Des Moines rivers.

[12] The Arikaras obtained horses earlier than did the Mandans and Hidatsas farther up the Missouri. All three tribes played important roles as middlemen in the diffusion of horses from the nomadic tribes south and west of the Missouri to nomadic tribes north and east of that river. Yet they retained few horses for their own use, and at no time during buffalo days was any of these horticultural tribes wealthy in horses. (John C. Ewers, "The Horse in Blackfoot Indian Culture," Bureau of American Ethnology *Bulletin 159,* 8–14, 23–28.)

stationary Indians are fond of fish. The roving tribes show but little relish for them. The Arickaras are also good swimmers,[14] venture out on floating cakes of ice when the Missouri breaks up in the spring and bring ashore the drowned buffalo drifting by. Many of these animals in attempting to cross the river in the fall before the ice is strong enough, break through. Often whole herds are thus drowned, which remain in the mud until the ice starts, when they are carried down by the current. Their carcasses are often piled up along the shore, impregnating the air with the odor of putrefied flesh for some distance around. Although these drowned animals are so much putrefied that the meat will scarcely stick together, and can be eaten with a spoon in its raw state, yet these Indians devour it greedily, even when other and good meat can be had. It is a horrid mess, producing an intolerable stench, and one would think sufficient to cause the worst diseases. Yet they suffer no inconvenience from eating it, which they do, men, women, and children, as much as they can cram down. If tolerably sound it is boiled a little, if too rotten it is eaten raw. In either case it is the most unnatural substance in the shape of food to be met with even in this wild country.[15]

At the same time this buffalo fishing is going on, drift wood is collected by the women, who sail out on the ice cakes, attach cords to floating trees which are hauled ashore by those on land. A great deal of wood is collected in this way, which is an object, as timber of every kind is very scarce near the village, and a good deal of time is required and some danger attended in procuring enough

[13] Tabeau observed that the old Arikaras were patient fishermen, although catfish were so scarce near their Grand River villages in 1804 that they caught very few. Their only method of fishing was the line. *(Narrative,* 91–92.) Construction and use of Arikara fish traps at a later period have been described in detail by Melvin R. Gilmore, "Arikara Fish-traps," Museum of the American Indian, Heye Foundation *Indian Notes,* Vol. I, 120–34.

[14] Tabeau considered the Arikaras "perhaps, the best swimmers in the world." *(Narrative,* 173.)

[15] Tabeau witnessed the salvage of a dead buffalo from the river drift in 1804. Although the odor was so high he found it impossible to go near it, he observed that the Arikaras ate part of the animal raw. *(Narrative,* 75.)

for fuel.[16] On the occasion and for the above purposes the whole village turns out, men, women, and small fry, so that the whole face of the river is alive with people, from shore to shore, leaping from one cake of ice to another, sometimes falling in or whirling by on the rapid current. It is a dangerous employment, yet they are so nimble, such good judges of the solidarity of the ice cakes, and such admirable swimmers that but few accidents happen.

These are their resources of living, and poor as they are, are greater than those of the Sioux and other tribes. If a person could abstract the idea of filth, or the filth itself from their cooking, the food offered to strangers in their homes is good enough.[17] Several really palatable dishes are served up, of which the sweet corn is the best. Boiled squashes when green are tolerable, though when dried are too bitter. They also make a pretty fair substitute for bread by parching corn and pounding it in a mortar. This is made into rolls and balls, dried, and carried along when they travel. It is pleasant to the taste, requires no cooking, and without any other kind of food will support life for a great length of time. A kind of hominy is also made of corn bruised in a mortar and soaked for a time in warm water, which is rather agreeable to the taste. They have a way of cooking a goose too that we do not remember to have seen in any cook book. They smear over the goose a thick coat of mud (that is over the goose as it is killed with feathers, entrails, and everything entire) after which the fowl is put in a hot fire, and covered over with live coals. Here it is left until the clay covering becomes red hot, then suffered to cool gradually until

16 Driftwood played a more important role in the economy of the Arikaras in earlier times when they lived downstream where timber was even more scarce. Trudeau claimed that "for fuel and the building of their cabins these nations use only the drift wood which is piled up by the rising waters of the Missouri." ("Journal," 22.) Tabeau noted that the Arikaras were "forced to change their habitations often for want of wood which they exhaust in five or six years," but the Mandans, farther upstream, were "more constant in their homes; because the timber begins to increase in their territory and the larger points are far better supplied with trees." (Narrative, 69–70.)

17 This is in agreement with Tabeau's caustic remark, "after having eaten almost a year with the Ricaras, one ought not to be allowed to be fastidious or disgusted." (Narrative, 174.)

the fire dies out. The shell is then cracked with an axe, the feathers and skin of the goose come off with the clay, leaving the flesh clean and well done. Catfish are also served in the same way, but the usual manner of eating these is boiled in water until they fall to pieces and compose a kind of soup which is drunk without any seasoning.

These Indians, although dull of intellect in many respects, show considerable ingenuity in manufacturing tolerably good and well shaped vessels for cooking out of clay, wrought by hand without the aid of any machinery and baked in the fire, though not glazed. These consist of pots, pans, porringers and mortars for pounding corn. They are of a grey colour, stand well the action of fire, answer their purposes, and are nearly as strong as ordinary potter's ware. For the shape of these vessels see plate.[18] For pounding corn or other hard substances they make also mortars of stone, working the material into shape by great labor and perseverance.[19] These utensils though clumsy appear to be preferred by them to metallic ones, for though the latter can now be had at a trifling cost, they continue the manufacture and will scarcely exchange them for others to us more convenient and durable. They also possess the art of melting beads of different colours, and casting them in moulds of clay, for ear and other ornaments, some of which are very handsomely done. The most common kind is of the shape and size drawn in the plate, the ground work blue, the figure white, the whole about ⅛″ thick and presenting a uniform glazed surface.[20] They also,

[18] This illustration was not with the Denig manuscript. In 1804, Tabeau noted that the Arikaras "make a very hard but coarse pottery which stands heat well." (*Narrative,* 149.) In 1811 an Arikara woman showed Bradbury a method of shaping pottery inside a basketry form. (*Travels in the Interior of America, 1809–1811,* Vol. V in Thwaites' *Early Western Travels,* 169.) Yet W. D. Strong found no traces of this method in his examination of sherds from the Leavenworth village site. (*From History of Prehistory,* 368–69, Plates 7 and 9.)

[19] Strong's trait list of the Leavenworth site includes "shallow mortars and mullers, rare." (*From History to Prehistory,* 369.) Thaddeus Culbertson saw "a small wooden mortar . . . sunk in the ground, for pounding corn" in the Arikara earth lodge in which he was entertained at Fort Clark in 1850. ("Journal," 98.)

[20] This plate was not with the Denig manuscript. However, Denig described Arikara bead-making in nearly the same words in *Indian Tribes of the Upper*

in common with the Mandans and Gros Ventres, make skin canoes which they use for hunting along and crossing the Missouri. The body of the boat is made of willows, bent round in the form of a basket and tied to a hoop of the same at the top, which hoop is about three or four feet in diameter. The hide of a buffalo, either fresh off the animal's back, or if dry, well soaked in water, is stretched over the frame, the hair inside. It is then turned upside down, dried, and sometimes smeared over with tallow. The whole is made of a single skin, can be carried by a woman on the run, and will cross three men over the Missouri even should the wind and waves be tolerably high. Usually these boats are propelled by the women, one in each boat, which also contains the meat of the same cow whose hide made the canoe. She uses a paddle in front making a pawing motion directly under the boat which turns half round to alternate sides at each stroke of the paddle. In this sort of navigation both men and women are very expert. Parties of both go for some distance up the Missouri in the summer when the hair of the animal is not seasonable, kill buffalo, make canoes of the hide, put the meat in and each one paddles his boat to the village. Fifty, sixty, or a hundred canoes can be seen, all loaded, manned or womaned by a single paddler, plying their way even in high wind down the rapid and dangerous current of the Missouri.

The domestic character and habits of the Arickaras are decidedly more filthy than any other nation on the Upper Missouri, but as most of their worst customs cannot for certain reasons be explained here, only a few will be hinted at as a sample of what might be shown were the barrier of decency withdrawn. In their dress they are greasy and slovenly, both men and women, and their hair is seldom untangled by a comb, though frequently, among the men, stuck together with gum in tufts, and these plastered over with clay, grease and paint, afford excellent pasture for ver-

---

Missouri (p. 413), and illustrated one type of ornament on plate 65 of that publication. Tabeau claimed the Arikaras were taught the art of melting and moulding glass beads by a Spanish prisoner. *(Narrative,* 149.) Matthew W. Stirling summarized the available information on this subject in "Arikara Glassworking, *Journal* of the Washington Academy of Sciences, Vol. **XXXVII**, No. 8.)

min, which grow to an immense size, multiply and replenish, spread over the cranium and clothes and even continue their explorations into every nook and corner of their cabins. They appear to be a distinct species of the kind, large and formidable, and no person except a native can withstand an attack of even a dozen or so. But these Indians seem rather to encourage them both in their manner of feeding them and providing confortable resting places in their matted locks and greasy robes. On almost any fine warm day, a stranger promenading in their village will see hundreds of lazy men lying down with their heads in the laps of their wives, who with the rapidity and regularity of a machine pick off and smash with their teeth these enormous crawlers, retaining the same in their mouth until enough is collected to spit it out in the shape of a ball as large as a good sized walnut. In this delicate and interesting operation, it may also be observed, they pick off only those that are full grown, which indeed are so numerous and easily handled that no search is required, though the smaller crop are left to grow, fatten, and afford amusement on future occasions. Now it is very well known that other nations are not exempt from this disgusting practice, but among them it is confined to a few elderly persons and even these only make occasional private hunts of the kind in their lodges. But among the Indians we now treat of, it appears to be a laudable custom which they are particularly anxious that strangers should witness, and for which there is no earthly excuse as fine combs can at all times be had.

Many of the Arickara families sleep indiscriminately together, the father beside the daughter, the brother with the sister, and this is the only nation among whom incest is not regarded as either disgraceful or criminal.[21]

There are neither handsome men nor women among them. The former have sharp, sneaking, thieving looks, shabby in dress, and

[21] Half a century earlier, Tabeau observed sexual relations between brother and sister among the Arikaras. He also found such relations between son-in-law and mother-in-law were customary in that tribe. (Narrative, 181–82.) The latter is particularly noteworthy in view of the strict mother-in-law avoidance customs among neighboring tribes which prevented these relatives from even speaking directly to one another.

ungraceful in their general deportment; and the latter coarse features, thick lips, short and thick set persons. Both young and old of either sex are more or less tainted with the venereal disease. This also makes its appearance in their children in the form of scrofula and other cutaneous eruptions, and these know no end. The iniquities of the parents are literally visited upon their children even to the third and fourth generations.[22] While on this disagreeable topic it might also be stated that the whole of the Arickara village, both within and without their habitations, presents a disgusting appearance. The spaces between the huts are seldom if ever cleaned, animal and vegetable substances in every state of putrefaction are scattered about, and the consequence of this is fluxes, dysentaries, scurvy, and other diseases prevail in the warm months, which sweep off numbers of every age and sex. All attempts on the part of traders to remedy these evils are of no avail, are viewed in the light of insulting interference, and only tend to make matters worse. Therefore, they plod on, show no disposition to improve, and are less likely than most tribes to be benefited by any missions or charitable institutions that may be devised for their welfare.

In 1824 (we are not certain of the date), but about that time, when the Arickaras occupied their village near the mouth of Grand River, and were killing every white man they could lay their hands on, Genl. Ashley descended the Yellowstone with a boat containing beaver etc., being the proceeds of his hunt in the mountains. The

[22] At the Arikara villages in 1795, Trudeau found "the foul distemper is more common here than the smallpox is in the northern countries of Canada. The Indians cure themselves of it very easily; they showed me some who six months ago were rotting away who are now perfectly cured." ("Journal," 31). Nine years later Tabeau found venereal disease especially virulent among the Arikaras. He claimed the natives were too ignorant and lazy to find plant remedies for their ailments. *(Narrative,* 183.) Both Trudeau and Tabeau were impressed by the looseness of Arikara feminine sexual morals. Lewis and Clark considered Arikara women "handsome." (Coues, *History of the Lewis and Clark Expedition,* I, 163.) But Tabeau wrote, "It is in derision or irony, that some travellers have called them the Circassians of the Missouri or else the present race has degenerated greatly." *(Narrative,* 174.) The earliest portraits of Arikara women were painted by George Catlin in the summer of 1832, and are in the collections of the Smithsonian Institution.

boat was managed by some thirty or forty persons. It so happened they ran aground directly in front of the Ree village and those Indians commenced firing upon them, in which skirmish seventeen of Mr. Ashley's men were killed, the rest escaping with the boat.[23] On reporting this outrage to the U. S. Government some troops were dispatched under command of Col. Leavenworth to chastise the Indians. The Sioux and mountain men joined the expedition and the whole formed a body of some three or four thousand men. On arriving near the village great preparations were made on the part of the whites for the attack, whole pieces of cotton were torn up into bandages for those expected to be wounded, and the Sioux allies led to believe an immense slaughter of their enemies (at that time) was to take place. The Sioux were full 1,500 men headed by their chiefs and half-breed interpreters. Great expectations were entertained by them of the destructive power of the artillery, and the strong hearts of the white soldiers.

In the meantime, the Arickaras barricaded their lodges and fortified their place as well as possible, placed their women and children in the cellars in the interior of the lodges. On the morning of the attack the Ree chief raised his flag on the top of his lodge, opened and spread before him his great medicine, lit his pipe, and by incantations invoked the interference of supernatural agency aginst this overwhelming force. The troops arriving near enough, commenced throwing some shells into the village, one of which knocked down the chief's flag, the next broke through his frail cabin and cut him in two in the middle during his solemn cere-monies for deliverance. The Sioux were commanded to stand back until such time as the Rees should evacuate the village. A charge was made into the village by the U. S. troops, headed by their officers and supported by the mountain men. But the enemy pre-sented no front, or rather none was seen, for each family was

[23] Actually Ashley's party was bound up the Missouri from St. Louis when this conflict occurred at the Arikara villages, June 2, 1823, in which thirteen or fourteen whites were killed or mortally wounded. Details of this battle are told in H. C. Dale's, *The Ashley-Smith Explorations and the Discovery of a Central Route to the Pacific, 1822–1829*, 69–77; and in H. M. Chittenden's *The American Fur Trade of the Far West*, I, 264–70.

holed up separately in their cabins, from which they fired, through holes pierced for the purpose, upon the advancing troops. How it happened, or for what reason it is impossible to imagine, but here the battle ended. In the charge a few soldiers were wounded and orders were issued for a retreat, or at least for a discontinuance of the conflict. The mountain men were dissatisfied with the result and requested permission to fight without the troops. The Sioux, also, supposing the whites were afraid, volunteered a rush into the village. But the commanding officer would not allow any one to act. His subordinate officers felt humiliated, high words ensued between them, as also some insulting remarks from the mountain men. At night the Ree village was guarded on the only side where escape was impracticable and the upper part left open. In the morning all had decamped and were not pursued, leaving to the expedition some spoils consisting of stone pots, horn spoons, and a considerable quantity of parched corn and pumpkins.[24] It appears that the officer had followed the instructions received from the Secretary of War, at least so it must be understood, for he gained, the journals of the day say, not only spoons and posts but "laurels" for his moderate and humane behavior on the occasion. Now however just or correct his course in a military point of view, the example has been very pernicious with regard to establishing the character of the white soldiery or indeed of whites of any kind for bravery. The Sioux then on the ground had been led to believe that a great and glorious display of the power of American troops was about to be made, in comparison with which their transient scalping was mere child's play—popguns and marbles, to their cannon and muskets. To this day a Sioux Indian cannot see a piece of cotton torn lengthwise without enquiring if bandages are wanted, and relating the anecdote of the great quantity of this article uselessly wasted on the eventful evening of the great battle with the

[24] Contemporary reports of Colonel Leavenworth's campaign against the Arikaras in the summer of 1823 are summarized in Dale *(The Ashley-Smith Explorations,* 77–85), and Chittenden *(The American Fur Trade,* 77–85). They differ in details from Denig's account. This campaign antedated by a decade Denig's entrance into the fur trade of the Upper Missouri. Probably his principal sources of information on this action were the oral traditions of the fur traders.

Arickaras. How can *they* otherwise account for the sudden cessation of hostilities than by imputing it to cowardice? What do *they* know of command, governmental instructions, subordination etc.? The fact was clear. Troops came some 1,500 miles to swallow up a nation, and after commencing an attack withdrew to let the enemy escape. Even among the troops concerned there were insinuations and insults thrown out against the officer in command, how then can the Indians be blamed for thinking the way they do? We repeat it. The result of the expedition ruined the reputation of all whites in the eyes of the Indians. Had the Arickaras then been taught a lesson by demolishing the village, and killing or conquering them thoroughly, the Sioux would also have profited by it, and the troubles now about to commence with the latter nation most probably never would have happened.[25]

The Rees though not much harmed were terribly frightened, they are cowardly wretches at best, and never stopped running until they reached the Platte River in the country of the Pawnees, from whom they had originally sprung. There they built a village and commenced their customary occupations, which suffered occasional interruptions from warparties of Sioux (Bruleés) whose camp was usually on the heads of *L'eau qui court* and White River. Not much information can be given regarding their operations while in that quarter. They however continued their depredations on and hostilities to all passing white men. At that time none but traders and trappers traveled in that quarter. But whenever they could catch a small party of them unprepared, they invariably killed them or stole their property. Things went on this way until 1838, when their continued aggressions made them so obnoxious to whites and Indians that they were again driven back to the Missouri. In the interim, while on the Platte, they caught the smallpox

[25] Denig's major contribution to the history of the Arikara campaign of 1823 lies not in his description of the action, but in his interpretation of its major result—the arousal of strong feelings of contempt for the military power of the United States on the part of the powerful and aggressive Sioux, which Denig believed were sustained until the beginning of Sioux hostilities on the North Platte at the time he wrote in 1855.

of which disease about three hundred of them died.[26] They arrived on the Missouri and took possession of their present village at the time when the smallpox of 1838 had nearly exterminated the Mandans who had built it, the few survivors left having abandoned the huts for those of their other village farther up. Though the disease was still raging when the Rees came, they, having had the infection, only lost a few children, and found themselves not only in possession of habitations ready built but far superior in numbers to the Mandans and Gros Ventres, who had formerly been their masters.[27] Both the latter nations, not being willing to live with

[26] Arikara movements during the nine years following the Leavenworth campaign have not been traced in detail. They massacred several parties of trappers near the Mandan villages later that summer and committed depredations on the Platte the following winter. (Dale, *The Ashley-Smith Explorations,* 85.) In June, 1832, George Catlin painted a view of the Arikara village on the Missouri "200 miles below the Mandans" from the deck of the steamer *Yellowstone.* A year later Maximilian saw the site of this village and stated that it had been abandoned for nearly a year. His description of the site as "two villages . . . on the west bank, very near each other, but separated by a small stream," located a few miles north of the mouth of Grand River, identifies it as the Lewis and Clark-Leavenworth site, to which the Arickaras had returned before Catlin passed it in 1832. Maximilian listed the reasons for Arikara removal from this site in 1832—fear of reprisals by the United States for their depredations on Americans, crop failure due to drought, and absence of large herds of buffalo in the locality. (In Thwaites' *Early Western Travels,* XXII, 335–36.) However, contemporary traders, more familiar with the military situation on the Upper Missouri, attributed Arikara removal to pressure from hostile Sioux. In fact their correspondence showed they had anticipated this move for at least a year, and were glad to see this troublesome tribe leave the Missouri. (Chardon's *Journal,* 205, 311–12.) Captain Ford, of Colonel Henry Dodge's Dragoon expedition, which met some Arikaras in June, 1835, noted that at that time the tribe had no fixed villages, lived in skin lodges, and subsisted entirely on buffalo, other wild game, and roots. He claimed they ranged on the Platte River from the forks to the mountains. ("Captain Ford's Journal of an Expedition to the Rocky Mountains [1835]," [ed. by Louis Pelzer], *Mississippi Valley Historical Review,* Vol. XII, 557–58.) In 1836, William N. Fulkerson, Mandan Sub-agent, reported that several Arikara families had not left the Missouri with the main body of the tribe, but resided among and intermarried with the Mandans. He had heard talk of Arikara plans to return to the Missouri, but hoped they would not do so "as this Country has been sufficiently stained with blood, shed by their treachery." (Chardon's *Journal,* 391.)

[27] Details of the Arikara return to the Missouri are well documented in the pages of Chardon's *Journal,* 80–194. They may be summarized as follows: In the

An Arikara Indian Village on the Missouri. From a painting by George Catlin, 1832.

THE BLOODY HAND, Arikara head chief. From a painting by George Catlin, 1832.

or near the Arickaras, removed a short time afterwards to *L'ours qui danse* on the opposite side of the Missouri about 65 miles farther up, and left their fields to the Arickaras.[28] These three nations are and for a long time have been at peace. As they pursue the same occupations and are about equal in horses and other property there is no advantage in being at war with each other, though the Mandans and Gros Ventres, being good warriors and better people in every respect, look down with contempt upon the Arickaras. But little sociability exists between these three tribes, few visits given or returned, and scarcely an instance of inter-marriage between them and the Arickaras.

The present number of huts in the Ree village is about 140 which

fall of 1836, the Arikaras sent two delegations from their camp "at the Black Hills" to ascertain the feelings of the Mandans at Fort Clark toward them. These delegations were received in most friendly fashion. The Arikaras wintered on the Little Missouri and northeastward as far as Turtle Mountain. On April 28, 1837, they arrived at Fort Clark, 250 lodges strong. The Mandans found quarters for most of them in their larger village. The remainder, some 20 lodges, took residence with the Hidatsas (Denig's "Gros Ventres"). They were welcomed by the Mandans and Hidatsas with feasting and dancing. In July smallpox broke out among the Indians in the vicinity of Fort Clark. By fall, Chardon reckoned seven-eighths of the Mandans and one-half of the Arikaras had died of the disease. On September 21, 1837, the remnant of the Mandans, fearing the Arikaras would unite with the Sioux against them, removed to the opposite side of the Missouri. After wintering south of Fort Clark, the Arikaras returned March 20, 1838 to take possession of the larger Mandan village. On June 29, a few Mandans who had remained with the Arikaras became incensed by Arikara theft of their women and moved upriver to join the Hidatsas. Next month, however, the Hidatsas moved downriver to the smaller Mandan village to be near the Arikaras for mutual protection against the Sioux. However, by spring of 1839, the Arikaras quarreled with the Hidatsas over the killing of a woman of the latter tribe, and both the Hidatsas and Mandans again moved upriver. Thus, a year after the Arickaras had been warmly welcomed to the Missouri by the Mandans and Hidatsas, they had alienated the friendship of those tribes.

[28] Dancing Bear Valley is on the south or west side of the Missouri River, opposite the site of Fort Berthold Indian village which was occupied jointly by the Mandans, Hidatsas, and Arikaras after 1862. Chardon traded with the Hidatsas at *L'ours qui danse* in 1845. (Chardon's *Journal*, 248.) The Arikaras remained at the former Mandan village until after Fort Clark was burned in 1861. Lewis Henry Morgan visited and described the abandoned village on June 4, 1862. (*Lewis Henry Morgan: The Indian Journals, 1859–62* [ed. by Leslie A. Whites,] 161–62.)

contain about six hundred persons, two-thirds of whom are adults.[29] From the local causes mentioned they do not increase fast, if any. Their children die off in far greater numbers than those of the roving tribes, from diseases arising from the filthy state of their abodes, from cholera infantum in the season of green corn, and from the impure air in their dark and damp hovels. Still, however, the men lose nothing by war like the prairie tribes. The Rees are no warriors, no fighters, not even good horse stealers, and knowing this wisely remain at home. The height of their ambition at war is to visit the mouth of the Yellowstone once a year or so and kill some stray inoffensive woman, or to waylay and murder an unsuspecting white man. Of late years two or three instances of the kind have happened at or near Fort Union. Some ten or twelve Arickaras found two of the Fur Company's men out hunting. Going up to one of them the leader of the party held out his right hand smiling, and shot the man with the left while shaking the other as a friend. The remaining man escaped by running. Thomas Jeffris, a trader of the Fur Company, and well known by them, was met by about 10 Rees a short distance from the fort, who smoked and talked with him some time as a friend and on leaving shot him through the head.[30] It is only by such cowardly acts as these the Arickaras are known as warriors. But such things occur seldom, and of late years have ceased altogether, not that they are getting any better, but more afraid. The presence of some of them at the Laramie Treaty in 1851, when they witnessed many passing trains of emigrants, and their former acquaintance with the troops, together with an instinct that tells them a day of retribution is draw-

[29] Alfred J. Vaughan, Indian agent for the Upper Missouri tribes, reported " . . . they have 60 lodges, number 14 to a lodge—making the aggregate of 840" in the Arikara village at Fort Clark in 1855. (*Annual Report* of the Commissioner of Indian Affairs, 1855, p. 73.) Thaddeus Culbertson estimated "200 lodges and 1,500 souls" in that village in 1850. ("Journal," 137.) The Arikara population of 392 males, 588 females, totaling 980 was listed in the Annual Report of the Commissioner of Indian Affairs, 1861, p. 213.

[30] Denig's letter to Alexander Culbertson, dated Fort Union, December 1, 1849, (in the collections of the Missouri Historical Society, St. Louis) mentioned that "The Rees killed Jeffris." Presumably the murder was committed shortly before that letter was written.

ing near, induce them to behave reasonably well towards the traders. They seldom leave the village if any meat at all can be had near it, work as little as possible, gamble and smoke all winter, and pass the summer in sleeping and catching catfish. They have none of the parade or manly exercises of other nations, not even gay dances nor soldier feasts, except when visited by the Sioux. Then they cut a sorry figure among their proud and warlike allies. The women, however, work hard, much more so than those leading a roving life. This together with hereditary or contracted disease soon breaks them down. A married woman of this nation not only looks old but really is so at thirty years. They have not many horses, neither do they use dogs much for carrying. Whatever work of this kind is done near the village is by packing on the backs of women, or if in summer by skin canoes. Regarding these Indians in their form of government not much can be said. They make some attempts to regulate hunts, which generally prove abortive, or after a short trial are abandoned and everyone hunts on his own account. But owing to their always having a supply of corn on hand, they are not subject to the same vicissitudes of living as other tribes, though sometimes they are hard up for meat. Their stationary habits have taught them a degree of economy in the article of provisions. They do not feast and waste like the migratory tribes. All raise some corn, and what little meat they can get on their hunts or around the village is husbanded with great care. Therefore, though not at all times flush, they seldom experience extreme hunger.

There is no wise ruler at this time at the head of the nation.[31] Several men of equal standing, or rather no standing, pretend to govern. But they impose no obligatory regulations on the rest. Each family is left pretty much to its own resources. There being no war spirit among them, no rule of precedence is followed. Indeed no man can show how or in what way he is superior to his fellows.

[31] Maximilian claimed that the principal chief of the Arikaras, when they left the Missouri in 1832, was *Starapat* (the Little Hawk with Bloody Claws). Nearly a decade earlier this man had killed a trader at the very door of his fort. (In Vol. XXII of Thwaites' *Early Western Travels*, 336.) This must have been the Arikara chief whose portrait Catlin painted at the Mandan villages in the summer of 1832. Catlin rendered his name "Stánau-pat, the Bloody Hand."

Success in war is the only road open to the chieftainship, and this being closed, no other attainments are sufficient to place one man in a higher position than another. And this is the reason they are so degraded and debased in their habits. Indians to be Indians must have war. Without it the young men have no occupation, no ambition, even if so disposed can do nothing to render their names and characters conspicuous. He, be he ever so brave, is classed with the rest and seeks distinction in circumventing the young women. Instead of being considered a great warrior he desires to be known as a great rake, he has no other choice, and his time is devoted to this purpose. The same spirit is visible in the elderly men. Thrown upon their own resources, with much idle time, they seduce each other's wives. This being almost the only occupation of the males, their minds become so debased that in the end they make victims of their own blood relations. In conformity with this state of things the virtue of all their women is at the lowest ebb, and for sale to any person who is so unfortunate as to make application. Now was there an opening to their ambition at war, or even large fields for operations in the chase as with the roving tribes, their diversions would take another channel. Distinction of rank would follow, and most of the evils we deprecate would give way to a laudable spirit of emulation.

ASSINIBOINES

THE CHIEF RIVERS running through the Assiniboine country are, first, the Missouri, which is so well known that it needs no description here. The next is Milk River, on the northwest boundary, a very long and narrow stream, rising in some of the small mountains east of the Missouri, and lakes on the plains, runs a southwest course, and empties into the Missouri about a hundred miles above the mouth of the Yellowstone. Its bed is about two hundred yards wide, though the water seldom occupies more than one-third of that space, except during the spring thaws, when for a week or two it fills the entire bed, and even overflows the valley. It is fordable on horseback the year round, except at the time above mentioned, or when swollen by continued rains, and it might even be navigated with Mackinaw boats, when full, though the undertaking would be attended with some risk, owing to the large quantity of drift-wood, snags, and other obstructions. The water in a high stage has a white and milky appearance,[1] caused by its running through beds of white clay, stratas of which are found running nearly its whole length, more especially near the heads of most of its tributaries.

The Rivière aux Tremble, or Quaking Asp River, empties into

[1] The early pages of this chapter are missing from the Denig manuscript. Probably they included a brief statement on the history of the tribe and a description of the Assiniboine country's boundaries in the early 1850's. They may have comprised the information appearing in pages 379–82 of Hayden's *Contributions*. The portion of the first paragraph of this chapter down to here has been taken from p. 382 of Hayden's *Contributions*.

the Missouri about 50 miles below Milk River, is about the length and breadth of the other, and takes its rise in the range of hills constituting the divide called the Woody Mountains, is fordable at all times except during spring freshets, or when filled by heavy rains, at which times it could be navigated with small Mackinaw or flatboats, if floating ice or driftwood would permit.[2]

Several creeks fall into the Missouri lower down on the east side called Porcupine, Big Muddy, Little Muddy, Knife River, etc., none of which contain much water and are of little consequence. These with other small coulees serve to drain the plains of the water caused by snow and rain. They are, for the most part, miry in their beds and only fordable on horses in certain places where gravel bottoms are found.

After these comes White Earth River on the eastern boundary of the district now being discussed, which is 100 miles in length and at the mouth a little over 100 yards wide. This, like the others, becomes very full from the melting of snow in the spring, but falls low enough in the course of the summer to be fordable in most places either on foot or horse. This stream could not be descended at any time by boat, though wooden canoes might come down in the months of April and May. It takes its name from a kind of fine white pipe clay that is found in great quantity about half way to its head, and is supplied by water from springs in the Coteau de Prairie.

The entire country occupied by the Assiniboines, or hunted in exclusively by them, the outline of which has been given, embraces an area of about 20,000 square miles and presents the same general features as the rest of the Upper Missouri territory on the east side of the Missouri River, from La Rivière aux Jacques up. It may be said to be one great plain, hills and timber only occurring where rivers run. Even streams are wooded only a short distance up, which leaves immense tracts over which the traveler may pass for days in succession without meeting tree or brush. In the valleys of rivers good land for tilling purposes can be found, but the level

2 Denig's Quaking Asp[en] River is Poplar River, entering the Missouri from the north in present Roosevelt County, Montana.

plains present a sterile aspect, and it is presumed do not possess good arable qualities. The soil for the most part is not deep, but light and sandy, and absorbs rain readily in level places. Where hills intervene they are either composed of clay of different colours or covered with stone of various kinds. When their formation is clay they are washed by the rain into many grotesque and singular shapes; when of sand the action of the water and heat of the sun cuts out and bakes large portions into stone, though of a brittle kind. In either case but little grass if found on these elevations, neither are they common except along the water courses.

Some of the grasses indigenous to the soil are very nutritious and particularly adapted to horses, horned cattle and sheep. Of this kind is the perennial prairie grass with which the level plains are covered, the fine blue grass that grows in the river valleys, and the short, very fine, curly buffalo grass found everywhere, but thickest at the base and on the sides of gentle eminences. The mountainous and barren surface of the country only terminates after crossing the Coteau de Prairie which divides the waters of the Missouri from those of the Red River of the North, where both the nature of the soil and its general appearance assumes an entirely different character, which will meet with description when the Cree district comes under consideration.

Though wood cannot be found in the Assiniboine plains and buffalo chips are used by the natives for fuel in the summer season, or at any time when not covered by the snow, yet water can at all times be had from small lakes, or rather large ponds. These are met with in many places on the prairie, are formed by melting snow and rain, have no visible outlet, but diminish by evaporation and saturation. They differ in size from 100 yards to 2 or 3 miles in circumference, usually contain tolerable good water, are surrounded by a border of tall flags and rushes, and in the fall are covered with innumerable quantities of wild fowl. A few small springs occasionally are seen, but most of them have a mineral taste and possess active cathartic properties.

Notwithstanding the unquestioned dull and dreary appearance always presented by naked and extensive plains there are no places that could reasonably be termed deserts. There are some marshes, pools and swamps, which, however, are not so close together or of a nature to form any formidable obstruction to travel. Neither do they seem to affect the health of the natives any farther than their being the abodes of hosts of mosquitos, which are very annoying to men and beasts.

This region does not appear to have undergone any great volcanic change, though pieces of pumice stone and rocks in a state of fusion are occasionally picked up, and several hills have been burning for years, calcining the stones and earth of which they are composed, emitting dense volumes of smoke of a sulphurous smell, but not producing any eruption.

The principal hindrance to foot travelers in this district is the innumerable family of cacti, some of which are armed with very long and strong points and ruin the feet of any one walking without strong soles to his shoes. The dogs also used by the Indians for carrying burdens over the plains suffer severely from these thorns though the older and more experienced have the faculty of perceiving and avoiding them even while running.

The climate of this latitude is pure and dry, and perhaps the healthiest in the world. In the months of April, May and to the middle of June, when east winds prevail, much rain falls. During the rest of the summer and autumn the weather is dry and moderately warm, except for a short time in July and August when it is intensely hot. Some very sultry days bring severe thunder storms accompanied by rain or hail, which in a few hours swell the smaller streams so as to overflow their banks, but with the ceasing of the rain they fall as suddenly as they rose. The Missouri and most of its tributaries inundate the neighboring valleys when rain falls for 10 or 15 successive days. This usually happens in the month of June when they are already pretty full of water from the melting snow at their heads, and is not a very frequent occurrence. Strong gales of wind also come from the west and southwest in the form of sudden gusts prostrating numbers of trees along the banks of the Missouri. But these only last a few minutes and are not common.

The short summer season allows vegetation but little time to decay, and the firing of the prairies, which happens more or less every year in different parts, burns up all old grass, fallen timber and underbrush in the points. Owing perhaps partly to these things and partly to the equal and temperate degree of heat and moisture, the air is pure and sweet, but few epidemics rage among the migratory Indians. Fevers are unknown and nervous diseases seldom are seen.

The transition from summer to winter is very sudden. No long time intervenes equal to the Indian Summer of the States. A few days is often sufficient to deprive the trees of leaves, freeze up the running streams, and clothe the yet partially green plains with a garment of snow.

The winters are variable, mostly very cold, with deep snow. In the severest cold the mercury freezes and the degree cannot be determined in this way. It often remains frozen for several days and for weeks ranging between 30 and 40 degrees below zero. The snow storms in these times are terrible and certain death befalls those who are caught on the plains. Every extreme cold winter Indians are frozen to death, instances of which will be found recorded in these pages when their traveling is alluded to. Other winters are mild, but little snow falls, though there is always a short spell of intense cold, mostly in the month of January. When the winter proves mild and open a disagreeable spring follows. Snow falls in May and March and April produce cold winds, rain, snow and sleet. Occasionally, however, the spring opens finely and the change from winter to summer is as sudden as from warm to winter weather.

The constant exposure to cold inseparable from the lives and occupations of the natives, sleeping on damp ground, wet feet and insufficient clothing bring on bronchitis, pulmonary afflictions, rheumatism, and sometimes quinsy. These do not often prove immediately fatal, but in many cases undermine the constitution. By a reference to the table of temperature kept at Fort Union we find the longest winter on record to be that of 1844, when the river closed the 9th of November and opened the 21st of April.

These Indians raise no livestock, though judging from that reared at Fort Union near the mouth of the Yellowstone the country is well adapted to grazing purposes. The grasses of spontaneous growth are very nutritious and their supply inexhaustible. The only difficulty appears to be the severe cold of winter and deep snow. If animals were housed and provided for during a month or two in winter, it has been proven that a hardier and better stock can be raised in this section than in warmer climates. Sheep especially would thrive well if properly cared for, as far as grazing is concerned, though the great number of wolves prowling about would form an objection. Large quantities of good hay can be cut either on the Missouri bottoms or in the valleys of other streams. By experiments made near Fort Union it has been ascertained that oats, corn, potatoes and all garden vegetables grow well in favorable seasons. The soil being light and sandy requires frequent rains to produce good crops, which happens about 1 year in 3, the others fail from drought and destruction by grasshoppers, bugs and other insects.[3]

The natural productions of the soil are few and such as no person but an Indian could relish. Wild turnips, artichokes, service berries, chokecherries, red plums, rose buds, bull berries, gooseberries, currents, sour grapes and a plant similar to garden rhubarb are principal fruits and are greatly sought after by the Indians. These are dried, cooked in various ways and considered by them great luxuries. Wild hops are found in abundance which possess all the properties of the cultivated hop.

When the Assiniboines moved to the Missouri and contiguous territory now occupied by them they numbered, as has been observed, from 1,000 to 1,200 lodges. These did not all come at the same time, but by bands at different periods from 1800 to 1837, when the whole may be said to have established themselves on their present lands except that portion which still remains in the British territory.[4] Their first interview with white people was when the traders

[3] These pioneer agricultural experiments by traders at Fort Union are of historical significance. This locality is northwest of the known limits of aboriginal agriculture on the Missouri.

of the Mississippi pushed their traffic as far as their camps when conjoined with the Sioux, at which time they were the poorest of all Indians, and used knives made of the hump rib of a Buffalo, hatchets of flint stone, cooking utensils of clay or skin, awls and other tools made of bone and arrow points or spear heads of stone.[5] Some of these articles can still be found among them, but most have been replaced by more durable metallic instruments obtained from the traders.

As soon as enough had arrived on the Missouri to afford a trading establishment the American Fur Company built a fort on White Earth River for the trade. This post was removed in a year or two and a large, substantial fort built 3 miles above the mouth of Yellowstone River on the east side of the Missouri.[6] It required

[4] In 1833, Maximilian remarked on the population and territory of the Assiniboines: "They live in 3,000 tents; the territory which they claim as theirs is between the Missouri and the Saskatchewan, bounded on the east to Assiniboin River, and on the west to Milk River." (In Vol. XXII of Thwaites' *Early Western Travels*, 387.)

[5] The Assiniboines separated from the Yanktonai Dakotas prior to 1640, at which date they were mentioned by Jesuits as a separate tribe. (In Vol. XVII of Thwaites' *Jesuit Relations and Allied Documents*, 240.) Sixteen years later Father Allouez remarked that the Assiniboines had long been "discovered" by the French. *(Relations*, XLIV, 249.) At that time they occupied the country around Lake of the Woods and Lake Nipigon. After the establishment of the Hudson's Bay Company in 1670, the Assiniboines visited posts on Hudson Bay to trade. Their hunting grounds shifted northwestward toward and beyond Lake Winnipeg. They became firm allies of the Crees and warred upon the Sioux. By the early eighteenth century they were serving as middlemen, trading European goods to distant Plains Indians who had no direct contacts with Whites. In 1738, La Vérendrye accompanied Assiniboine traders to the Mandan villages on the Missouri, where he observed their exchange of firearms and ammunition, knives, kettles, and awls for Mandan corn, tobacco, buffalo robes, and other articles. *(Journals . . . of . . . La Vérendrye and His Sons* [ed. by L. J. Burpee], 332–33.) Assiniboine hunting grounds were extended westward and southward. In 1755, Anthony Hendry located the Eagle Indians, an Assiniboine division, as far west as the present Province of Saskatchewan. *(York Factory to the Blackfeet Country: The Journal of Anthony Hendry, 1754–1755* [ed. by L. J. Burpee], Royal Society of Canada *Proceedings and Transactions*, 3rd ser., Vol. I, Sec. II, 351). In 1804, Lewis and Clark learned that one Assiniboine band, the Big Devils, roamed the plains between the Missouri and the Saskatchewan rivers above the Yellowstone and the head of the Assiniboine River. This was the southwesternmost extension of the Assiniboine range reported at that time. (In Vol. VI of R. G. Thwaites' *Original Journals of Lewis and Clark*, 104.)

[6] The returns from Kenneth McKenzie's winter post at the mouth of White Earth

some years to bring these wild savages to anything like order. Guns, ammunition, knives and other things had to be furnished them gratis, horses sold cheap and every inducement held out to them to work and improve their condition. Although wretchedly supplied either with arms, clothing or other necessary articles, and subject to extreme want at all times, yet they were so lazy and improvident and their wants were so few that many years passed before the proceeds of their hunt did much more than pay the expenses of their trading establishment. Besides this they were of a thievish and malicious disposition, not bloodthirsty but tormenting the traders by stealing their horses, robbing and abusing the men in their employ, killing the domestic cattle of the fort and in short annoying them in every way. They were inconscionable beggars. Having been supplied with many things to induce them to work, they did not see why everything could not be had without any trouble on their part, and any refusal to supply their demands resulted in retaliation in some of the forms above mentioned. This state of affairs kept gradually growing worse until the fort gates were closed upon them and they were made to trade within close range of loaded cannon and lighted matches.

In the course of a long time, however, and by the unmitigated exertions of a few sensible traders, they were brought to pursue a correct course, and at the present date may be ranked among the best Indians in the N.W. Territory. Traders can stay in their camps or white travelers traverse their country with every security of life and property, though in either case some payment would be expected. They appear to look upon every person as a source from which benefit is to be derived, care but little for individuals or principles if some gain is realized. This runs through the whole course of their operations, either among themselves in camp, at

---

River were so encouraging that he moved upriver and established Fort Union above the mouth of the Yellowstone the next fall (1829). The chief of the Rock Band of Assiniboines is credited with having requested him to build his post at that location. (Larpenteur, *Forty Years a Fur Trader*, I, 108–109.) The most detailed description of Fort Union as a fur post was written by Denig for John James Audubon, July 30, 1843. *(Audubon and His Journals,* II, 180–88.)

the fort with traders, or in their peace makings with other nations. It is more or less the great motive of all savage nations. It forms the basis of all their transactions or even their tribal organization, and will be better understood when pursuing that portion of this work where their manners and customs are treated in detail.[7]

The first calamity by which this nation was cast down was the smallpox of 1838, which has been already alluded to in the history of other nations. This disease made its appearance in Fort Union when the steamboat arrived in the month of June with the annual supplies of the post. No Indians were then near except the wives of the engagees of the Fur Company in the fort, every one of whom caught the infection. In a short time 30 persons were laid up. When the first band came, they were met a mile from the place by good interpreters who represented to them the danger of going near and goods were brought out with the view of trading with them at a distance. All efforts of the kind, however, proved unavailing. They would not listen, and passed on to the fort, and 250 lodges or upwards of 1000 souls contracted the disease at the same time, which during the summer and fall reduced them to thirty lodges or about 150 persons old and young. Other bands coming in from time to time caught the infection, some of which remained at the fort where the dead were daily thrown into the river by cart loads. Others attempted to run away from it. The different roads were dotted with carcasses and occasionally lodges standing in which whole families lay dead. A singular characteristic of this disease was that two-thirds or more died before any eruption appeared. This event was always accompanied by hermorrhages from the mouth and ears. Except in some few cases of the distinct kind, the fever always rose to a pitch of frenzy, in which state many committed suicide or died in other horrid forms. An Indian near the fort, named the Little Dog, after losing his favorite child, proposed to his wife to kill the whole family before they were so much disfigured as to present a disgusting appearance in the future world.

[7] This portion of Denig's writings is not with the manuscript in the Missouri Historical Society. He may never have completed the detailed description of Indian manners and customs, which he had planned, before his death in 1858.

71

She agreed with the stipulation that he should kill her before the children as she did not wish to witness their death. The man then went to work deliberately, shot all his horses and dogs, then his wife, then cut the throats of his two children and lastly blew his own brains out.

It was an awful time for the poor Assiniboines. Run where they would, remain where they might, they carried the disease with them. With those who remained about the fort remedies were tried but in few if any cases did success follow. They were bled and died, purged and died. Every kind of care was taken of some old and tried friends. Still nothing but death was the result. A solitary instance here and there of a healthy woman or child who had a mild attack, recovered without any assistance. Before all were prostrated the Indians tried their own remedies, but none appeared to be in the least beneficial. They continued dying until the middle of the ensuing winter, when the disease having spent itself, ceased. Out of the upwards of 1000 lodges of Assiniboines but 400 remained. Of these 200 were saved by having been vaccinated in former years by the Hudson's Bay Company. These only lost some children and others who had not applied this preventative.[8]

Among the rest relationship was nearly extinguished, all property lost or sacrified, and generally very old or very young persons were the only ones who recovered. Most of the principal men having died, it took years to recover from the shock. Young men had to grow up, remnants of bands had to be collected, new leaders to be formed, property to be had. In fact, under all these adverse circumstances so slow has been their increase that during a period of 17 years but 100 lodges have accumulated. Nevertheless, through all these distressing and trying scenes the Indians have behaved remarkably well toward the whites. Although aware they were primarily the cause of the disorder being brought among them

8 Denig's account of the smallpox epidemic among the Assiniboines in 1837–38 is that of an eyewitness. According to Larpenteur (*Forty Years a Fur Trader*, I, 131–35), Denig, himself, had the smallpox at that time, his case "ending favorably." Denig described this epidemic more briefly in *Indian Tribes of the Upper Missouri*, 399–400. According to Larpenteur the Assiniboines were reduced to less than half their former numbers by the spring of 1838.

yet nothing in the way of revenge took place either at the time or afterwards. Neither was insult or reproach heaped upon those whom they had every reason to blame as the authors of their misfortune. Indians only resent smaller evils resulting from comprehensible, human agency. National calamities are attributed to the powerful hand of the Great Spirit and submitted to in awe and silence.

When in this stage of adversity, and after the disease had entirely disappeared, one of their chiefs formed a daring project to retrieve their ruined fortunes. This man was old. He had had the smallpox when in the British territory and therefore escaped at the present time. His name had undergone several changes in the course of his lifetime, as is their custom when fortunate achievements entitle them to this distinction. The first name by which he was known was *Chat kâh* or Left Handed, usually called "The Gauche" by the French traders or Indian interpreters. Afterwards this name gave way before that of *Tah to'ka nah,* or the Antelope, from some exploit in which he distinguished himself, and lastly *Me'nah u hi'nah,* or He Who Holds the Knife, was the title bestowed upon him on the occasion described in the following brief sketch of his life and character.

About the year 1776 and from that time till 1800 the band now known as the band "du Gauche" inhabited the English country, and the man above named, then a child, had recovered from the smallpox of that period. By some means, when a young man, he gained possession of poisonous drugs by the use of which he removed several persons who had offended him in various ways. This he accomplished in such an adroit and secret manner as to lull suspicion, but always predicted their deaths before hand. This in the course of time led the Indians to believe that he was inspired with the spirit of prophecy. By a continuance of this course and risking other predictions he worked himself up to the chief of the band in a few years and was more feared for his supposed supernatural powers than any other Indian of modern times. He made no scruples of administering poison to any of his people who stood in his way to power, and had, it is said, several agents to aid him in his nefarious practice. The simple minds of the Indians at that time and their complete ignorance of deleterious drugs rendered them easily imposed upon. Thus the Gauche increased in popularity through fear of his power. Still, however, something more was wanting to render his power absolute. It was necessary that he should lead parties to war or be suspected of being wanting in personal bravery. Now this was no easy matter, for the Gauche was an arrant coward and had as yet never struck an enemy. Perhaps he presents the only instance among the tribes where a man became a chief and was invested with supreme authority though destitute of every particle of personal daring.

To remedy this and meet as well as he could the demands of his people as their leader, he struck out into something new in their manner of warfare. He pretended to turn the tide of victory in their favor by his medicine ceremonies. For this purpose he made a huge drum out of a hollow log, a skin head on one end, which with the rest of the instrument was covered with rude drawings of monsters, said by him to have been revealed in dreams and to possess a magical influence over his people on every important occasion. The band over which he ruled consisted of upward of 250 lodges among whom good warriors were found. These were all assembled at the sound of the drum whenever the Gauche's medicine intimated a favorable time for war expeditions, and he usually started at the head of such a force as was not likely to suffer defeat. On the excursions this chief took no arms but had his drum carried along. He was not encumbered with anything but his medicine pipe and always rode a fleet horse.

What means this man had to gain information regarding the location and numbers of his enemies is not known but the fact can be well attested that he did know and that his predictions were invariably fulfilled. Whether his men fought better under their superstitious belief in his powers and prophecies, or whether he arranged the attack with the sagacity of a good warrior is uncertain, but his party always came off victorious in their battles with the Blackfeet, even against superior odds.

During these engagements the Gauche usually took up a position

CRAZY BEAR, Assiniboine head chief. From a pencil portrait by Rudolph F. Kurz, 1851.

THE LIGHT, an Assiniboine Indian en route to and returning from Washington. From a painting by George Catlin, 1832.

alone, if possible on a hill, and always at a respectable distance from the battleground. Here he went through his medicine ceremonies with his pipe and drum, invoking the aid of the supernatural powers with every appearance of intense devotion. The day was commonly decided in his favor, but when defeat followed and he perceived his party in full retreat, he hastily packed up his drum and pipe, mounted his swift horse and was the first to fly. In the few instances during a war of many years that this chief was obliged to run away, he always made out to throw the blame on some of his people or on some defect in his magic instruments. In this way and by repeated success this man acquired a standing among the whole nation of Assiniboines far beyond anyone then existing or since brought into notice. His very name was sacred. Even yet, although he has been dead 14 years, they seldom can be induced to mention his name, or when anyone plucks up courage enough to do this it is only done in a whisper.

When in the height of his power, and his people confirmed in their belief of his prophecies, a circumstance happened which aided greatly to substantiate his interests, conferring upon him at the same time that distinguished honor among Indians which entitles them to change of name. His camp was placed a short distance up the Rivière aux Tremble and had been for some time at rest from their war excursions, but were waiting patiently for the sound of the magic drum to recall them to their favorite pastime. One night it came booming on the breeze while all were sound asleep, and the warriors hastily and willingly rose to obey its summons. The music continued until all had arrived and great was the crowd inside and around the large lodge of the chief, though no noise nor indecorous behavior was observed. Each waited until the leader thought proper to deliver himself of the intelligence his medicine imparted.

The Gauche was a man of few words. Even these were often of an ambiguous nature, somewhat in the form of the ancient oracles leaving a chance of escape in the event of his non-fulfillment of his predictions. The amount of his expressions on this occasion was that while the camp slept a body of Gros Ventres of the Prairie had passed by on their way to a smaller camp below, and that their absence from their homes would be a favorable opportunity of making an attack. The warriors were ordered to prepare and when day broke a force of 400 or 500 men were ready for the expedition.

They started, headed by their chief who promised success. This was readily believed as the tracks of the war party that passed by had been seen in the morning. They reached the place foretold by the chief, found a small camp of Gros Ventres of the Prairie, whom they exterminated and reaped great spoil. This they accomplished without any loss as most of the men of the camp were absent on the war expedition referred to. The party returned loaded with scalps of women and children and well supplied with horses.

When about half way back to their village a thick fog arose one morning. The party separated into several divisions unable to see each other, but continued their march in a homeward direction. In this partial obscurity those in front came in sudden and close contact with the returning Gros Ventres war party and a fight ensued. The Assiniboines behind and scattered rushed forward when the firing was going on, and the enemies, perceiving themselves engaged with a superior force, endeavored to escape, but in doing so met their opponents in all directions. At the beginning of the affray the Gauche was behind with a few others. They, pressing forward, were soon lost sight of. In this situation he endeavored to reach his people but came in contact with some of the enemy. The chief as usual had no arms. They, perceiving this, rushed upon him with their knives. Now the Gauche was a strong man and handled with ease the one who grappled him. But others came. He received some stabs and would have been killed but for the timely arrival of some of his people. The enemies fled at their approach except the one held down by the chief, from whom he wrested his knife, buried it in his breast and tore off his scalp. This was done in the presence of his own people, who afterwards called him "He Who Holds the Knife." The result of this skirmish being in favor of the Assiniboines, the fame of the Gauche rose to a still higher pitch.

In the ensuing summer a war expedition on a large scale was planned against the Blackfeet to which some bands of Cree Indians were invited to join. Their entire force amounted to between 1,100 and 1,200 warriors, who, pursuing the directions and under the command of the Gauche in person, massacred 30 lodges of the Gros Ventres of the Prairies. By his usual good fortune he arrived with his warriors at a time when all the men of the village except eight or ten were out hunting. The few men in camp defended themselves bravely but all were killed, also every woman and child found there, who numbered about 130 souls. This was a terrible massacre. The children were killed and tormented to death in every possible variety of savage warfare. Many were roasted alive by a pointed stick being run through the body and planting it in the ground before a hot fire. No prisoners were taken, no mercy shown. But one or two boys escaped to bring the dreadful intelligence to the ears of their people. A great many horses were also taken by the Assiniboines on this occasion. One warrior counted 14 children for his share in this work of destruction.

By such lucky hits as these the Gauche was enabled to sustain his position as the leader of the band, and indeed the whole nation, until the smallpox of 1838 interposed its destroying agency. The whole of the band caught the disease almost at the same time, which soon reduced them from 250 lodges to about 30 lodges, and these occupied by 150 persons old and young. The chief, having had the disorder in former times, escaped, but found himself in command of about 60 persons able to bear arms, mostly old men and young boys.

Notwithstanding this great reverse of fortune his warrior spirit did not leave him. Hearing that the Mandans had suffered so severely by the same disease as to be incapable of defense, he formed a daring project for their extinction. His plan was, to visit the Mandan village with the pipe of peace, and after entering it on friendly terms, to fall upon the inhabitants knife in hand at a given signal, and after killing them possess themselves of all the horses and other property belonging to that people. The whole was well planned, kept secret, and would have succeeded but for a circumstance of which the Assiniboine was unaware. The Arikaras, a numerous tribe, had left their homes on the Missouri, been for years residing on the Platte River, and having had the smallpox there, did not contract the disease after they returned to any great extent. About the time the Gauche started on his way to the Mandans these (the Rees) suddenly came to and took possession of the lower village of the Mandans, that they had abandoned.[9]

The Gauche, ignorant of this, presented himself before the Mandans, taking his usual place on the hills and sending forward most of his party, which consisted of 52, with the pipe of peace. The former nation, anxious to make a peace with their hitherto hostile neighbors, eagerly embraced this occasion, and came out some distance to meet the deputation. A halt was made on the prairie. The parties met, seated themselves and proceeded to open negotiations with the pipe. Now the formula of peace making between two savage nations is somewhat tedious. The ceremonies with the pipe, the speeches, etc., usually take the best part of a day to get through with. During this time it seems something had been done or said which led the Mandans to believe their supposed friends meditated some treachery. They, therefore, secretly sent off an express to the Arickaras requesting their presence. The distance is not far and in a few hours the latter made their appearance in great force. The Assiniboines, seeing the plans broken, ran away, were followed by the Rees and Mandans, and about 20 of them were slain. The Gauche, having the start of his position, escaped.[10]

From this time his power ceased as a ruler, though he was feared for his other qualifications. Shortly after this he predicted his own

[9] The Arikaras took possession of the former Mandan village near Fort Clark, March 20, 1838. (Chardon's *Journal,* 153.)

[10] Other accounts of this action state that it was the Hidatsas rather than the Mandans who were aided by the Arikaras against the Assiniboines, and that the latter's losses were greater than were reported by Denig. In his *Journal* (167–68), Chardon dates the battle July 12, 1838, identifies the leader of the Assiniboines as "He That Holds the Knife," and states that sixty-four of his men were killed and eight women taken prisoner in this action. Five years later, Audubon was told of this battle in which "La Main Gauche" left seventy warriors killed and thirty wounded on the prairie in the year following the smallpox epidemic. (*Audubon and His Journals,* II, 156.)

death to the hour, several days beforehand. It happened at the time specified by him, although not preceded by any disease or approaching dissolution. The conclusion was that he took poison, which was long supposed to have been in his possession, and kept for the fullness of time. Since his death the band headed by this man has received additions from other bands and from some of the Assiniboines of the north, but still preserves the name of this renowned leader.[11]

The present divisions of this Nation are the following:

1. Wah tó pah an da to Gens du Gauche	100	lodges average 4 persons
2. Minne she nák a to Gens du Lac	60	lodges average 4 persons
3. É an tó an Gens des Roches	50	lodges average 4 persons
4. We ché ap pe nah Gens des Filles	60	lodges average 4 persons
5. Wa tó pap pe nah Gens des Canots	220	lodges average 4 persons
6. Wah zé ab or To kúm pe Gens du Nord	30 to 50	lodges average 4 persons

$$520 \times 4 = 2,080 \text{ souls}$$

Several smaller bands are also found near the Mountain du Bois,

[11] During his lifetime this chief was well known to traders and travelers in the Upper Missouri country. Larpenteur met him when he went to trade at Fort William early in 1833. (*Forty Years a Fur Trader*, I, 56–59.) Maximilian witnessed the attack of a large Assiniboine and Cree force under his leadership upon a small Piegan trading party outside Fort McKenzie, August 28, 1833. He referred to this chief by the name of Knife-holder, and claimed that he changed his name to "*Tatogan* (the antelope)" after this battle. Maximilian learned that in the following fall this chief "offended on account of the battle at Fort McKenzie had gone northwards with a hundred tents to the English, in order to trade with the Hudson's Bay Company." (In Vol. XXIII of Thwaites' *Early Western Travels*, 146–53, 204.) Additional information appears in the biographical sketch of this chief which Denig wrote for Father De Smet. (*Life, Letters, and Travels*, III, 1,111–41.) In that account, Denig stated that The Gauche died at Fort Union in the autumn of 1843.

but these, for the most part belong to and reside in the English territory.[12]

The Gens du Gauche above named inhabit that part of the district described along the Woody Mountains on the west side in summer, often moving westward to the heads of the Rivière aux Tremble, and towards fall place their camp at or above Big Muddy River or along the first named stream. In this direction along the east shore of the Missouri wintering houses are built by the Fur Company for the convenience of the Indians and collecting the buffalo robes and other skins they raise by hunting. These are tolerably good hunters, have some pretty fast horses which they get from the Gros Ventres of the Prairie, with whom a peace has existed for the last 3 or 4 years. A good many horses are also supplied them by the Fur Company in exchange for their skins.[13]

Since the death of the chief who has been made the subject of the foregoing article, the band has been portioned out as it were

[12] In addition to the six Southern Assiniboine bands listed above, Denig recognized the "northern Assiniboin, 250 or 300 lodges, rove the country from the west banks of the Saskatchewan, Assiniboin, and Red Rivers in a westward direction to the Woody Mountains north and west among spurs of the Rocky Mountains east of the Missouri, and among chains of small lakes through this immense region. Occasionally making peace with some of the northern bands of Blackfeet enables them to come a little farther west and deal with those Indians, but 'peace' being of short duration, they are for the most part limited to the prairies east and north of the Blackfeet range." (*Indian Tribes of the Upper Missouri*, 396.)

The number and names of Assiniboine bands were imperfectly recorded by early writers. Lewis and Clark named but three bands, terming them tribes. (In Thwaites' *Original Journals*, I, 221; VI, 104.) Alexander Henry named twelve Assiniboine bands, found mainly near trading posts in Canada and totaling 880 lodges in 1809. (Alexander Henry and David Thompson, *New Light on the Early History of the Greater Northwest* [ed. by Elliott Coues], II, 522–23.) Maximilian listed eight Assiniboine bands in 1833. (In Vol. XXII of Thwaite's *Early Western Travels*, 387–88.) But the ethnologist, Robert H. Lowie, obtained from informants a list of seventeen bands among the Assiniboines. ("The Assiniboine," American Museum of Natural History *Anthropological Papers*, Vol. IV, Pt. 1, pp. 33–34.)

[13] Denig translated the Indian name of this band "Those Who Propel Boats." (*Indian Tribes of the Upper Missouri*, 430.) David Rodnick claimed this band was known as Big Devils to John McDonnell (1793) and Lewis and Clark (1804), and after Denig's time was named the Mountain Village Band. He found descendants of this band on Fort Belknap Reservation, Montana, in 1935. (*The Fort Belknap Assiniboine of Montana*, 34.)

to several men of equal standing who govern their different parts when separated in summer, but when all are assembled for winter operations they are ruled in a body by The Whirlwind.[14] This man exhibits no distinctive feature from others in his position. He is known as a good warrior, has conducted war expeditions with success, and behaved bravely on many occasions. These acts, together with his family connections, entitled him to precedence as is usual with the roving tribes.

The Gens des Canots are commonly found along the White Earth River, extend their travels in the summer season as far north as the heads of La Rivière aux Souris, Grand Coulee and Pambinar River.[15] Indeed the entire extent of country east of Fort Union as far down as the Great Bend is hunted by them at different times. But owing to the absence of wood on this great plain they are obliged to place their camp on or near the Missouri in the winter season. They are usually found at that time either on White Earth River or above that point where trading houses are established and they are dealt with in the same way as the others. Some 15 or 20 lodges of this band trade at the posts of the Hudson's Bay Company or with the half-breeds of Red River who visit their camp during the winter with dog sleds loaded with merchandise. These Indians of later years have been much troubled with Sioux war parties, have been run away from their customary hunting grounds which, it is believed, will before long be occupied by that great and warlike nation.

In proportion as buffalo recede from the Sioux country, that people are forced to follow them and being numerous must displace weaker tribes to provide for their own subsistence. Every year the battles between the Sioux and Assiniboines become more frequent,

[14] Denig listed "La Main qui tremble" as chief of the Gens du Gauche in c.1854, and mentioned Whirlwind as a noted warrior. (*Indian Tribes of the Upper Missouri*, 402–31.)

[15] Alexander Henry listed a Canoe Band of Assiniboines, numbering 160 lodges in 1809. (*New Light*, II, 552.) Maximilian named the "*Otaopabine* (les gens des canots)" as an Assiniboine band in 1833 (In Vol. XXII of Thwaite's *Early Western Travels*, 387.) Descendants of the *Wato'pabin* were located by Rodnick on Fort Peck Reservation, Montana, in 1935. (*The Fort Belknap Assiniboine*, 34.)

but as the latter are on the alert no great damage has as yet resulted. A few killed on both sides or some horses taken off generally determines the success of these collisions. The band now being discussed suffer more than others from their approximate location and have been obliged to consolidate by joining with or establishing near other portions of their people farther west. This part of the nation is poorly furnished with horses. When by great exertion and a considerable lapse of time they have accumulated animals either by trade with the Company or by exchanges with their people, they are visited by Sioux or Blackfoot warriors who sweep off the whole. This being the case, but little trade is had with them for skins. Neither do they show any great disposition to improve their condition, considering it hardly worth while to amass property, particularly horses, which are liable at any moment to be taken from them.

The chief of this band is The Rattle Snake, a very good Indian, and of course endowed with the usual qualifications necessary to a savage ruler.[16]

The remaining bands mentioned are scattered over the intervening region between the locations of the two already spoken of, move about near the divide in warm weather, approaching the Missouri in the fall and stationing themselves on its banks or low down on some of its tributaries. These bands commonly make their winter hunt near the Rivière aux Tremble and along that stream, but when traveling over the unwooded plains permits, proceed as far north as the Cypress Mountains. Some of them, especially those called Les Gens du Nord, go still farther and make their trade either at some of the Hudson's Bay Company's posts on Assiniboine River or with the Red River half-breeds.[17]

[16] Denig stated *"Wo'a-see-chah,* or Bad Animal, known to traders by the name Le Serpent, is a war leader and chief of Les Gens des Canots . . . I believe he has never killed many enemies but has murdered in quarrels two of his own people, is considered a sensible man, very friendly to the whites, judicious in his government of his band, and also a person whom it is not desirable to aggrevate too much." *(Indian Tribes of the Upper Missouri,* 402.)

[17] Denig listed the Gens du Lac of the above table as Gens du Nord, "thus named because they came from that direction in 1839 . . . though their original appelation

The ruling chief of the whole nation is named *Mau to weet ko,* or the Foolish Bear, who has always been considered a good and sensible man and lately confirmed in his office by the Commissioners at Laramie Treaty.[18] He is somewhat more elevated in his opinions than most of his people, but does not rank so high as a warrior as some, though he has on occasions shown an utter contempt of danger before his enemies. He is a mild, politic man, looking to the interests of his people and viewing with suspicion anything inconsistent with them. Even when a very young man he had a voice in council, respect was paid to his opinions, and he now conducts the affairs of the nation with great credit to himself and satisfaction of his followers. He uses every exertion to bring his people strictly to conform to the stipulations of the treaty and, we believe, has succeeded in this as well, if not better than, any other chief connected by that alliance.

He is a sterling friend of all white men and his speeches exhibit considerable mental powers. At all events his whole mind is given to produce a good understanding between his people and the United States Government. It is pleasant to perceive good and amiable qualities in a leader among these rude tribes. The majority of such men are nothing more than savage warriors, listened to and obeyed through the principle of fear or extensive relationship. But this

was Gens du Lac." He designated the sixth band of the above table The Red Root Band, and told of its organization as the result of separation from the Canoe Band since c.1844. *(Indian Tribes of the Upper Missouri,* 430–32.) Rodnick identified the Red Root Band as the Red Buttock Band of Assiniboines, located in Canada in 1935. *(The Fort Belknap Assiniboine,* 34.)

[18] Maximilian met *"Manto-Uitkatt* (the mad bear)"*, one of "several distinguished men of the Assiniboins," at Fort Union, October 20, 1833. (In Vol. XXIII of Thwaites' *Early Western Travels,* 202.) Larpenteur considered him "the greatest chief of the Assiniboines." *(Forty Years a Fur Trader,* I, 184.) Rudolph F. Kurz met this chief after his return from the Fort Laramie Treaty Council of 1851, and drew several pencil portraits of him at Fort Union. *(Journal,* plates 7, 32, 34.) In 1854, Father De Smet received a letter from this chief requesting him to send Catholic missionaries to the Assiniboines. *(Life, Letters, and Travels,* III, 934–35.) According to James J. Long, a modern Assiniboine, Crazy [Foolish] Bear died northwest of Fort Union during a smallpox epidemic, at seventy years of age. ("The Fort Benton Journal, 1854–1856 and the Fort Sarpy Journal, 1855–1856" [ed. by Anna McDonnell], Montana Historical Society *Contributions,* Vol. X, 291.)

man has neither. He belongs to the band called Gens des Filles, which is one of the smallest portions of the nation, and his immediate kindred are very few in comparison with many others in subordinate command.[19] Still the whole of them feel that he has more intelligence and is in other respects better able to regulate their affairs both with whites and other nations. Consequently the chieftainship in his hands is not a post of contention as would otherwise be the case if war alone had been the cause of his elevation.

When the circular issued by Col. Mitchell, then Superintendent of Indian Affairs, was explained to the Assiniboines by A. Culbertson, Esq., Agent of the American Fur Co., not a single Indian except The Foolish Bear would consent to go. They did not wish to risk themselves among the large body of Sioux on whose ground the treaty was to be held. Besides the road to Laramie being up the Yellowstone in the summer, when that river is literally stocked with Blackfoot war parties, their deadly enemies, did not present flattering views of their safe arrival. Indeed the trip was one of extreme danger to all concerned, and nothing but the good council and great exertions of the above named gentleman induced the Indians to undertake it. After the Crazy Bear had determined on going several others joined the expedition. In due time, however, the deputation returned safe. But the chief on his arrival at Fort Union was fated to mourn the loss of some of his relatives. During his absence his son had been killed by the Blackfeet, his child died, and his wife hung herself.

To anyone well acquainted with the superstitious notions entertained by Indians of misfortune under those circumstances it would be surprising to learn that the chief did not destroy himself, or resign his authority, which commenced under such unfavorable auspices. It is the invariable custom of savages to throw the blame of any calamity on whites, particularly if any papers are passed

[19] Alexander Henry wrote that the "Little Girl" Band of Assiniboines numbered two hundred lodges and inhabited "Rivière la Souris, the Moose Hills, and Tête à la Biche" in 1809. *(New Light,* II, 522.) Maximilian listed "Itscheabine (les gens des filles)" as an Assiniboine band in 1833. (In Vol. XXII of Thwaites' *Early Western Travels,* 387.) Rodnick found descendants of the Girl's Band on Fort Peck Reservation, Montana, in 1935. *(The Fort Belknap Assiniboine,* 34.)

or handed to them before the accident occurs. They look upon these things as a judgment for being considered in some measure contrary to the will of the Great Spirit. Though much grieved at what had happened, yet he behaved like a man, and as soon as he could recover sufficient spirit proceeded to make known to his people the spirit of the treaty.

It also happened that the first annual presents of goods promised at the treaty did not arrive the ensuing summer. Neither did any agent make his appearance on the part of the Government until the middle of the next winter when Mr. Culbertson was especially appointed and came up from St. Louis for that purpose. In the long interim the nation became dissatisfied, ridiculed the chief. They said he had been trifled with, laughed at, and they did everything they could to turn him against the Government. His name was harangued throughout the camp as one who had come back from the White's country with a lie in his mouth, or had sold their lands for a handful of goods. The old chief stood alone against his people and maintained the equanimity of his temper. He never swerved a particle but placed implicit faith in the Government, though he had a hard time of it with his people. However, when the gentleman above named came and issued out ten thousand dollars worth of goods as the Government's presents for the first year, the Indians were struck dumb and those who before reproached now flattered their ruler. On this occasion he made a speech which bears evidence of the solidity of his views.[20] Since the time above mentioned the nation has received its presents yearly. This has tended to increase the respect always manifested towards the "Bear." His people are disposed to listen to his council and pretty generally conform to his decrees, though he possesses nothing like arbitrary power.

After according all this merited praise it is rather painful to state that, although a man of nearly fifty years, his amorous propensities are so great as to cause a great deal of difficulty with several of his band. On one or two occasions his life has been in danger from intrigues carried on with the wives of some of his soldiers, and it

[20] Denig recorded this speech, presumably in its entirety, in *Indian Tribes of the Upper Missouri*, 598–600.

is often said that this course if persisted in must eventually lead to his overthrow.

After The Foolish Bear, the leader of the Gens des Roches is perhaps the principal war captain. His name is *To káh ke á non ot,* The First Who Flies.[21] He is the son of the old chief known as *Wah hé muzza.*[22] The whole of this old man's family have been and those now living still are desperate men.

The first was named The Light, who visited Washington City by General Jackson's orders during his administration. On his return to his people loaded with presents and honours from the President he assumed a high tone of manner and action. He related

[21] Kurz noted that "Le Premiere qui Vole" was Denig's brother-in-law, who had counted more coups and had more followers than had Foolish Bear, and who might have been head chief of the tribe "but for his impetuous temper." *(Journal,* 242.) De Smet mentioned that this Indian traveled with him to the treaty council at Fort Laramie in 1851. *(Life, Letters, and Travels,* III, 1117.) Denig himself wrote that "First Who Flies" had "frequently led parties to battle and showed such recklessness of danger that his name stands high as a warrior; has also killed two of his own people who were concerned in the murder of his brothers; was at the Laramie Treaty and since behaves himself with great moderation; is one of Crazy Bear's principal soldiers and supports; and should the Bear die would undoubtedly take his place as chief of the tribe." *(Indian Tribes of the Upper Missouri,* 401–402.) This man's great-grandson, Joshua Wetsit, was chairman of the Tribal Council on Fort Peck Reservation for many years, and was this editor's able interpreter on that reservation in 1953.

The Gens Des Roches Band was referred to as the "Stone or Rocky Assiniboines, who dwell about the Skunk Wood hills or Montagne de Foudre ("Thunder hill"), numbering forty lodges, by Henry in 1809. *(New Light,* II, 523.) Maximilian listed the "Jatonabine (les gens des roches)" as an Assiniboine band in 1833. (In Vol. XXII of Thwaites' *Early Western Travels,* 387.) Rodnick located the Stone Band in Canada in 1935. (The *Fort Belknap Assiniboine,* 34.) The Canadian Indian Census of 1944 listed 769 Indians living on the Stony Reserve near Morley, Alberta.

[22] *Wah hé muzza* (Iron Arrow Point), claimed to have recalled the separation of the Assiniboines from the Sioux and to have met Lewis and Clark on the Missouri in 1805. The first claim was patently false. Nevertheless, he was a prominent Assiniboine chief known to traders as Le Gros François. He was said to have fathered fifty children by his several wives. (De Smet, *Life, Letters, and Travels,* III, 1176.) He died at an advanced age some years prior to 1850. After his death his body was laid out in his lodge and the lodge closed tight in accordance with his orders. He had said "he wished to remain above ground in order to see and hear his children all the time and to have the spot rendered remarkable by his being there." (Denig, *Indian Tribes of the Upper Missouri,* 401–402, 573.)

to his ignorant and gaping enquirers the strange sights and customs he had seen in his travels. He described the magnificent houses, large ships and innumerable hosts of white people, enlarging upon their powers and riches, which to the untutored minds of his hearers appeared as the relation of the fables handed down from their ancestors. Day after day and night after night this man described the wonders of machinery, the fine horses and carriages, furniture, dress and all the display of eastern cities. In all this the Indian told the truth, and less than the truth, for their simple minds could not grasp the tithe of what he recounted. But he was not aware that he engendered a spirit of envy among his hearers. However, this was the case. They envied the means of people so much more comfortably situated than they, and were vexed that only he had been allowed to see and partake of the profusion. When the novelty of his stories had worn off, some began to doubt his word. This ended in his killing one, shortly after which he was shot by the brother of the deceased.[23] The Indian law of retaliation

[23] The tragic death of this Indian following his visit to Washington is one of the best known stories of the Indians of the Upper Missouri. George Catlin painted his portrait in St. Louis while he was en route to Washington in 1831. Catlin accompanied him upriver on the steamboat *Yellowstone* on his homeward journey the following summer, and painted a double portrait contrasting his clothing and appearance en route to and returning from Washington, as well as writing a colorful account of the events leading to his murder. *(Letters and Notes,* I, 55–56; II, 194–200.) However, Denig's own account of this man's travels and violent death probably is much more accurate. (De Smet, *Life, Letters and Travels,* III, 1177–85.) Maximilian met this Indian at Fort Union in the summer of 1833, and again on October 20 of that year, at which time he was first chief of his band of forty-two lodges, and an orator of outstanding ability (In Vol. XXIII of Thwaites' *Early Western Travels,* 20–21, 201.) It is apparent, therefore, that he survived his trip to Washington by more than a year. Larpenteur claimed that following his death "he was brought to Fort Union and buried . . . in a tree. In the summer a requisition for Indian skulls was made by some physicians from St. Louis. His head was cut off and sent down in a sact with many others." Catlin erroneously named this man *"Wi-jún-jon,* The Pigeon's Egg Head." However, Larpenteur referred to him as *"Lya-jan-jan* (the Shining Man)." Joshua Wetsit, a descendant of his brother, told me that his name fully translated meant "something transparent and bright" so that Denig's "The Light" was a reasonable translation. For a more complete account of his life see John C. Ewers, "When the Light Shone in Washington," *Montana, the Magazine of Western History,* Vol. VI, 2–11.

requires the next of kin to revenge the death, and his brother, named le Sucre, killed the offender. In the course of another year he was killed in turn by some of the relatives and this imposed the revenge of his death on his next brother who was named The Broken Cloud, who, after killing the other, was himself slain a short time afterward. Now the one whose name occurs at the beginning of the sketch shot down the murderer of his brother last named, since which retaliation had ceased on the other side, most probably from an inferiority in number.[24] This man has behaved bravely on several war expeditions against enemies and raised his name as high if not higher than any of the warrior class. However, he has given up war of late years, was at the Laramie Treaty and since his return conducts himself well both with whites and his own people.

There are many good leaders of war parties, or soldiers as they are called, among this nation, sketches of whose lives would present the usual bloody character of Indian warfare, but are too numerous to be entered into largely. Of these is one named *Wah ké un to*, or The Blue Thunder, of the Gens des Canots who is not over 28 years of age but has raised himself to distinction by going to war upon the Sioux alone and bringing home scalps and horses. He has also headed several large war excursions with success and is generally liked by his own people.[25] Others of the same kind are known by the names of The Knife, Grey Eyes, Wind Blanket, etc., who are leaders and camp soldiers.[26]

The general disposition of the Assiniboines has been alluded to. In the first years of their residence on the Missouri they were

[24] Denig wrote that this feud ended when "the smallpox epidemic [of 1837] settled the affair by taking off the offenders on the other side." *(Indian Tribes of the Upper Missouri, 453.)*

[25] Denig gives an almost identical characterization of The Blue Thunder in *Indian Tribes of the Upper Missouri,* 402.

[26] Denig listed "Les Yeux Gris" (Grey Eyes) as chief of the Gens des Filles Band, and "Le Robe de vent" (Wind Blanket) as chief of the Gens du Nord (which is the Gens du Lac of this manuscript) in 1854. *(Indian Tribes of the Upper Missouri, 431.)*

famed for being lazy, thieving, ignorant and malicious. They had but little home regulation, governed by very precarious and insufficient laws, and did not respect the private rights of their own or any other people. By a judicious and well regulated trade, however, they have been greatly changed for the better. They may now be reckoned among the best Indians of the Upper Missouri. Their domestic arrangements and dress have also undergone great improvement. What was once filthy skin clothing has given way before good and handsome apparel of American manufacture, which enables both sexes of all ages to appear tolerably neat and clean. The laws by which the camp is regulated are radically the same as other roving tribes.

Up to the date 1844, the nation was surrounded entirely by hostile tribes. The Crow Indians were on the south, the Blackfeet on the west, the Gros Ventres of the Prairie on the northwest, the Minnetarres on the east, and the Sioux on the southeast. The Crees were their only allies and the country inhabited by the latter was the only road open to them for hunting when game failed in their own. Notwithstanding all this they defended themselves well. They are considered good warriors, are famous for a sudden rush on enemies, for their horse stealing qualifications and, when brought to a stand, are known to fight with almost unequaled desperation.

In their wars with the Crows the Assiniboines usually were beaten, but often succeeded in bringing away large bands of horses. The Crows, having nothing but scalps to gain, seldom pushed the war into the country of the latter. They preferred remaining at home and guarding their numerous herds of horses from the attacks of this and other tribes. But when horses are stolen they invariably pursue, mostly overtake, and being generally encamped in large bodies, usually follow the enemy in such force as to insure their certain destruction should they come together. In these skirmishes the Assiniboines suffered considerable losses, so much so that when overtures for a peace were made in 1844 by the Crows the other readily accepted the proposal. In a few years these two nations became good friends, often camped and hunted together, the Crows giving the others a good many horses, hunting in their company and furnishing them with hides and meat. This peace still exists and enables the Crows to visit the Gros Ventres village for corn.

Hostilities between the Minnetarres and Assiniboines ceased about the year 1844, both nations having found out the uselessness of contention, though when at war some bloody battles were fought between them. It was on one of these occasions that the present chief, The Foolish Bear, gained his name. A small camp of Assiniboines were attacked while traveling by a large force of Gros Ventres. The "Bear" and a few others remained between them and their people, fought desperately and kept the enemies off until the women and children of the camp reached the woods of the Missouri where they were safe. The conduct of the chief on this emergency was said by his people to resemble the furious and fearless actions of a crazy bear, hence his name.

Another singular circumstance happened in a skirmish between these two tribes which may as well be noticed. A small war party of Assiniboines on their way to the Gros Ventres met a large body of the latter coming upon them. The scouts of the Gros Ventres discovered the opposite party first and they concluded to conceal their main force under the brow of a hill while they sent a few forward as a decoy to bring the Assiniboines into a snare. The stratagem succeeded. After a few shots the Gros Ventres fled. The others pursued until they found themselves within a few yards of the main body of the enemy. The Assiniboines, being all on horseback and the others on foot, as soon as they perceived the superiority of force to be against them, wheeled their horses and got away with the loss of a few men. One elderly Assiniboine was on a wild horse which he was unable to turn, and the animal dashed forward and into the thickest of the enemy. The rider, finding himself in the midst of them thought he might as well employ his time to the best advantage. Being armed with a long lance he killed and wounded 13 in passing among them. His horse got out behind, took a circuit around and reached the rest of his friends without either it or the rider receiving any hurt. The fact was the enemy stood too thick, were in each others' way, and by some almost miraculous means both horse and man escaped the many balls and arrows fired at them. This individual was afterwards known among his people as He Who Had the Fast Running Horse.

A great many battles distinguished the war period between these two nations, but in the end both were willing to make peace. The Assiniboines preferred to get corn from the others, and they to be left quiet to pursue their hunting and agricultural operations. Neither the one nor the other party had ever had many horses, therefore, the principal object of their war not being obtainable by either, both were pleased to meet on friendly terms and exchange commodities in place of scalps. Both this peace and the one with the Crows will be likely to continue as there appears to be no advantage in any party to break them. Some few interchanges of women have taken place between these tribes, but the females thus given are not of the most virtuous or desirable kind.

The principal theater of war for the Assiniboines has been in the Blackfoot country. The numerous bands of horses possessed by this nation present irresistible temptation to the Assiniboines who have but few animals of this kind. The Gros Ventres of the Prairie, being the nearest people in that direction, most of the fighting is done with them. Other bands of the Blackfeet are generally located farther west, but these are commonly found on or near Milk River, the northwest boundary of the Assiniboine country. This portion of their enemies was about 300 lodges with whom war was kept up without intermission until about 1851. Since that time a precarious peace has existed. When at war, however, parties were always out on both sides and many bloody struggles took place with various success. Upon the whole the balance of damage has been decidedly against the Assiniboines.

In 1850 a party of 52 of the latter stole a number of horses from the Gros Ventres of the Prairie above Milk River and made off with them. The others gave chase and brought them to a stand on a plain some 5 or 10 miles from camp, where they forted as well as they could with stone in the absence of timber. The whole camp turned out and the firing was kept up the best part of the day on both sides. Before evening every one of the Assiniboines was killed, though not without a loss of 15 or 20 of the opposite party.[27] This was the most extensive slaughter of late years, but smaller numbers were killed frequently by other bands of the Blackfeet with whom no peace has yet been made. The annual loss on either side cannot be much less than from 40 to 60 men.

After the above massacre and after the Laramie Treaty the Assiniboines made peace with the Gros Ventres of the Prairie and were well received in their camp. Each year since they have continued their visits, were well entertained, and always returned with horses and other property had from their new friends. During the 4 years this peace had lasted the number of horses given to the Assiniboines by the Gros Ventres of the Prairie cannot fall short of four or five hundred. Some of these were bought by the former people but the greater part were bestowed for the purpose of promoting friendly relations. The Gros Ventres show great anxiety to preserve peace, have never been to war against the others since their friendly connection commenced, but the Assiniboines were not united enough among themselves for this end. In the course of time a few individuals become dissatisfied and leave their homes secretly for the purpose of stealing the horses they could not get by peaceful means. This is by no means the general desire of the nation, nor even the desire of a large portion, but amongst most tribes there are always some whom it is difficult to control. In this way several small expeditions of Assiniboines each year have started ostensibly with the view of presenting the pipe of peace and begging horses from these people, but secretly with the understanding that should a favorable opportunity offer to steal a large number. Hence the Gros Ventres have been vexed and duped several times, often keeping the others in their camp for a month, entertaining them in the best possible manner and having their

[27] In a letter to Alexander Culbertson, dated December 1, 1849, Denig wrote, "Les Gens du Nord, & Band du Gauche have but a few days past had 52 young fellows killed by Piegans on the Maria River. Loss of Blkft. 25 dead. This is the greatest blow the Assiniboines have received for years and will severely hurt the making of robes in those bands." (Letter in Missouri Historical Society.) This action, therefore, must have occurred late in the year 1849, and the enemies may have been Piegans rather than Gros Ventres.

horses stolen by them when departing. Of late this double game has been practiced to such an extent that the Gros Ventres have killed 4 Assiniboines whom they found prowling around their camp. This, it is thought, will lead to the breaking up of the peace generally, but it may be settled in some other way. The Gros Ventres of the Prairie do not want war with them. They have nothing to gain and everything to lose by it.

With the Blood Indians, Piegans and other bands of the large Blackfoot nation the Assiniboines are yet at war, but negotiations are afoot which may lead to a temporary peace.[28] Heretofore every winter the Blackfeet war parties visit the Assiniboines' camps, run off what horses they have and often get killed in the attempt. The others do the same. Thus the poor horses often change owners twice or thrice a year.

This is the cause of the slow increase of the Assiniboines since their reduction by smallpox in 1838. The nation being small and continually losing men at war, with others from disease, and the old in the course of nature, it is not likely they will be able to hold out much longer as a distinct people, but may exist some length of time if united with the Crees.

The damage done at war by the Arickaras, either to the Assiniboines or any other nation, is very trifling, mostly limited to the killing of a defenseless woman or child. But of later years the Sioux have become more formidable than they formerly were. It is believed that the great diminution of buffalo in the Sioux country will compel that nation to seek subsistence farther west. The district watered by the last 100 miles of the Yellowstone River offers great inducement for a hunter population. At this time the entire south side of the Missouri as high up as the Musselshell and as low down as the confluence of the Little Missouri of the Big Bend, extending for 100 miles into the interior, is unoccupied by any

---

[28] Denig probably referred to the negotiations of Isaac I. Stevens, governor of Washington Territory, with the Blackfeet tribes, which resulted in a treaty between the United States and the Blackfeet in October, 1855. But this treaty did not put an end to Blackfoot-Assiniboine warfare. (See John C. Ewers, *The Blackfeet: Raiders on the Northwestern Plains,* 205–25.)

Indians.[29] This is one of the best game districts in the world. The surface of the country is rolling, diversified by small patches of wood and green meadows over which the buffalo graze in immense numbers undisturbed except by passing war parties of the Sioux and Blackfeet. The extensive forests along the large and broad valley of the Yellowstone are well stocked with elk, deer and grizzly bear, while antelope are seen in thousands on the neighboring hills. Both on this river and the Little Missouri the bighorn sheep are found in bands where the country is broken into clay eminences. Every stream swarms with beaver, excellent fish can be taken in quantity, and wood and water can be had in traveling at all seasons. Most of the soil, judging from the spontaneous productions, is fertile and would produce several kinds of grain and other vegetables. At least it is better than that on the northern side of the Missouri. Neither the Crows nor Assiniboines can be induced to remain here. Both have made the attempt and both have been obliged to leave on account of the numerous Blackfoot and Sioux war parties who consider this their favorite range. But the Sioux are numerous and could defend themselves in this region while the Assiniboines, being the weaker party, would be driven northward to their ancient home.

The Assiniboines are tolerably good hunters, both on foot with the gun and on horse with bow and arrow. But they are lazy and improvident. They will not purchase guns, or if they do, exchange or give them away to other nations. In a party of 50 hunters or warriors not more than 10 or 12 guns could be counted. They depend on their horses to catch the buffalo, and when these are stolen or dead they are at a loss how to live. Besides, they have not many horses, cannot keep them from being taken by the numerous parties of enemies by whom they are surrounded. Even when guns

[29] The portion of this unoccupied tract between the Little Missouri and the mouth of the Yellowstone was a part of the area defined as Mandan, Hidatsa, and Arikara territory in the Fort Laramie Treaty of 1851. The portion extending westward from the Mouth of the Yellowstone to the Musselshell was included in Assiniboine territory as defined by that treaty. (Charles C. Royce, *Indian Land Cessions in the United States,* Bureau of American Ethnology *Eighteenth Annual Report* [1896–97], 786–87.)

are given them they take no care of them, cut them off, or give them away to the first person who flatters them a little. It is not unusual to see a war party start with lances, war clubs, axes, tomahawks, bows and arrows and other primitive weapons to contend with the well-armed, superior numbers of Blackfeet. The consequence of this negligence is that at war they get killed and at home starve half the time. They do not seem to keep up with the age of advancement in the same degree as other nations who have had fewer opportunities. It is but a few years since any of them could be persuaded to wear a coat or pantaloons, or even a hat or shirt. Neither have they any mechanical genius. Their saddles, dresses, utensils are all made in the same way as they were made in the days of stone axes and bone awls. They see and know well enough that something better can be done, particularly when iron tools are furnished them and every sort of material can be had, but they will not exert themselves and even ridicule other nations for imitating the manners, dress and manufactures of whites.

Now the Blackfeet and Crow nations perceive at once the convenience and utility of European articles, especially portions of clothing, horse gear and other things. They readily throw aside the cord and use a bridle for a horse's mouth, will pay well for a saddle. They pride themselves on the cut of their coat, in a fur cap or com boots, if they can get them. But the Assiniboines stick to their old customs, use a paunch for a water bucket, a horn for a spoon, bowls made of wood and mallets of stone wrought in the same way and applied to the same purposes as they were at their creation. The last few years, however, have changed this in a measure. Individuals are becoming more civilized, the general community more industrious, and the large present given them by the Government has formed a taste for flour, coffee and other things before abjured by them. They are infinitely better in their disposition than formerly and more cleanly in their habits, dress, lodging, etc., than they were in the first years of the trade. But we wish to be understood that this is only comparatively. They are yet far behind the other tribes who have not had the same advantages.

These Indians subsist entirely on the proceeds of their hunts.

95

Buffalo is the principal animal killed, which is found in greater numbers through their territory than in other districts. The meat of this, either fresh or cured by drying, is their principal food. A good many indigenous fruits and roots aid considerably in their support at times when buffalo are too far from camp. The skins of the quadrupeds killed by them serve for clothing, lodges or are exchanged with the Fur Company for articles of use and comfort assorted to suit their necessities. Owing to several causes pointed out they seldom have a large supply of meat in their homes, living for the most part on rather short allowance. But at times when buffalo are plenty and near constant, feasting is general in the camp. It also sometimes happens that from an entire disappearance of these animals they are distressed by actual famine. This was the case in 1846, when they ate up their dogs and horses, and in some instances devoured their own children.[30]

They have but few horses and these are required to transport their tents and children when traveling.[31] Dogs are used to a great extent for carrying burdens. But these cannot carry heavy burdens and when killed for food their means of migrating are withdrawn, particularly when in winter the snow falls to such a depth that horses cannot proceed. This inability to carry destroys the desire to lay up provisions and militates against any economy in the article of meat. They are compelled to follow the buffalo at all times when over one day's travel from their camp. In this respect

[30] However, Denig "only witnessed one season in twenty-one years where they were driven to this necessity," i.e. cannibalism. (*Indian Tribes of the Upper Missouri,* 584.)

[31] In spite of the fact that the Assiniboines began to obtain horses before the middle of the eighteenth century, they were always poor in horses in buffalo days. Lieutenant Bradley estimated that "about the year 1830" the Assiniboines averaged two horses per lodge, whereas the Gros Ventres averaged five per lodge, the Piegans ten, and the Crows fifteen horses per lodge. (James H. Bradley, "Characteristics, Habits and Customs of the Blackfoot Indians," Montana Historical Society *Contributions,* Vol. IX, 288.) Denig claimed that in a large Assiniboine camp "at least one-third of the men have no horses that they can catch." (*Indian Tribes of the Upper Missouri,* 456.) Elderly Assiniboine informants, who recalled the last decade of buffalo days, told this editor that it was rare for an Assiniboine family to own more than four or five horses at that time.

they are worse off than the tribes who live in stationary wooden huts as the Mandans, Arickaras, etc., who can and do take good care of provisions. Their moving habits also prevent the accumulation of much baggage. All useless articles must be thrown away to make room for the more necessary implements. Thus personal property cannot be acquired to any amount. Even their horses, the mainstay of their existence, are very precarious stock, being subject at any moment to be taken away by the hostile tribes in the neighboring territories. These things united produce a carelessness of character and an apathy of disposition which runs through most of their actions.

In their personal appearance they are not remarkable for their beauty or homeliness. The men average about the middle height, usually have a determined, dogged look, especially when in a strange place. In their homes, however, they are more sociable. Each master of a lodge preserves a degree of dignity in his family and exhibits a determination to be respected. They do not play or joke much with their women. Neither do they enter into useless quarrels or recriminations. Trifling differences are settled by the decision of the master in a tone of authority and more serious quarrels are ended by sudden application of the tomahawk. They are affectionate to the children, urbane to strangers, distant in their manners to each other, unless to kindred, and very revengeful when roused.

There are but few handsome women among them, and virtue is still a rarer commodity except in very young females.[32] In these matters, however, they are very sly and modest. Nothing of the

[32] George Catlin's painting of the wife of "Wi-jun-jon," executed at Fort Union in the summer of 1832, probably the earliest portrait of an Assiniboine woman, is in the collections of the Smithsonian Institution. However, a young Swiss artist, Peter Rindisbacher, who was a member of the Earl of Selkirk's colony on Red River in Canada from 1821 to 1826, depicted members of this tribe in some of his scenes. His water colors "Drunken Frolic amongst the Chippeways and Assiniboins" and "Mode of Chasing the Bison by the Assiniboins, a Sioux Tribe, on Snow Shoes," are in the collections of the United States Military Academy, West Point, New York. John Francis McDermott discussed the life and work of this artist in "Peter Rindisbacher: Frontier Reporter." *The Art Quarterly,* 129–44.

bold and baldfaced vulgarity of the Arickaras and Crows is visible. They do not seem to be an amorous people. Marriages are often contracted for the first time at 25 and 30 years of age.

In conclusion, it may be well to observe that no insuperable difficulties appear to prevent the bettering of their condition by a partial education and instruction in agricultural operations. If war with other tribes could be stopped, or a good stationary residence found, most of them could with ease be brought to pursue a more profitable and moral course of life.

CREES

THE HISTORY, government, employments and opinions of all migratory tribes assimilate in many instances, though in other respects each differs materially from the other. To avoid repetition as much as possible we have adopted the plan, as stated before, of presenting any peculiarities *not* common to all in the abstract sketches of each before entering into a minute and general review of their character and habits.[1] The nation now about to be considered, together with their employments and country they inhabit, impose upon us a somewhat lengthy description from the fact that in many things they do not resemble the others.

A great difficulty is experienced at the commencement of the history of any of these tribes in endeavoring to trace their origin to a remote period. From a people where no written data exists, and whose only method of preserving their national history is oral tradition, very little of ancient date can be extracted aspiring to the dignity of truth. Their traditions handed down through several generations, diversified and embellished by the fancies of the narrators, become confused and fabulous. Farther back than the year 1760 all appears obscure, or at least their statements of events said to have happened before that time differ so materially as to be unworthy of note. From that period, however, most of their acts

---

[1] The reader is reminded that Denig planned to follow his individual tribal accounts with detailed descriptions of the manners and customs common to all of the tribes of the Upper Missouri. There is no indication that Denig was able to complete the latter part of this ambitious project before his death in 1858.

. . . social government can be traced with a tolerable degree of certainty.[2]

The Crees were originally a part of the Chippeway nation, which is proven from the similarity of language. Even yet they are so mingled with the latter as with difficulty to be considered a distinct people. The name for their nation in their own language is *Nai ah yah' og*, which being interpreted means "those who speak the same tongue." They are called by the Assiniboines *Shi é yah*, by the Sioux *Shi e á lah*, and by other surrounding tribes as the Crows, Blackfeet and Gros Ventres nearly the same, differing only in the pronunciation of the word, *Shi é yah*. This word has nearly the same significance in the Assiniboine as that of *Nai ah yah' og* among the Crees. With other nations it has no meaning further than an appellative for the Cree tribe.[3]

. . . say they inhabited a district much . . . north than their present location.[4] Their range at that time was along the Athabaska, Slave, Rainy and Great Bear Lakes, stretching towards Hudson Bay, but never reaching the latter place. The Chippeways at that time spread out towards Lake Superior, Lake of the Woods, even as low down as Lake Michigan and Prairie du Chien. The time when and cause why the Crees separated themselves from the Chippeways and formed a distinct nation is now lost. Most probably the division was very ancient and arose from some family feud so frequent in their primitive mode of government. Or it may have been they

[2] A word or words are missing from this sentence in the Denig manuscript.

[3] The name, Cree, is a contraction of the French-Canadian corruption (Kristeno) of the name *Keethisteno* given these people by the Chippewas. There is no *r* sound in the Cree language. Umfreville (1790) regarded the Chippewas as descendants of the Crees because of their similarity of language and traditional alliance. In historic times many Chippewas have lived among the Crees. (David Mandelbaum, "The Plains Cree," American Museum of Natural History *Anthropological Papers,* Vol. XXXVII, Pt. 2, p 180.) The Indians of Rocky Boy's Reservation, Montana, numbering 1,165 in 1950, are primarily descendants of Plains Crees and Chippewas who fled to the United States after the Riel Rebellion in Canada in 1885. Plains Crees also are settled on some twenty-four reserves in the Canadian Provinces of Saskatchewan and Alberta. (See the map in Mandelbaum, "The Plains Cree," Fig. 1.)

[4] The words missing in this sentence are supplied in Hayden's *Contributions* (p. 235), as follows: "Prior to the year 1700 the Crees say they inhabited a district much farther north than at present."

were induced by superior hunting advantages in the northern direction where even yet the country abounds in game and the rivers and lakes are well provided with beaver, fish and wildfowl. Whatever the cause of the disunion was, it is now not remembered. After long and bloody wars with the northern tribes they were obliged to retreat south westerly, where in the 1760 we find them along the banks of the Saskatchewan and Red Rivers and around the shores of Lake Winnipeg. The Assiniboines joined them in this district and entered into a league offensive and defensive against all surrounding tribes except the Chippeways. About the year 1800 most of their Assiniboine allies left them for the Missouri and Yellowstone Rivers, although to this day some 200 or 250 lodges remain with the Crees in the British Territory.[5]

The present boundary of the Cree Nation is nearly as follows: on the north and northeast by the Saskatchewan and Red Rivers, on the south and east by Pembinar River, thence west to the Coteau de Prairie or divide, from that point along the Coteau through Woody, Cyprus, Tinder, Moose and Prickly Pear Mountains to or nearly to the head of the Saskatchewan, thence down that stream to its confluence with Lake Winnipeg and around that lake to its eastern extremity.[6]

This is the section claimed by them as their own, although they

[5] The Plains Crees, in whom Denig was primarily interested, were a historic offshoot on the numerous Cree bands who lived in the forests between Hudson Bay and Lake Superior in the seventeenth century. Armed with English guns by the Hudson's Bay Company prior to 1690, the Crees proceeded to arm the Assiniboines and to make an alliance with them before 1700. This enabled both tribes to push westward out of the woods onto the plains. La Vérendrye's mention (1730) of the "Cree of the Prairies" is the first definite reference to Cree Indians living on the plains south of the Saskatchewan. Crees and Assiniboines continued to move westward and southward in the face of Sioux and Blackfoot hostility until they reached the upper Saskatchewan and the valley of the Missouri by or before 1800. This movement, and the accompanying transformation of a portion of the Crees from Woodland to Plains hunters, has been traced by Mandelbaum ("The Plains Cree," 169–187).

[6] This definition of Cree territory indicates Denig's primary interest in the Plains Crees. He excludes from consideration the numerous and scattered Woodland Crees, also known as Swampy Crees, who lived north of the Saskatchewan and east of the Red River.

do not confine themselves to hunting within it but are as frequently found west of their boundary in the country of the Assiniboines, particularly if buffalo are not numerous in their own. Occasionally their robes are bought by the traders of the Missouri but most fine furs collected by them are carried to the posts of the Hudson's Bay Company established in their territory. The Crees are surrounded on the east by the Chippeways, on the southeast and south by the Sioux, on the southwest by the Assiniboines, and on the west and northwest by the Gros Ventres of the Prairie and Blackfeet. With the Assiniboines and Chippeways they have been for many years and still are at peace, but with the other tribes named they have carried on an inveterate war beyond the recollection of any one now living.[7]

The principal river in their country is the Saskatchewan, called by the halfbreed voyageurs La Rivière du Parc, which takes its rise from springs in the Rocky Mountains east of the Missouri, runs generally a northeastern direction and empties into Lake Winnipeg. By a tolerably correct estimate of its navigable length for mackinaw boats, it may be set down as 1,200 miles. Sixty-seven days are required to reach the last post of the Hudson's Bay Company near its head, which, averaging 18 miles per day would come near the length stated, and from the head of navigation to its sources is said to be about 150 miles. It is boated at all times to within that distance of its head, where a post named Fort à Cape Pierre is found, at which point the goods of the Bay Company intended for the trade of the Crees in that vicinity are landed, and which is the last fort on the river being as high as the boats can proceed. There are other trading houses from that place down the stream. This river is about 300 yards wide in the middle of its length, but at its mouth it is nearly a mile in width, usually from

---

[7] From the time of their first mention by Jesuit missionaries in 1640, the Crees were at war with the Sioux. Cree-Blackfoot warfare followed Cree penetration of the Plains in the eighteenth century and continued with little interruption until the extermination of the buffalo. The last large-scale battle between the Crees and Blackfeet was fought near present Lethbridge, Alberta, in 1870. In this battle the Blackfeet routed the Crees, killing more than two hundred of them. (Ewers, *The Blackfeet*, 260–61.)

ten to fifteen feet deep. Its navigation is obstructed by 160 rapids and falls of various heights, at all or most of which the goods up or packs of furs down are carried round on the backs of the voyageurs, the bales being made to weigh 95 pounds each. The merchandise with the boats are transported by the men round the dangerous places, but where smaller rapids occur the goods only are carried while the boats being empty are gently let down the stream.

Assiniboine River flows from the north side of the Montagnes du Bois and after running through several lakes and joining Red River, as marked on the map annexed, discharges into Lake Winnipeg.[8] Its entire length, including the lakes, is estimated at 400 miles. In this stream there are no rapids. It is navigable throughout with the mackinaw boats in which the goods and peltries of the Hudson's Bay Co. are carried to the different trading posts along it.

Red River is a branch of Assiniboine River debouching into it about 80 miles above its junction with Lake Winnipeg. This is called La Fourche where is established a large fort of the Hudson's Bay Company.[9] The principal fork of the Red River takes its rise in Red Lake, is commonly from 50 to 60 yards wide, pretty deep, with but a slow current. The other branch heads in Lake Traverse and joins the first about 100 miles above the mouth of Pembinar River. This branch is called by the natives the Plat Coté. It is not navigable with boats except during spring freshets, and even then is not safe.

Pembinar River rises in Turtle Mountain, its source soon forming a lake, after which it passes through four other lakes of small dimensions. It is a long, crooked stream, full of rapids and not navigable by any craft larger than a bark canoe. It empties into Red River eighty-one miles above its mouth. Extending a con-

[8] This map does not accompany the Denig manuscript in the Missouri Historical Society.

[9] This was Fort Garry, built in 1835–36 on the site of the present city of Winnipeg. It was one of the best constructed and most important posts of the Hudson's Bay Company.

siderable distance up the stream is the settlement of the halfbreeds on the American side of this district.

The Rivière aux Souris owes its origin to springs rising in the Coteau de Prairie. It is a long and very crooked stream, so much so that after seven days travel down it not more than 30 miles in a right line are gained. Its length is estimated at 600 miles. Its width varies from 100 to 150 yards, but is very shallow except when filled by spring thaws, at which time loaded mackinaws could descend. Assiniboine River receives its water 90 miles above the mouth of Red River, and its course being through the locations of several bands of Cree Indians and halfbreed hunters, no less than five trading posts of the Bay Company are found along its banks.

The foregoing are the principal streams in the Cree Country, although there are many others running into them whose sources and courses, together with their pecularities, could be traced if required but which are not necessary to the main object of this work. Along the valleys of all, and indeed throughout the whole of this district, are found a great many springs of excellent water, many of which would afford power for machinery. Others are impregnated with saline and sulphurous substances and from some a great quantity of good salt is produced by the natives. Nearly all the lakes of the larger class are deep enough to admit of running steamboats and are at certain seasons covered with incredible numbers of wild fowl. Fish too of various kinds, some of which are of excellent quality, are taken in great quantity by the natives when stationed on their borders.

All the territory claimed by the Crees, with the exception of a few square miles near its southeastern boundary, is beyond the parallel 49° North Latitude and consequently forms a portion of British America. The general surface of the country is what is called rolling, though there are extensive level prairies in some parts of it. It would seem to be a gradual descent of land from the base of the Rocky Mountains east of the Missouri including several other mountains of smaller note, these giving rise to the rivers and creeks running in every direction throughout the interior, thereby cutting up the land. At the bases of most eminences from which springs flow are found marshes, called muskegs by the inhabitants, which vary in extent from a few miles to a day's travel across, according to their supply of water and its inability to find an outlet. These swamps are for the most part covered with long, strong grass, growing very thick—six or eight feet high, sometimes mingled with rushes. But the ground though humid is not miry and can in most places be traveled over on horseback. All the rivers are well wooded in their valleys and on their bluffs and often for many miles inland where the soil is damp and adapted to the growth of trees. On the level plains also forests of timber are met with which become more frequent and dense as the northern limit is approached. Upon the whole there is more prairie than woodland but it does not present the monotonous barren aspect of other territories before described. The soil is of an excellent quality as has been proven by the agriculturalists settled along the banks of Red River, Pembinar River and the small band of Cree Indians who raise maize and other vegetables at Tinder Mountain.[10]

The halfbreed settlement at the forks of Red River contains at this time upwards of eight thousand persons many of whom cultivate and raise livestock to a great extent, but owing to their farms being subject to inundations from Red River during the spring thaws, by which many animals and other property are destroyed, a good many have removed to Pembinar River on the American side where they live by hunting and tilling small portions of land. More of these people will soon follow and in a few years a city will spring up in this wilderness. There is at present a population of some three or four hundred distributed along the banks of Pembinar River, besides some forty or fifty families living in a newly laid off town. Even at this early day the place boasts both Catholic and Presbyterian churches, a school, grist and saw mills, with several stores and trading establishments. Indeed the country presents many good features which cannot long fail to attract the attention of those restless emigrants in search of lands flowing with milk and honey. Wheat, oats, barley, corn and potatoes together with most garden vegetables grow well and produce abun-

[10] See footnote 15.

105

dant crops. But as yet no market being found for the surplus grain and stock the attention of the settlers on the American side has not been directed much to agricultural pursuits. Their principal source of sustenance is derived from hunting buffalo and selling the meat and skins to the traders of both settlements. Those on the English side dispose of a portion of their produce to the Bay Company who ship it farther north where breadstuffs are not raised. But only a small part of what they could and do produce is thus sold. The remainder is consumed by their families. The want of a market is much felt. It is a great hindrance to their operations besides forcing them to adhere to the hunter's life in quest of skins and furs which bear the ready price denied the proceeds of the soil.[11]

It is believed the entire Cree district is arable, both prairie and woodland, although the latter is perhaps not so rich as low prairie. The different grasses are of the very best kind, tender and fine except that immediately on swamps which is tall, coarse and unfit for use. Some of these marshes, however, are covered with small rushes which are said to be more nutritious food for animals than any kind of grain. The poorest kind of horse will fatten if let run twenty-five or thirty days among these rushes. Notwithstanding the high altitude of the country domestic animals are not housed during the severe cold of winter and those left to graze at large are said to be invariably in better condition than others kept in stables and fed on grain. Horned cattle and horses are reared in abundance, also some sheep, but the latter are not yet much attended to. In fact, the section now being noticed is known to be one of the best grazing and grain growing portions of North America.

---

[11] At the time of his visit to the Red River settlement in the summer of 1846, Paul Kane reckoned its population at 3,000 whites and 6,000 half bloods. The latter were descendants of white men employed by the Hudson's Bay Company and Indian women. (*Wanderings of an Artist Among the Indians of North America*, 50–51.) A brief history of the settlement and a detailed description of its appearance in 1857, two years after Denig had visited it, appears in Henry Youle Hind's *Narrative of the Canadian Red River Exploring Expedition of 1857 and the Assiniboine and Saskatchewan Exploring Expedition of 1858*, I, 172–232.

Where springs or streams are not convenient water can be obtained by digging from ten to thirty feet in level places, but on elevations wells would require to be deeper. The water thus found is free from any mineral taste and suitable for all household purposes. The places designated as marshes are not useless or irreclaimable. On the contrary the waters forming the swamps could be collected and made subservient to agricultural use. The soil is commonly of the very richest kind and would soon repay the expense of draining did the increase of population require that labor.

In most places where the country is thickly timbered, the undergrowth is a kind of moss and bushes, but little or no grass, and it is only in such places the soil sustains any damage from the action of fire. The moss forming the sod is reduced to cinders, the roots destroyed and many years are required to replace its coat of green, which, like the preceding, is destined to be burned whenever the fire passes in that direction. The soil of the prairie, however, receives no such injury. Being covered with grass deeply rooted, only the stalk burns, the heat is swept away by the wind, the roots retain the living principle and soon after another crop springs up, more lively and thick than the former owing to its having been freed by the fire from all briars and decayed vegetation. Wooded districts suffer greatly on these occasions. Whole forests are often deadened which require centuries to replace by young sprouts. In fact the old trees must first fall then be again buried before others can grow to perfection.

Firing the prairie is not a custom resorted to by the Indians to facilitate hunting, as is generally supposed. Nothing they desire less and their laws to prevent it are severe in the extreme. It effectually destroys their hunting by driving away all game and renders the country unfit for pasturage during the winter, especially if burnt late in fall. These fires mostly originate in the carelessness of hunters, travelers or from the petty malice of individuals. Occasionally it is done by passing war parties. Sometimes the flames are very destructive and sweep over districts several hundred miles in all directions until extinguished by rain, snow or contrary winds. Both men and animals run great risk of being consumed if caught by the fire among the tall and thick grass growing on swamps when the water in them is frozen.

The only appearance of volcanic action in the Cree Country is the burning of hills containing beds of lignite. The earth in these places becomes red and whatever stone or other substances are there undergo various changes. No pumice or lava is found that would denote eruptions and these subterraneous fires are not common. Perhaps not more than three or four could be counted in the whole region.

The climate may be set down as variable, not as regards heat and cold, but wet and dry. Cold and constant northeast wind in the spring brings long and settled rains. From the beginning of May to the last of June may be termed the wet season. In July and August there are no steady rains for days without interruption, but terrible and sudden thunderstorms come from the west and southwest which in a few hours swell the smaller streams to their full, though seldom to overflowing. Red River being the grand reservoir of all the others is the only stream that inundates the surrounding country. This is caused by the melting of deep snow in the spring, never by rain alone. Severe tempests never last longer than an hour or two. When the clouds roll on, the sun shines and shortly after the prairie is as dry as before. These storms are frequent in the summer months, but the autumn is dry and pleasant. Frost occurs every month in the year, though about the 10th of September it is cold enough to destroy the vegetation. October ushers in the winter with snow. The rivers close up about 1 November and remain frozen until the middle of April or first of May. Much snow falls in the months of December, January and February. The air is very cold. The thermometer seldom rises above zero, but ranges from that point to 50° or 55° below it. The shortest day of the year is something less than seven hours and the longest a little over nineteen hours. During the winter north and northwest winds prevail which always bring snow. At that season south and west winds denote clear weather. All traveling and hunting by the natives is done on snow shoes, using dog sledges for transportation. The snow is too deep for horses to make their way through it.

The general health of the inhabitants is good. Fevers and nervous diseases or any inflammatory complaints are unknown, although exposure for a long time to the intense cold air brings on chronic rheumatism and catarrhs which often terminate fatally.

Before the smallpox of 1776 or 77 made its appearance among them the Crees numbered about 800 lodges, one half of whom were supposed to have died of that disorder.[12] Since that time they have been slowly on the increase, particularly those bands who are too remote to suffer from invading foes. At the present date, 1855, their whole number may be put down at 1,000 or 1,100 lodges, which, averaging 4 souls to a lodge would make a total of between four and five thousand persons.[13] These, like most of the tribes in the Northwest Territory are separated into clans or bands occupying different districts for the greater convenience of hunting. The names and numbers of these bands are as follows:

Cho cab, or band of Eyes Open, bearing the name of the chief who governs it, consists of 100 lodges or upwards, reside in the neighborhood of Lac Qu'Appelle, live in skin lodges, hunt, and trade their skins at the posts of the Hudson's Bay Company.[14]

Páy e si e kan, or Striped, are 40 to 50 lodges, rove and hunt near Tinder Mountain, inhabit skin tents, and deal with the same traders as the first mentioned band.

Pís cha káw a kis, or Magpies, count 30 or 40 lodges, are stationed at Tinder Mountain, live in log cabins covered with earth, till the soil to some extent and raise considerable quantities of

[12] See footnote 21.

[13] Clark Wissler, following Palliser, estimated the population of the Western Crees, chiefly those residing on the plains west of Lake Winnipeg, at 11,500 in 1858. However, this estimate may have included some Woodland Crees. ("Population Changes Among the Northern Plains Indians," Yale University *Publications in Anthropology,* No. 1, 9-10.)

[14] This was the *Katepoisipi-wiinuuk,* Calling River (Qu'Appelle) Band, also known by the names of later prominent chiefs, Loud Voice's Band and Fox's Band. In 1913, Cree informants told Skinner that this was the most important Plains Cree band. (Allanson Skinner, "Political Organization, Cults, and Ceremonies of the Plains-Ojibway and Plains-Cree Indians," American Museum of Natural History *Anthropological Papers,* Vol. XI, Pt. 6, 517–18). Descendants of this band now reside primarily on the Crooked Lake Reserve in the Province of Saskatchewan.

maize and potatoes, hunt buffalo in the winter season and get their supplies from the English posts of the interior.[15]

Kee as koo sis, Small Gulls, reside on and around the fourth lake from Lac Qu'Appelle, live in skin lodges, were formerly numerous but have been greatly reduced by continued wars with the Blackfeet, they being the nearest of all the bands to this large and fierce nation of enemies. At this time their number is thought not to exceed thirty or forty families.

1. *Wick yu wám kam muse nái ka tah,* The Painted Lodge.
2. *Mus quoi káh ke noot,* He Who Shoots the Bear with Arrows.
3. *Ah pís te kái he,* The Little Eagle.
4. *Mus quoi cáw e páh weet,* The Standing Bear.

The above are the names of four chiefs who govern each a small band which takes the same name as its leader. These live near each other in the country about the Fort de Prairie and trade at that place. They count in all about 130 or 140 lodges and occupy skin houses.

Band of *Ma tái tai ke ók,* or Plusiers des Aigles, the chief of this name is also known among the traders as Le Sonnant, heads about 300 lodges who move through and hunt the country along the Woody Mountains, sometimes trading on the Missouri but more frequently at some of the Hudson's Bay Company's posts.

Band of *Shé mau káw,* or La Lance, hunt near and in Cyprus and Prickly Pear Mountains, occasionally visit the Missouri to dispose of their skins, especially if opposition runs high and goods are cheap. Otherwise they prefer dealing with the English traders in their own country. This is the largest division, contains 350

15 Mention of this horticultural settlement far north of the area of aboriginal corn cultivation is of special interest. Probably this band began to reside in earth lodges and to till the soil only a few years before Denig's (1855) mention of them. Evidence of recent Cree adoption of horticultural practices was observed by Hind in September, 1857. (*Narrative,* II, 145.) At Prairie Portage on the Assiniboine River he visited a half-blood Cree who had cultivated Mandan corn, obtained from Indians on the Missouri, for two years. A neighboring Cree Indian had raised corn successfully for four years.

lodges which are of skin construction and well manned by good warriors.

Several smaller portions of the nation are found every winter at and west of the Woody Mountains, usually led by respectable men such as the Red Fox, Iron Child, *Mus ké gan* etc. These mostly trade their robes on the Missouri but carry their fine furs, wolf skins, dried meat and tallow to the traders of the Bay Company, from whom a much higher price is obtained for these articles.[16]

Besides the foregoing there are about 200 lodges more who are not formed into bands, but scattered along Lac de l'Isle Croix, where they subsist by hunting reindeer, moose, fish and wildfowl. They inhabit skin tents in summer but build log and bark huts for winter residences and seldom more than one cabin is found in the same place. These are the poorest of all the Crees.

From close inquiry it does not appear that at any ancient date any great or wise chief ruled the nation. They were formerly more detached and divided than they are now, forming small camps of 20 or 30 lodges of their own immediate relations, subject only to parental authority. This was no doubt the reason why they could not sustain their position near the numerous tribes northward, but were compelled to place, by their removal, several hundred miles of uninhabited territory between themselves and other more war-like nations. Many recitals of individual bravery and contest are told by them, when in their scattered situation they fought with the hordes of enemies by whom they were surrounded. There can be little doubt but the entire loss by war in remote times was greater than at present, although the incidents happened in so many places distant from each other and with such small portions that nothing like extensive massacres took place. These like other nations, by the introduction of the horse and firearms, were en-

[16] Plains Cree bands were loose, shifting units, often referred to by the names of their current leaders. Not only did the bands acquire new names after changes in leadership, but their membership changed with shifts in residence on the part of individuals or families from one band to another. Their numbers also were augmented by recruits from other tribes. Mandelbaum named the eight principal Plains Cree bands of the 1860–80 period after the territory generally occupied by each, although the limits of the range of each band never were defined clearly. ("The Plains Cree," 166–67, 221.)

abled to hunt and locate in large bodies capable of defense and subsistence.

The first Europeans with whom they recollect dealing were the English traders from the north, who, wishing to open a trade, made a treaty having for its object establishment of trading posts through their country.[17] In consideration of the traders paying an annual rent they were allowed to build forts in several places. This sum is yet paid to the Crees by the English and is to continue as long as the Hudson's Bay Company exists.

As each of the bands mentioned has its separate chief, there is no one person who could be considered the national ruler. Their locations are usually distinct from each other, require different regulations for hunting, trading and traveling. Each band is in a measure independent of the others in its domestic arrangements. Nevertheless there have been times when numerous assemblies took place including most of the nation, particularly when large war expeditions were about to be formed. Should such a meeting be convoked at the present day the chief named *Shé mau káw* or La Lance would unquestionably take precedence in the council as he unites in his person the powers of a great medicine man and great warrior, has often been successful against his enemies, which has the effect of inspiring his people with implicit belief in his prophecies. This man is now 60 years old, governs his band with wisdom and still heads large war parties, although usually at that age the chief relinquishes this right in favor of some young and rising warrior. He has also distinguished himself in making several peaces with some bands of the Blackfoot nation at different times, none of which, however, lasted longer than a good opportunity to gain some advantage over each other.

Cho cab or Eyes Open is also a chief of note among them, not

---

[17] Establishment of Hudson's Bay Company posts on Hudson Bay in 1670 inaugurated English trade with the Crees. The Crees had been accustomed to trade with the English for more than a century and a half before the American Fur Company built Fort Union near the mouth of the Yellowstone on the Missouri and began to attract some of the Crees to that post. George Catlin claimed that the Cree bands who traded at Fort Union in 1832 totaled 3,000 souls. (*Letters and Notes,* I, 57.)

so much as a warrior but as a prudent financier in matters regarding trade, knowledge in leading the camp and placing his people in situations where good hunts can be made. His band, residing for the greater time at or near Lac Qu'Appelle, is seldom subject to depredations from enemies. His duty as a leader, therefore, is to look out for the welfare of his people, to see they amass property, live comfortably and hunt with order, also to go at their head when they visit the fort to trade and endeavor to secure their general advantage by making the best bargain he can for them.

The third in rank, although he was formerly the first, is Le Sonnant who was a greater warrior and a tyrant among his people. Supported by extensive relationship and possessing the fame of a medicine man he was much feared by his followers. Even now, though a very old man, he takes a prominent part in all councils, is much listened to by his band and no doubt would be one of the principal men to be consulted in the event of making a purchase of any of their lands. He is a sterling friend of the English, abjures all acquaintance with Americans, endeavors to hinder his people from trading on the Missouri and never comes there himself except to beg. His days as a warrior are over but as a councilor his voice is yet respected.[18]

There are many soldiers or leaders of war parties among them, some of whom have distinguished themselves often in battle, and of these perhaps *Ma kái ah shís* or The Red Fox stands most prominent, is considered a capable leader and a wise and respectable man. *Pe wób quoi a shis* or The Iron Child, *Wah wísh a caut ée* or The Handsome Leg, *Pái pásh e quon áil* or Plumet Caille,[19] *Ah*

[18] In the fall of 1833, Maximilian met "the celebrated medicine man or conjuror, *Mahsette-Kuinab* (le sonnant)," who "is highly respected among his countrymen, because his incantations are said to be very efficacious." He was adept at the Algonkian shaking-tent rite and his medicine was "the skin stripped off the head of a bear," which he wore upon his head on ritual occasions (In Vol. XXIII of Thwaites' *Early Western Travels*, 200–201.) Carl Bodmer, the talented Swiss artist who accompanied Prince Maximilian, drew Le Sonnant's portrait, although he had difficulty in getting his subject to sit still because "he was suffering severely from an affection of the eyes."

[19] Kurz met the Cree chief, Le Plumet Caille, when the latter came to Fort Union to trade in the fall of 1851. (*Journal*, 228.)

áh to wish kín e síc or Eyes on Each Side, are all camp soldiers and sub chiefs leading portions of bands in the absence of men of higher standing and guiding parties to war. The one last named was taken to Washington City in company with an Assiniboine and other Indians by General Jackson's orders during his presidential administration. He is a scheming, mean beggerly Indian and on his return proved himself unworthy the attention bestowed upon him. It appears to have been the wish of the President to impress upon the minds of the Indians present the power and extent of the Government, its desire to befriend all good nations and ability to punish the bad. After counciling with them, giving them good advice and loading them with honors and presents he sent them back to their people. The fate of the Assiniboine deputy has already been described. He was a man of truth and would not bear contradiction. The Cree now written of named Eyes on Each Side, fearing a similar end, or at least profiting by experience, told all lies, represented the Americans as but a handful of people far inferior in every respect to his own. In thus flattering their vanity he gained their good will, passed for a man of sense, still lives, is pretty generally despised by traders, although he has some influence among his own nation.[20]

After the Crees had established themselves in their present district in the year 1776 or 77, the smallpox came among them, which is still fearfully remembered by a few old men yet living from whom we learn that about 1,200 persons died of the disease. The nation was reduced from 800 to about 400 lodges and these but

[20] George Catlin painted a portrait of this man, who was better known as "Broken Arm," at St. Louis when this Indian was en route to Washington in 1831. Maximilian saw him at Fort Union a year after his return "wearing a medal with the effigy of the President hung round his neck." In Thwaites' *Early Western Travels,* XXIII, 13.) Larpenteur traded for robes in the camp of "Broken Arm, the great chief of the Crees, who had been to Washington," in 1844. *(Forty Years a Fur Trader,* II, 412–13.) Perhaps Denig's low opinion of this Cree Indian may have been somewhat colored by the fact that this man was unimpressed by the white man's wonders seen on this trip to Washington, while his Assiniboine traveling companion, the brother of one of Denig's wives, was murdered by his own people for trying to tell the truth about the great marvels he had seen in the white man's country. (See Ewers, "When the Light Shone in Washington," 2-11.)

thinly peopled.[21] There is yet to be seen a mound near the mouth of the Assiniboine River embracing an area of several hundred yards in circumference and ten to twenty feet high, being the cemetery of nearly an entire camp of 230 lodges who died of the infection. The natives to this day look upon this depository with horror and on no consideration will they consent to its being opened under the apprehension that this terrible disease, though buried for nearly a century, might again spread among them.[22]

Another visitation of this malady happened in 1838, but owing to the good management of the Hudson's Bay Company most of the nation were preserved by introducing vaccine matter and persisting in its application for several years previous. Still many young children died who had not been vaccinated, with some few grown persons whose superstitions would not admit of its being applied.[23]

The next calamity was the measles which appeared among them about 12 years since when a great many children and old persons were cut off, though in general adults recovered, many of whom, however, died afterwards from diseases of the lungs caused by the measles. The halfbreed settlement on Red River suffered severely at the same time from the same distemper.

Another singular accident is said to have happened about forty years ago of which the following are the particulars. A camp of

[21] Denig's dating of early events frequently was inaccurate. The smallpox was most virulent among the Plains Cree in 1781–82. The epidemic spread from whites to the Sioux and Chippewas and from them to the tribes living to the westward on the plains. (*David Thompson's Narrative of his Explorations in Western America, 1784–1812* [ed. by J. B. Tyrrell], 109, 321–23.)

[22] On August 19, 1800, Alexander Henry saw the many old graves at the mouth of the Assiniboine and stated "this spot having been a place of great resort for the natives in 1781–82; and at the time the smallpox made such havoc many hundreds of men women and children were buried here." (*New Light,* I, 46.) Chris Vickers, of Baldur, Manitoba, has informed the editor that this site is now in the heart of the city of Winnipeg. The north bank of the river, on which the Indian cemetery was located, is much higher than the south bank, giving the former a mound-like appearance.

[23] Hind wrote that the Hudson's Bay Company introduced vaccine inoculation after serious epidemics in 1816, 1817, and 1818, "and small-pox has been unknown in this country since." (*Narrative,* II, 143.)

between thirty and forty lodges were situated near the bank of Assiniboine River, say distant one or two miles. From this village an Indian eloped with the wife of one of his friends. The husband pursued, which the other perceiving set fire to the long grass and the wind blowing in the direction of the pursuer he was soon overtaken by the flames and with his horse burned to death. The fire continuing soon reached and surrounded the camp, which being but lately planted among thick dry brush, nearly all the occupants perished. Some, taking time by the forelock, seeing the volume of flame coming in the direction of the village, absconded on fleet horses and saved themselves by plunging into the river.

Another place is still shown where the Crees gained a victory over the Sioux. It is situated near the mouth of Pembinar River and is a mine underground in which several hundred Crees were concealed. A small party enticed the Sioux to follow them retreating towards the ambuscade, who, as soon as they came near were surrounded by their hidden foes and cut off to a man. The Crees claim to have killed upwards of 100 Sioux in this battle.

On the occasions of the diseases spoken of, we hear of no renowned leaders to whose sagacity or wisdom they were in any way indebted for their partial preservation. The nation, as usual with the prairie tribes, had to resort to incantations and other remedies of their medicine men. The drum, rattle, vapor bath with various decoctions of roots were all tried in turn, but few were saved and they most probably would as well have recovered if left to themselves. In general nine out of ten who caught the smallpox died. Among them there were many whose last moments would have been much more comfortable if undisturbed by the loud drummings and frightful yellings of the medicine men.

With regard to the event of war, however, there have been, no doubt, good leaders among them as at the present time. But the fame acquired by the most successful savage warrior is short lived, often entirely forgotten, or at least seldom alluded to in the old age of the gallant chief who wisely planned and fearlessly led large expeditions. When decrepid and infirm, borne down by the weight of years and wounds, instead of being respected he serves for the butt and ridicule of the camp. Those who once feared him mock and his past deeds vanish before those of younger men and of more recent date. The ambition to rise is too general, the claims to rank too much divided to admit of a lasting reputation being bestowed upon any one man. Besides, each aspirant to power considers only his own merits, is jealous of the rest and regards their just praise in the light of detraction from his own abilities. Bad rulers only sometimes leave a name to posterity through the principle of superstitious fear.

The Cree Nation have many means of subsistence not obtainable by other migratory Indians. Some of the bands when situated around the borders of the lakes in this district collect quantities of wild rice which they can either eat or exchange for other commodities. To gather this grain nothing more is required than to push their bark canoes through the water in which it grows, bend over the stalks and strip it off with the hand. Afterwards it is threshed in a simple manner and winnowed by the wind. It makes excellent soup, is very palatable and not greatly inferior to the cultivated kind.

Fishing and hunting wild fowl also occupies a great part of their time. Most of the lakes are well stocked with either. The former are taken with nets of various kinds which they make very strong and suitable for all seasons. Even under the ice fish are caught all winter and the supply is inexhaustible. Of these the white fish are the best, though there are a great variety of other sorts. Wild fowl are very numerous and living on the wild rice renders them exceedingly fat in the fall. On the approach of winter immense numbers of ducks, geese, brants, etc., are killed, cleaned and frozen. In this state they are laid away for winter use. Both these and fish are often salted should warm weather prevent their preservation in a fresh state. From the above employments a good deal of profit is derived by the nations by selling these articles to the halfbreed inhabitants. They also afford supplies of provisions much desired in a country where fresh meat is not always to be had.

The greater part of the nation, however, depend chiefly upon hunting buffalo and other game for food, clothing and the purposes of barter. Buffalo robes always command a good price, are ready sale and enable them to get supplied with the most costly and necessary articles for their existence, such as horses, guns and metallic cooking utensils, which they could not obtain by returns of fish, fowl, rice, sugar and other articles produced by them. This large and useful animal, whose hide is so much sought after and forms the staple of the Indian trade, is found in innumerable herds through nearly the entire extent of the Cree Country. They appear in full as great numbers at this time, 1855, as at any period during the last 20 years, though there is little doubt but the whole number is rapidly decreasing and those remaining confined to a small range, having entirely abandoned other sections where a few years back they were found in abundance. As yet, however, there is no scarcity of them in the Cree district except perhaps in some of its most northern limits where, it is believed, they never were much accustomed to roam. The severe cold of the winter and deep frozen snow on the plains forces these animals to seek grazing and shelter in the woods, along streams and in broken country protected by hills from the wind. But during the summer months they remain on the plains, around lakes where good grass and water are convenient. At that time they are not much hunted, the skins are not seasonable and the Indians then subsist on fish and wild fowl. In the beginning of September the hunting commences which is continued without interruption until the middle of March, in which space of time the Crees, being excellent hunters, lay in a large stock of buffalo robes, skins of smaller quadrupeds, dried meat, tallow, pemmican etc. These they carry to some of the Hudson's Bay Company's posts, or sometimes, as has been stated, to the Missouri traders. But these Indians give a decided preference to the English market especially for their fine furs. When competition runs high on the American side and merchandise is sold very cheap they sell their robes to them. Otherwise they dispose of their whole trade at the British posts.

Though the buffalo are the principal game hunted, yet other skins and furs are collected, more especially by the bands occupying the wooded districts northward. These trap and kill wolves, fisher, marten, foxes, wolverine, muskrats, lynxes, hares, rabbits, badger, skunk, ermine and occasionally a few otter, beaver and black bear. All of these skins are much desired by and bear a high price with the English traders in proportion to their scarcity and the labor required to procure them.

Wolves are very numerous throughout the whole Northwest Territory, and are of three kinds, the large white, large grey back and small prairie wolf. They follow in the wake of the buffalo in bands of several hundreds waiting an opportunity to strangle some small calf or mired grown animal. When hard pressed by hunger they will attack a full-sized cow or bull and by dint of great perseverance torment and tire the animal to death. Wolves are trapped and killed in many ways by these Indians. The most common is the deadfall, constructed by small pickets driven in the ground and a trigger baited with meat supporting a heavy log. The wolf in endeavouring to get the meat displaces the prop and the log falling upon him breaks his back. Another mode is by digging a pit about 8 feet deep, which is covered with a revolving door well concealed with grass or snow. The bait is placed in the middle, which the wolf tries to reach by marching over the door. This gives way downward, the animal is thrown in and the covering rises to its place. When two or more are thus caught they commence fighting and the noise attracts others until a dozen or so are penned the same night. This trap is sometimes made on the side of a hill with a high fence around the base below enclosing the carcass of a buffalo, in which great numbers are taken. When hunting on the plains the Crees often kill and skin a buffalo, then dig out a hole in the snow of sufficient size to contain one or two men. The hide of the buffalo is placed over the hole in an upright position which in a few minutes stiffens and presents the appearance of an animal standing. This is placed a short distance to the windward of the carcass. The hunter is hidden within and when the wolves come to eat the meat he shoots them down through holes made in the buffalo hide. The wolves, neither seeing nor scenting the men, pay little attention to the firing. The hunter is protected from the cold and often kills a dozen or two before they discover the trick. These he skins, buries the hides in the snow and returns for them the next day with his dog trains.[24] No diminution is apparent in these animals when compared with former years. The probability is they increase in a ratio equal to their means of subsistence and the surplus die off by hunger and madness. The larger sized skins are worth 3/0 Sterling and the smaller 1/6 at the Hudson's Bay Company posts. Red, cross, silver grey and kit foxes are hunted by all the Crees and are more or less to be met with in every part of their territory. But of late years a great reduction is felt in their numbers, particularly in the silver grey and cross kinds. These are now but rarely seen and owing to their scarcity the price of a single skin has risen in a short time from 1 pound to 4 pounds Sterling for the first named fox. The other is rated about half that value. Red foxes are still caught in considerable numbers, though they are by no means as plenty as formerly. Grey kit foxes are yet abundant. Thousands of them are killed by the Indians each year. They are trapped by the deadfalls, as described, and their taking forms the principal occupation of the smaller boys in the winter season. The price of a skin is about 1 shilling.

Fisher and marten are peculiar to the wooded districts. The fur of the latter is in great demand. It is a small animal about the size of a large squirrel and varies in color with the season. The fisher is about the size of a red fox, black fur, with the end of the hair white. Neither are very numerous but the fisher is the most rare and its skin brings about 4/6 Sterling.

Muskrats are very prolific. Most of the small lakes and swamps teem with incredible numbers. These formerly were a principal article of traffic but of late years the price of the fur has so depreciated as not to compensate the Indians for the time and labour of killing and skinning them. Consequently they have been for years on the increase. At several of the Hudson's Bay Company's posts muskrats form a considerable item in the bill of fare. The natives also live upon their meat often when more desirable flesh cannot be had. They can be preserved either by drying in the sun

[24] Mandelbaum mentioned only the baited, deadfall trap as a Plains Cree method of taking wolves and coyotes. ("The Plains Cree," 198.)

or by salting, and many are eaten in both ways. Although the meat is not very palatable, yet the supply is abundant and may be considered a great source of subsistence among the savage tribes whose principal aim is to secure a sufficiency of animal food.

Beaver, though formerly plenty, may be considered as nearly extinct in the country of the Knisteneau. At this time the animal is scarcely to be met with except in the northern portion where the regulations of the Hudson's Bay Company regarding the hunting of it have been exercised for a long time. They allow the Indian to trap certain streams at stated seasons and prohibit the successive hunting of any place for two or three years. The country in which that animal abounds is parceled out into hunting portions which are worked in rotation each third year, leaving them the intervening two years to accumulate. In this way these animals are and will be preserved for a great length of time. But it appears these laws have never been enforced with the Crees of the interior and refer altogether to the portions farther north. The moose was once found everywhere in their country but now is confined to solitary places in the woods. It is a shy animal difficult to kill and in the territory under review seldom met with. The reindeer is still more so being only seen occasionally by that portion inhabiting the extreme northern limits. Of the two the skin of the former is the most valuable.

The wolverine or *car ca jou* is the same animal called the glutton in natural history. They also are becoming rare in comparison with what they were some years since. They are very cunning and are a great nuisance to trappers and hunters whom they follow at a distance and set off their traps when they leave. Its habits are well known. It is a timid animal possessing keen sight and scent, not swift of foot. The skin is worth about 4/6 Sterling.

Hares and rabbits are hunted mostly by the boys. Of each great numbers are killed. In some parts the former are driven into pens by circular hunts when they succeed in enclosing two or three hundred at a throw. The skins of both are salable at a low price. They are also wrought by the natives into caps, mittens and woven into coarse durable blankets for their own use.

The other animals named are not extensively killed. Otter are uncommon, black bear not numerous and elk and deer so few as scarcely to be considered a source of profit to this nation.

It is customary with the traders of the Hudson's Bay Company to facilitate hunting by crediting these Indians with a small amount of necessary articles for their occupations, varying the same according to the character of the individual credited. Indians of established reputation, who have always paid their debts, can get advances to the extent of 30 plues while others of a doubtful cast must be satisfied with barely a sufficiency to enable them to prosecute their employments, say from five to ten plues. A plue is an imaginary amount used to value skins equal to about 2/ Sterling. The proceeds of all hunts are reckoned into plues and the prices of merchandise fixed to conform to that standard by which arrangement the natives are able to calculate with certainty how much of each article they will receive for their skins. The accounts of the traders are kept in this manner:

DR.	LE SONNANT				CR.			
1854	To 6 ft. Blue Cloth	8 Plues	1855	By 10 Muskrat Skins	1 Plue			
Augt.	" 1 " Scarlet "	3 "	Mar.	" 1 Large Beaver "	4 "			
	" 1 3 pt. Wht Blanket	7 "		" 1 Small " "	2 "			
	" 20 Loads			" 10 Otter Ea. 2	20 "			
	Ammunition	1 "		" 6 Cross Fox " 4	24 "			
	" 1 ft. N.W.			" 2 Silver " " 5	10 "			
	Twist Tobacco	1 "		" 1 Buffalo Robe	3 "			
	" 1 N.W. Gun	15 "			—			
	" 1 Horse	30 "			65 Plues			
		—						
		65 Plues						

Now although a plue is normally valued at about 2/ yet it must not be inferred the actual value of that amount is paid in merchandise at prime cost with expenses of importation and a fixed advance per cent added. All articles of trade are reduced to a standard price made proportionately higher or lower as they are necessary to and indispensable for the Indians. Yet care is taken not to rate too high such things as guns, ammunition, horses, traps and other

THE BROKEN ARM, a Cree Chief who went to Washington. From a painting by George Catlin, 1831.

LE SONNANT, a Cree chief and medicine man. From a lithograph by Carl Bodmer, 1833.

things absolutely required for hunting purposes. In that case most of the Indians not being able to procure them their hunts and consequently the best interests of the traders would suffer. But such commodities as tobacco, cloth of gay colors, beads and other ornaments bear very high prices in proportion to their actual cost. Therefore we see in the foregoing bill a N.W. Gun, the prime cost of which in England is seldom less than 20/, sold for 15 plues, while half a pound of tobacco worth 6 pence brings 1 plue.[25] The Indians themselves keep no accounts neither pictorial nor otherwise. The small amounts for which they stand indebted are notched on a stick, each notch counting a plue. But if in this way they are not recollected, their memories are refreshed by the traders when they have the means to pay.

The tendency of every fur trade is towards extinction of the game and diminishing the value of the country for hunting. Some animals such as beaver, otter and muskrat may be perpetuated by the enforcement of laws as is done by the Bay Company. But it is owing to the habits of these animals confining them to certain localities these means become feasible. Buffalo, wolves, foxes and other migratory quadrupeds could not be thus protected. Neither do we see any way of preventing their ultimate extinction except the abandonment of the trade entirely, and reducing the natives to their primitive state of arms and means.

By diversifying their operations and parceling out the country

[25] The northwest gun was a smooth bore flintlock introduced in the Indian trade by English traders and later offered to the western tribes by the American Fur Company and other firms in the United States. Peculiar characteristics of this gun were a counter-lock plate of cast brass in the form of a dragon or sea serpent and a large trigger guard permitting the trigger to be pulled by a mittened finger. This was the most common firearm among the Northern Plains Indians prior to the introduction of breech-loading rifles in the late 1860's. As late as 1872 the muzzle-loading flintlock was in general use among the Crees. (Charles N. Bell, "The Journal of Henry Kelsey," Historical and Scientific Society of Manitoba *Transactions,* Vol. IV, 28.) A gun of this type, obtained from Cree Indians near Moose Factory and manufactured by Parker Field and Company of London in 1868, is in the United States National Museum. (Cat. No. 387,266.) The most comprehensive study of this weapon is that of Charles E. Hanson, Jr., "The Northwest Gun," Nebraska State Historical Society *Publications in Anthropology.* No. 2 (1955).

into hunting districts the Bay Company have done much toward the preservation of some kinds of animals and more for that of their Indians and halfbreed allies by their judicious government and well regulated trade. Thanks to the good sense of the British Government for granting them a charter of monopoly and investing them with the power of judicature by which both Indians and white settlers are kept in due subordination, crime prevented and punished, industry encouraged. By a wisdom gained of long experience the employments of the inhabitants are directed in useful channels and their moral and physical condition improved. Vaccination has been introduced and persisted in until the greater number of Indians are secure from that terrible malady, the smallpox. Ardent spirits are not dealt in to any extent. The skins of animals not taken in season and not duly prepared are not received in trade. No system of concubinage is tolerated about their establishments. Their servants must either marry lawfully or remain single. Churches are raised, schools and factories formed. In short, everything is done that could be to advance the interests of the persons in the country over which their government extends. We speak of this Company as it is *now,* not as it was many years ago. No doubt they encountered difficulties in bringing the savages to subjugation, in overcoming their prejudices and introducing industrial and economical habits. But these they have surmounted and the result has been beneficial.

No portion of the Northwest Territory treated of in these pages produces much in the way of antiquities. Nothing is ever seen that would denote its having been the residence of any other than savage tribes, nor are there any works of human industry that would induce the belief it had been the abode of civilized beings at a remote period. The only objects worthy of attention in this respect are the mounds of earth mentioned, but these have been formed within the last century and are known to contain the bodies of those Cree Indians who died of smallpox in 1776. Hundreds of corpses lie beneath them, or rather the tumuli are composed of many separate burials alongside and on top of each other. There are persons yet living who contributed to their structure by interments of their friends and relations.

During a second visitation of this disease in 1838, several other depositories of the kind were made which, owing to there being fewer victims, were consequently smaller but are nevertheless testimony of the nature of these formations which have been made the subject of argument by different historians. Ordinarily Indians are not buried in heaps because when not visited by fatal epidemics they rove in quest of game, do not remain long in one place, and are healthy people and seldom more than one or two graves are seen near any of their transient encampments. Even where large villages have wintered the interments do not often exceed ten to a dozen bodies. But when pestilence such as smallpox prevails, attacks the whole nation at the same time, they are disabled from travel and obliged to remain stationary until the disease finishes. Thus hundreds are consigned to the same general burial ground. In former times the Indians, for want of proper tools, could not excavate to a sufficient depth. Therefore each individual was interred near the surface and the spot covered with a large quantity of rock, wood and earth to protect the body from birds and beasts of prey. The desire of all Indians is to be placed near their deceased relatives or even on top of them, which course would eventually build up a large eminence. In the course of time this could be covered with sod or even trees. It is evident the extensive mounds found in different parts of this continent have been raised in this manner, where large villages of Indians were located and selected a spot for their cemeteries. The size of some of these tumuli is nothing extraordinary. They perhaps took a century to form. But where a numerous population existed and were swept off by a pestilence, each interment contributing its quota of earth and rock, a mountain would soon appear. Usually much superstition is attached by savages to burial places. They are invested with a kind of sacred character and they will put themselves to great inconvenience to transport their dead many miles to lay them with their deceased friends. The spirits of the departed are supposed to associate in the same manner as those of the living. It is generally looked upon as a great misfortune to be obliged to inter a body in a solitary place. Therefore, it may be presumed these places of depository received additions as long as the nation existed undisturbed in that quarter. The excavation they make, if any, is scarcely of sufficient depth to cover the body, which with the envelopes and implements is often of considerable bulk, and the pile of earth, rock, etc. raised around and heaped on a single carcass is in form of a cone fifteen or twenty feet in circumference and three to six feet high. It has always been the custom and still is with the North American tribes to bury with their dead, if a man, his implements of war and the chase, if a woman, her working tools and utensils, and if a child its toys, clothes and ornaments. Most of their primitive tools were made of bone, stone, wood or clay. If, therefore, these depositories were carefully opened and the different *strata* of burials examined, they would exhibit the different stages of advancement in making these utensils; that is, supposing they had advanced, which is not likely. The examination of these rude instruments, even at the present day when they have the assistance of metallic cutting tools to make them, disclose no ingenuity nor artifice whatever. Neither are they superior to those anciently formed. The best of their primitive utensils are nothing more than might be expected from uncivilized man compelled to exertion by his necessities to sustain life. The only change we find to be the sudden abandonment of these implements as soon as they were enabled to procure those of more useful and durable kind from traders.[26] The ancient arms and utensils used by the Crees were similar to those already pointed out in the notices of other nations.

[26] At the time of Denig's writing (1855) the Indian mounds of the Ohio and Mississippi valleys had attracted widespread interest in scientific circles in this country. E. G. Squier and E. H. Davis' classic of American archeology, "Ancient Monuments of the Mississippi Valley," was published as Volume I of the *Smithsonian Contributions to Knowledge,* in 1848. Denig may have read that book. On his visit to Columbus, Ohio, in the summer of 1855, he may have seen the collection of artifacts assembled by Squier and Davis in the Ohio State Capitol. Nevertheless, Denig's interpretations of the mound builders appear to have been conditioned primarily by his knowledge of the burial customs of living, nomadic Plains Indians.

Pots of various kinds were made of clay and stone.[27] Arrowpoints, spear heads, dagues, knives and axes were wrought from flint. A kind of knife was also formed of the buffalo hump bone. Small bones of the moose and sturgeon served for fish hooks. Thread for line and nets was made out of a weed called by them *Shá a sip*. With the fibrous roots of the red cedar (*Wat tab,* Cree) they sewed their canoes constructed of birch bark. Spoons, called *Miquoins* by the natives, were easily had from buffalo horns and the broad, flat antlers of the moose furnished them with handsome and durable pans.

Of all these there still remain some specimens but most have given way before more convenient articles of European manufacture. Bone fish hooks and awls with the two sorts of thread above named are still in use and are preferred by them to those introduced by the traders. They also cling with great tenacity to their horn spoons, perhaps for the reason they are larger and better adapted to serve their capacious stomachs.

The process of manipulation by which these things were wrought was by chiseling one stone with another until the flint knife and axe were obtained with which other instruments were formed. Stone of different degrees of roughness and the inner or hollow part of the leg bones of animals served the purpose of filing and polishing. It was doubtless a long and tiresome employment but their necessities compelled them and practice and perseverance did the rest. The art is now lost or at least discontinued. But we are informed it was not confined to individuals as a trade. Each warrior made his own arms or employed some old man to do it whose active days being over was doomed to toil indoors for his daily support.

These Indians work very handsome pipes of various kinds of stone and a great variety of shapes. The material used is a kind of marble admitting of a very high polish and of jet black, blue, grey

[27] In 1913, Skinner found that Plains Cree informants knew that their people formerly used clay kettles, "but no one remembers how they were made." He examined camp sites on the northern bank of the Qu'Appelle River near the eastern end of Round Lake and found "numerous tiny postsherds." ("Notes on the Plains Cree," *American Anthropologist,* new ser., Vol. XVI, 79.)

or transparent green color. The shapes of these pipes often represent men and animals with considerable elegance, at times giving the pipes three distinct heads of different patterns, though never constructed for more than one stem. Red pipestone such as used by the Sioux is found in the most northern portion of their district, though not in quantity. The kind above mentioned are the handsomest and most durable.[28]

In most matters requiring mechanical ingenuity this nation is more expert than other tribes herein written of.[29] Their bark canoes are often elegantly shaped and they show a neatness in the construction of the paddles for same not equalled by any tribe except the Chippeways. Their traps, snares, nets, fishing tackle, dog trains and harness all show great skill and are adapted to their several purposes with a correctness and propriety that exhibits studied construction. Most of them make good carts which they join together without a particle of iron. They will last several years and carry a weight of 1,000 pounds over the plains. The greater number of them use carts in traveling in the summer season.[30] A few of the natives aspire to be regular mechanics. Having by some means acquired tools to a small extent they repair kettles, make tin cups

[28] Mandelbaum described Plains Cree pipe-making methods on the basis of information obtained from Indians in 1934–35. ("The Plains Cree," 216.) A mid-nineteenth-century Cree pipe bowl is illustrated in Hind's *Narrative*, II, 140.

[29] The mechanical skill attributed to the Crees by Denig must have been in part acquired by prolonged, close contact with whites and half-bloods. Half a century earlier, David Thompson wrote of the Crees: "They have no genius for mechanics, their domestic utensils are all crude, their snow shoes and canoes show ingenuity which necessity has forced upon them, the state of everything with them rises no higher than absolute necessity, and in all probability their ancestors some hundred years ago, were equal to the present generation in the arts of life." *(Narrative,* 94.)

[30] This was the Red River cart, much used by the fur traders and half-bloods of present Manitoba for land transportation before the days of railroads. It was a development from the first carts used by traders at the mouth of Pembina River in the fall of 1801, which, according to Alexander Henry, who was trading in that area at that time, had wooden wheels 3 feet in diameter, each of a solid piece cut from the end of a log. "These carriages we find much more convenient and advantageous than it is to load horses, the country being so smooth and level that we can use them in every direction." *(New Light,* I, 191.) Yet the carts used in Denig's time were equipped with spoked wheels as were the ones seen at Pembina in 1861 by Lewis Henry Morgan and described by him. (*The Indian Journals,* 123.)

and other utensils out of old pans or worn out sheet iron buckets. Some are tolerably good blacksmiths, can repair a gun lock, cut a screw, make knives, grates, scrapers for dressing skins and other things not requiring welding or tempering. One old man in particular deserves to be remembered here. He is a musical instrument maker. With a knife and file he makes a pretty fair fiddle and bow. Out of the entrails of small animals or sinew he forms strings. With the instrument when completed he can play several airs with some skill, which he picked up from the halfbreed settlers among whom fiddling is going on the best part of the time.[31] The making of cradles for infants also gives employment to some. These are often handsomely carved, painted and otherwise adorned. The child being tied on is protected from bruises by falls by a hoop across the upper part from which also descends a thick veil to exclude the sun's rays. This is carried on the back while traveling and is a very safe machine in their rough and rapid movements.

The women also of these people claim our notice for their industry and expertness in several ways. In some portions of the most northern points where buffalo robes are not to be had they use a covering of rabbit skins. These are cut in strips, rolled up in the shape of cordage and connected by a bark chain are woven into a blanket so firm as to be impervious to rain and to protect their persons from the most severe cold of these high latitudes.[32] Mats are made of rushes which form a good substitute for carpets and are in general use for their beds. All kinds of garmenting are very neatly wrought both on skin and cloth with silk, beads, porcupine quills, feathers and moose hair. Some portions of dress thus ornamented are neatly executed and look very gay and brilliant. Even the different colors of flowers are in this way represented with a great degree of correctness.[33] They make large quantities of sugar

[31] As Kurz observed in 1851, Denig himself played the fiddle. This may account for his interest in a Plains Cree fiddle maker. (*Journal,* 124.)

[32] A method of weaving rabbit skin blankets known to aged Plains Cree Indians in 1934–35 was explained and illustrated by Mandelbaum. ("The Plains Cree," 214.)

[33] Plains Cree informants claimed that only geometric patterns of decoration were executed in bead and quillwork before floral designs were introduced from the east by half-bloods. (Mandelbaum, "The Plains Cree," 219.)

from the sap of the box elder tree, using large baskets of birch bark to contain the juice while being collected. This is a considerable source of revenue during the early days of spring. All skins dried or dressed by the Cree women are better handled than those of other nations, particularly their buffalo robes and wolf skins. In fact both men and women of this tribe are seldom idle, are naturally active and industrious besides having a shrewd eye to their comfort and prosperity. Their employments do not seem so distinctly separated and defined as is usual with roving tribes. Indeed the Crees have attained a degree of civilization but little if any inferior to most border populations of white people.

When the spring opens sugar making, fishing and wild fowl hunting is pursued. The summer is devoted to making household utensils and clothing. The fall is employed in killing fowl, taking and selling fish, procuring wild rice etc. As soon as the hair and fur of animals becomes seasonable hunting operations are commenced, when they move into the interior of their country where buffalo are found and station their camps as has been stated. They are excellent foot hunters, perhaps the best in North America, and shoot their northwest guns with nearly the certainty of rifles. They lose no time in their camps when hunting commences. By daybreak they are out and persevere until they are successful. The snow being very deep, both men and women travel on snowshoes, the one to kill the game the other to drive the dog sleds and aid in bringing home the hides and meat. Even the smallest boys trap wolves, kill rabbits and hares and foxes, besides herding the horses. The labors of the sexes are thus divided: The old men remain indoors, make pipes, bows, pans, spoons, snowshoes, nets and other fishing tackle. The middle aged hunt, make their dog trains, harness, saddles, traps, prepare the bark and frame for birch canoes which the women sew on and gum. The men make paddles, both by turns maneuver the boat. The women dry, stretch and dress skins, cure meat, make pemmican cords and grease, cook, make clothing and other things mentioned. The young men hunt, go to war, gamble and seduce women.

In their personal appointments both sexes present different appearances at certain seasons. While hunting, and indeed at all times through the winter, they wear skin clothing. A coat of buffalo skin with the hair turned inward ties up close to the chin and descends to the knees. The head is covered with a cap of same or rabbit skin, hair inside, made so as to cover the head back of the neck and all the face except the nose and eyes. It is usually ornamented with tufts of skin resembling horns. Long mittens and moccasins are of red calf skin, hair inward, with skin leggings and blanket breech cloth. Over the body is belted a buffalo robe. Fire apparatus is tied to the belt, powder horn and shot pouch on his back, gun in hand well covered with skin, knife in belt secured by scabbard and long snowshoes on his feet. This forms the costume of the Cree hunter of the plains.[34]

The clothing of the women is of the same materials and made in every respect like that of the men except a short frock instead of the skin coat.[35] The dress of both sexes above described is not thrown off or changed, neither is it in any way cleaned from the time the hunting commences until the ensuing spring. Long before this time, however, it is covered with dirt, saturated with grease and becomes the abode of innumerable hosts of vermin. But after their return to the trading posts and the proceeds of their winter's work are exchanged for blankets and cloth of various colors the camp looks gay and lively. Both young and old of both sexes lay aside their filthy habiliments and adorn themselves in those of European manufacture. A profusion of ornaments is worn. Most parts of dress are garnished in some of the forms before referred to and a general neatness is exhibited leading one to suppose that

34 Whether Cree men wore the skin coat in aboriginal times is questionable. However, James Isham, who knew the Crees in the vicinity of Hudson Bay in the second quarter of the eighteenth century, considered this garment typical of the "ancient wear and apparel of the natives." (*James Isham's Observations on Hudson's Bay, 1743* [ed. by E. E. Rich], Champlain Society Publications, Hudson's Bay Company, Ser. 12, p. 109.)

35 The Cree woman's dress was a long slip supported by straps over the shoulders. Isham observed that Cree women near the Hudson Bay posts were making their dresses of trade cloth as early as 1743. (*Observations*, 109–10.) Kurz described and sketched skin dresses of this style worn by Plains Cree and Chippewa women who visited Fort Union in 1851. (*Journal*, 156, plates 23, 36.)

they were an entirely different people. This cleanly appearance, however, only lasts a short time. Their employments are of such a nature as soon to soil dress. As different suits are never thought of nor any washing done the brilliant colors of English goods become gradually obscured by dirt so that in the fall a new supply of winter clothing is as desirable as the spring exchange.

In their houses also the Crees are by no means as cleanly as the Assiniboines, though they are more companionable with their women. These are consulted and advised with on all occasions and possess more influence over their husbands than those of the other nation. Polygamy, though not forbidden, is generally not practiced. The majority have but one wife.[36] Their laws with regard to their authority over women are more just and rational than among other tribes. The husband is allowed to thrash his wife with a small stick three times. If she still proves incorrigible she is sent to her parents who are obliged to refund payment. This only extends to women who have no children. Those who have must behave themselves. Indeed their disposition is mostly found out and position determined before they have issue. A mother is seldom flogged and few women are ever killed for infidelity to their husbands. Most difficulties in these matters can be settled by a high pay and the owners of such women have the happy disposition of considering it little more than an ordinary domestic grievance.

This nation is not quarrelsome among themselves. Few disputes terminate in bloodshed, though they are celebrated for their horse stealing propensities. Individuals will steal horses from different bands, though the number taken does not amount to more than two or three, which they usually give up if pursued and overtaken. Nothing like droves of horses are robbed from each other. The general voice is against these proceedings but among all tribes there are some unruly characters.

Their intellectual capacities may be set down as superior to

[36] David Thompson, writing of the Plains Crees before 1812, observed that, although some men had as many as three wives, polygamous marriages commonly resulted from a man's taking responsibility for a dead friend's widow, sister, or daughter. (*Narrative*, 93.)

the surrounding nations. By association with white settlers they have acquired a good deal of practical and useful knowledge, understand to some extent the value of money, are good judges of the qualities of merchandise, count with facility and show great shrewdness in their dealings. They practise economy in their domestic life, trade only useful articles, take good care of provisions and make the most they can of everything. The majority reckon up the value of their hunt and consult their wants before they enter the store and cannot be enticed to buy articles which they do not need. They are not very great beggars, are reasonably fond of rum, and think it no harm to cheat or steal if they are able to avoid detection. In general they are liked by the traders as they are not so passionate and troublesome as other tribes. Each one minds his own business, places his whole attention to gain, seldom takes offense and departs as soon as his objects are accomplished.

Their knowledge of the globe with its natural divisions into seas, continents, islands etc., is very limited. The earth they take to be a great plain and they know there are many lakes which contain islands, for their own country is full of them. All nations are well enough acquainted with the natural features of their own lands but they can form no idea of the extent of other territories. They cannot realize the earth as a whole, though they think it very extensive. The ocean they believe is a large lake from the descriptions given by voyageurs. Some of these Indians have been and still are employed as boatmen by the Hudson's Bay Company. They have been as far as the Atlantic in a north direction. But this advantage has happened to few and the rest are not disposed to give implicit credit to the tales of travelers. They have in fact no knowledge or belief in the existence of greater districts than those known by them and contiguous to their own. The Earth however is supposed to be flat and circular, joined around the edge to the Sky, which is a solid mass of blue earth supporting the plane in the same way a basket is suspended by the handle. The Sun, they say, is a body of light and heat. This is the *Great Master of Life* which gives light and heat to all things and is the future residing place of the spirits of men. This body is self existent, is in fact the Almighty who goes round the earth every day overlooking the affairs of men. To it all sacrifices and prayers are made when of sufficient importance to invoke its aid and no other or greater idea of a Great Spirit is entertained. The moon they conceive to be another world receiving light from the sun and stars. It is a secondary object of worship. In these two luminaries Indian paradise is supposed to be located. Stars are small lights attached by cords to the Sky and hang down from it. They are not thought to be other worlds but ornaments and lights to this and the upper regions. The Milky Way is called *The Chief's Road* or a division separating the sky into two portions, which was done by some Great Spirit Chief set forth in their traditions but which are too long to be recorded here. When the Sun is in eclipse they say a portion of the material is burned out, dead. This is what is meant by a "dead sun." But they harbor no superstitious fears of eclipses being the forerunners of great misfortune as do other nations and look at the extinction of a part as the natural consequence of a burning body, which, as it exists of itself has the power to re-illumine.

The North Star is named the Stationary Star, the Ursa Major "The Tail of Stars." These are all that have particular names attached. They are also aware of the revolution of the Great Bear round the Polar Star and can tell the watches of the night in this way with tolerable certainty. The Aurora Borealis is called The Dance of the Dead who are supposed to be enjoying themselves in the upper regions. Meteors are stars dropping out of their places by the burnings of the cords that hold them and which extinguish as they fall. There is no particular opinion expressed regarding Comets. These are looked upon as stars or lights of another shape. Neither does their appearance or that of meteors have any influence on their fancy or religion.[37] Indeed these Indians seem not to fear

[37] David Thompson interpreted the Cree regard for heavenly bodies thusly: "The Sun and Moon are accounted Divinities and though they do not worship them [they] always speak of them with great reverence. They appear to think [of] the Stars only as a great number of luminous points perhaps also divinities, and mention them with respect; they have names for the brightest stars, as Serius, Orion and others, and by them learn the changes of the season, as the rising of Orion for winter, and the setting of the Pleiades for summer." *(Narrative,* 84.)

any natural phenomena except thunder, which is thought to be the flapping of the wings and screaming of a large bird, represented on their lodges and medicine envelopes in the form of an eagle. Wind is believed to be produced by its flying. Flashes of lightning are the reflections of the Sun or stars from its bright and golden plumage. When strokes of lightning are felt they are said to be caused by a Thunder Stone cast down by the bird. All storms, tornadoes and hurricanes are brought about by its agency. Fair winds, gentle breezes, calm and pleasant weather are tokens of its good humor, the reverse evidence of its wrath.[38]

Clouds they are aware are formed by mists which rise from the surface of lakes and swamps in the shape of fog. The fine particles of water adhere in the air and descend in rain, snow and hail, the latter being congealed rain by passing through regions where cold thunder stones are piled up. The rainbow they explain as the reflection of the Sun from a cloud of water in the same way as the reflection from the surface of a mirror, the colors of the bow naturally belonging to the Sun.

Their idea of Creation, though not very clear, is very original. We see no allusion made to a Creator or to anything except the Sun *as a body* and *material substance,* also the Moon in a lesser degree. These luminaries, together with the arch of the heavens and all the earth apart from animated nature, never had a beginning, exist of themselves, and never will have an end. In the beginning of *life* upon earth a kind of Genii or Medicine men were hatched out of the ground by the heat of the sun and to *these* supernatural powers are accorded. They made as in sport small images out of mud and clay resembling men, beasts, fish, birds and every living thing as their fancy dictated and threw them about in all directions. These were impregnated with life by the sun's rays and grew until they attained their present size, retaining the

[38] The thunderbird concept was widespread among the tribes of North America and this mythological creature is described in many of their legends. (In Vol. II of Maria Leech's *Standard Dictionary of Folklore, Mythology and Legend,* 1,112.) This creature was graphically portrayed in Indian religious and decorative art. (W. J. Wintemberg, "Representations of the Thunderbird in Indian Art," Ontario *Archaeological Reports,* Vol. XXXVI, 27–37.)

various forms given them by the Genii. Thus in the course of time were all living things made, while trees and all vegetation pushed and grew from the earth of their own accord as fungi are produced.

These are the elements of their belief, the particulars usually being wrought up and enlarged upon in the shape of tales and allegories, some of which are of interminable length and if recorded would afford no additional information. The ceremonies of their worship being the same as other tribes will be laid down elsewhere. The object venerated is only h—— from which it may be concluded that the Crees like . . . of the Persians are the true worshipers of the Sun.[39]

This tribe had no word signifying a year. Neither is there any stated number of days forming that period of time. Each month begins when the new moon appears and ends when it is no more seen. During the few days the planet remains invisible it is said to be dead. They . . . .[40]

[39] Several words of this sentence are missing from the Denig manuscript.

[40] Thus Denig's account of the Plains Cree Indians in the Missouri Historical Society manuscript ends in an unfinished sentence. The back of the page is blank. Yet on page 246 of F. V. Hayden's *Contributions* this sentence appears complete: "They cannot even tell how many days make a moon, and all subdivisions of time are denoted by the different phases of the moon, as "moon on the increase" (first quarter), "half moon" (second quarter), "more than half round" (third quarter), "full or round moon," "decreasing moon," "small moon," "dead moon." Hayden then listed the Cree names for the thirteen moons of the year, for periods of the day, and describes the Cree method of counting. There is every reason to believe that this information was supplied by Denig.

V : OF THE

CROW

NATION

CROW RELATIONSHIP TO THE HIDATSA

THESE PEOPLE were once a part of the Minnetarees or Gros Ventres, with whose history the reader has already been made acquainted.[1] They resided with them, they say, at different places along the banks of the Missouri, where the remains of dirt villages are still to be found. But about 80 years since a quarrel arose which divided them. The cause of the division was this. The nation was governed by two factions each headed by a separate chief, both of whom were desperate men, and nearly equal in the number of their followers. Jealous of each other and striving after supreme command, many difficulties and differences arose from time to time, 'tho they never had proceeded to extremes on these occasions, there being always a sufficient number of wise heads and good hearts to quell such disturbances. But this course of things could not possibly last. Therefore, at a hunt where both chiefs were present with their followers, and a great many buffalo had been killed, the wives of the two leaders quarreled about the manifolds or upper stomach of one of the cows. From words they came to blows, from blows to knives, in which scuffle one of the women killed the other. The relations on both sides took part. The nation armed, each headed by one of the above-named chiefs, and a sharp skirmish ensued in which several were killed on both sides. The result was that about one-half left those on the Missouri and migrated to the Rocky

[1] There is no chapter on the Hidatsas in the Denig manuscript in the Missouri Historical Society. Probably it appeared in the pages missing from that manuscript.

Mountains, through which wild and extensive region they continued to rove.[2] Why they are called Crows we cannot say. The word *Ap sar roo kai,* which is the name they give themselves in their own language, does not mean a crow more than any other kind of bird, the interpretation being simply anything that flies.[3] The language of the Crows has undergone some change since their separation from the Gros Ventres, though enough resemblance remains to identify them as the same people. They have little or no difficulty in conversing with each other. This difference of dialect may arise from association with surrounding nations and incorporating some of their words into their own language.[4]

[2] Lowie has pointed out that "the alleged reason for the secession occurs among the traditions of other tribes and cannot be uncritically accepted as historical." ("Social Life of the Crow Indians," American Museum of Natural History *Anthropological Papers,* Vol. IX, Pt. 2, p. 183.) Denig's dating of this separation, as published by Hayden *(Contributions,* 391) has been credited to the latter by more recent writers. Now we know this dating was provided by a man who had far greater knowledge of the ethnohistory of the Upper Missouri than did Hayden. Mere separation from the Hidatsas does not explain Crow abandonment of the semisedentary life typical of the Missouri River horticultural tribes in favor of the nomadic-hunting existence typical of this tribe when first met by white men. If Crow separation from the Hidatsas occurred after horses were introduced into the Upper Missouri region, Denig's dating may not be much too late. If it occurred earlier and the Crows remained earth-lodge dwellers for a period after the separation it may have occurred a century or more earlier. In 1877, on the basis of Hidatsa tradition, Washington Matthews estimated that the Crows separated from the Hidatsas "doubtlessly, more than one hundred, and probably not less than two hundred years ago." *(Ethnography,* 39.) As one of several possible interpretations of the Hagen site near Glendive, Montana, where buffalo scapula hoes, pottery, and a single earth lodge site were found, William Mulloy has suggested its occupation by the Crows in process of transition from a horticultural to a hunting economy. ("The Hagen Site, a Prehistoric Village on the Lower Yellowstone," University of Montana *Publications in Social Science, No. 1,* 99–102.)

[3] An early mention of the Crows by that name appears in the journal of the fur trader, Jean Baptiste Trudeau, among the Arikara Indians in 1795. "A war party of the Ricaras arrived on the fifth of June with the scalp of a man of the Crow Nation, a people who live near the Rocky Mountains." ("Journal," 22). Trudeau also learned that "a Canadian, named Menard, who, for sixteen years has made his home with the Mandan . . . has been several times among the nation of the Crows in company with the Gros Ventres [Hidatsas]." (Trudeau's "Description of the Upper Missouri," 175.)

[4] The affinity of the Crow and Hidatsa languages was recognized by fur traders

138

HE-WHO-JUMPS-OVER-EVERYONE, a Crow warrior. From a pencil sketch by George Catlin.

Crow Indian encampment on the Little Big Horn River. From a painting by J. H. Sharp, 1908.

DESCRIPTION OF THE CROW COUNTRY

The country usually inhabited by them is through the Rocky Mountains, along the heads of Powder River, Wind River, and Big Horn, on the south side of the Yellowstone, as far as Laramie's Fork on the River Platte. They also are frequently found on the west and north side of that river as far as the head of Muscleshell River, and as low down as the mouth of the Yellowstone.[5] That portion of their country lying east of the mountains is perhaps the best game country in the world. From the base of the mountains to the mouth of the Yellowstone buffalo are always to be found in immense herds. Along that river elk may be seen in droves of several hundred at a time, also large bands of deer both of black-tailed and white-tailed species. Antelope cover the prairies, and in the badlands near the mountains are found in great plenty bighorn sheep and grizzly bear. Every creek and river teems with beaver, and good fish and fowl can be had at any stream in the proper season.

The once almost fabulous country of the Rocky Mountains is now so well known as scarcely to need description. The scenery of the district now under consideration does not materially differ from that in other parts of their range. The same high, stony peaks and eternal snows are seen, intersected with fertile valleys and rich land. Most of the rivers whose sources are in these mountains

in the first decade of the nineteenth century. In 1805, the French trader, François Larocque, noted close resemblances between these languages and listed a comparative Hidatsa-Crow vocabulary of 21 words to prove his point. (*Journal of Larocque from the Assiniboine to the Yellowstone, 1805,* Canadian Archives *Publication No. 3.,* 68–69.) In the next year Alexander Henry wrote, "The language of the Crows is nearly the same as the Big Bellies." (*New Light,* II, 399.) Matthews suggested that even in the period when the Crows lived in close proximity to the Hidatsas they may have spoken a slightly different dialect from the latter. (*Ethnography,* 39.)

[5] While at the Crow camp on an island in the Yellowstone River a few miles east of present Billings, Montana, September 14, 1805, Larocque recorded the earliest known definition of Crow territory. "They told me that in winter they were always to be found at a Park by the foot of the Mountain a few miles from this or thereabouts. In the spring and fall they are upon this River and in summer upon the Tongue and Horses River." (*Journal,* 45.) "Horses River" is present Pryor Creek. Today the Crow reservation lies within the area occupied by this tribe a century and a half ago.

are clear, rapid streams formed from springs which widen into lakes of different sizes according to the nature of the obstruction the water meets with in its descent. In their course through the valleys some of them assume a muddy appearance caused by the falling in of alluvial soil. The spaces between the spurs of the mountains are well covered with rich, grassy field flowers, shrubs, and trees, presenting many beautiful landscapes well worth the painter's pencil. The high ranges of mountains appear to consist of three different portions. From the base, one-third the distance up is well covered with tall pines, poplars, and other trees of large growth. This part of the ascent is also varied by occasional level places well clothed with verdure. The middle or second third is composed of gigantic rocks piled one on the other, often overhanging in such a manner as to present a frightful appearance to the travelers below. Through these rocks stunted cedars and pines, with other shrubs and vines, push their way, taking root where apparently there is no earth. At the end of this part vegetation ceases, and snow commences which continues to the summit. This snow is perpetual, 'tho part of it melts annually, which loss is supplied the ensuing winter. Yet it is presumed no thaw takes place on the summit, but on the sides some distance down. When the snow accumulates on the projections so as to lose its balance it is precipitated below in the form of avalanches something like those of the Alps, taking on its way large rocks and increasing in size as it goes along. Trees give way before it until it finds rest in the lower places where it aids to form the sources of rivers. Snow slides are also common by which piles of snow miles in extent are detached and force their way into the valleys or at least as far as the thickly timbered section. Many parts of these mountains along Powder River and the Big Horn appear to have undergone volcanic action. Pumice stone and different rocks in a state of fusion can be picked up. There are also large towers of melted sand 20 or 30 feet high, some of which can be met with in the valleys isolated from any rock, and surrounded by green prairie for miles every way. Other ridges of hills seem to have been entirely calcined, convulsed by some eruption, after which the rain has washed them into that grotesque appearance known as Mauvaise Terre, which has already been referred to in treating of the Sioux district. Some of the springs near the head of the Yellowstone are bituminous, sending forth a substance like tar, which is inflammable. Others are sulfurous, and one or two boiling. The water in the last is hot enough to cook meat well enough to fit it to be eaten. The Indians describe others to be of a poisonous nature to animals, 'tho the same water is said not to affect the human species. Many beautiful specimens of petrified marine shells, fish, snakes, and wood are to be found along the banks of the Yellowstone and its tributaries, even some distance in the interior. Some of these do not belong to any known living animals of the kind in this country, which would seem to prove that these mountains have at a former period been submarine. Most of the tributaries of the Yellowstone are well wooded; 'tho that river is only well timbered about one-third the distance from its conflux to the base of the mountains, where the pine growth commences, the lower part being altogether cotton-wood and the points getting larger from the mouth of Powder River to its junction with the Missouri. The soil is good along the valley of the Yellowstone from the mouth to the Big Horn. Indeed most of the valleys near the mountains through which streams run are fit for tilling purposes, 'tho the want of timber in the interior would always prove a bar to the country's ever being thickly settled by an agricultural population.

The Yellowstone, like the Missouri, rises to its full every spring, owing to the melting of the snow on the lower parts of the mountains. This rise usually comes on about the middle of May and continues till the middle of June, when it commences falling unless kept up by heavy rains. During this high stage of water steamers of light draft might navigate it to the first rapids which are about 150 miles from the mouth. The ice commonly gives way about the first of April, and when broken up suddenly by pressure of water from the mountains, it forms dams quite across the valley raising the water 50 or 60 feet and inundating the neighboring country. The Crow Indians are greatly in fear of the water on these occasions, and suffer severely when taken unaware. The writer was eyewitness to one of these breakings up early in the month of February. About 130 lodges of Crows were encamped on the bank of the Yellowstone where the valley is 3 miles wide to the nearest hills. The water came down upon them in the night so suddenly that they barely escaped with their lives by running to the hills. But the land near the bluffs is lower than that on the bank of the stream, consequently in running that way they encountered water, wading and swimming through it carrying their children. They lost their whole winter's hunt, besides nearly all their arms, ammunition, and other property. When the water fell it left immense quantities of ice piled up around their lodges, which were dug out with great difficulty. Their entire loss on this occasion could not be much less than 10 or 12 thousand dollars' worth of merchandise. A few years ago the American Fur Co.'s fort at the mouth of the Big Horn was inundated in the same way, and a great deal of merchandise and peltries destroyed. This river is, when high, very rapid and dangerous to navigate on account of the rocks, snags, and other obstructions. Mackinaw boats descend it, but every year furs are lost and men are drowned.

POPULATION AND MAJOR DIVISIONS

The Crow Indians live in skin lodges like the rest of the migratory tribes. They were formerly about 800 lodges or families, but from the usual causes of diminution, sickness, and war, are now reduced to 460 lodges. These are separated into several bands each governed by a chief, and occupying different parts of their territory.[6] Their present range and divisions are nearly as follows.

[6] Larocque estimated Crow population at some three hundred lodges in 1805, having been reduced from two thousand lodges by a succession of destructive smallpox epidemics. "Since the great decrease of their numbers they generally dwell all together and flit at the same time and as long as it is possible for them to live when together they seldom part . . . though at such time and as long as they are not liable to be attacked they part for a short time." *(Journal, 55–56.)* Prior to Chief Rotten Belly's death in 1834, his rivalry with Long Hair resulted in a split of the tribe into two divisions, the River and the Mountain Crows. ("The Bradley Manuscript," Montana Historical Society, *Contributions,* Vol. IX, 312–13.)

That band headed by "The Big Robber" usually make their winter hunt on the head of Powder River, and of late years take their furs and buffalo robes to the trading houses along the River Platte in the spring from which they obtain supplies to continue their operations, and move back to winter quarters early in the fall.[7] Another portion, led by "Two Face," is the largest band of the Crows, consisting of about 200 lodges.[8] These generally move about through Wind River Mountains and deal with the American Fur Co.'s traders located up the Yellowstone. The next part of any consideration is that which acknowledges "The Bear's Head" as its leader and which travels along the Yellowstone from the mouth to its head, sometimes passing the winter with the Assiniboines and trading at Fort Union, but more frequently selling the proceeds of their hunt to the traders in the upper part of their country.[9]

Zenas Leonard, the fur trader, found the Crows in "two divisions of an equal number in each" in the fall of 1834. (*Adventures of Zenas Leonard, Fur Trader* [ed. by John C. Ewers], 139.) In 1856, Indian Agent Vaughan estimated Crow population at 450 lodges. (*Annual Report* of the Commissioner of Indian Affairs, 1856, p. 80.) Edward S. Curtis was told of an incipient third division of the Crows, the Whistle Water clan, who, about the year 1850, hunted apart from the other Mountain Crows on the headwaters of the Big Horn and Powder rivers. (*The North American Indian,* IV, 43.) Presumably this was Denig's "Big Robber's Band."

[7] Kurz called this chief "Big Robert." He considered him the head chief of the Mountain Crows, and Rottentail head chief of the River Crows in 1851. Rottentail did not attend the Fort Laramie Treaty Council that summer, so that Big Robber was selected by the government as head chief of the tribe. (*Journal,* 212, 240.) Big Robber was killed in battle in 1858. (*Annual Report* of the Commissioner of Indian Affairs, 1858, p. 91.)

[8] Two Face's Camp traded at Fort Sarpy in April, 1855. The following spring a trader named Scott convinced Two Face that the government annuities at Fort Union contained smallpox, and that he should take his trade to the Platte. His camp was en route to the Platte when Agent Vaughan reached the Crow country that summer. Vaughan sent runners to Two Face and he returned and agreed to receive annuities for his division of the Crows at Fort Union. (In McDonnell's "Fort Benton and Fort Sarpy Journals," 120, 122, 178, 186–87.)

[9] Bear's Head traded at Fort Union in the fall and winter of 1851–52. Kurz referred to him as "the chief in command of the soldiers . . . a warrior of great ability and renown." (*Journal,* 213, 251, 260.) The "Fort Sarpy Journal" makes frequent references to Bear's Head's trade at that post in the early months of 1855, and of his trade at Fort Union in March, 1856. The journalist described Bear's Head

INTERTRIBAL RELATIONS

The whole nation have a rendezvous every summer, when after performing several national solemnities which will be mentioned, they move across the mountains to exchange the greater part of the merchandise traded for horses. This traffic is carried on with the Flat Heads in St. Mary's Valley, or with the Snake and Nez Percé Indians on the headwaters of the Yellowstone.[10] With the natives named, the Crows have been at peace for a long time. Also for the last few years, since 1850, they have been on meeting terms with the Assiniboines. But their natural and eternal enemies are the Blackfeet on the west and the Sioux on the east, with both of whom war has continued from time immemorial without being varied by even a transient peace.[11]

RAIDING FOR HORSES

The Crows are perhaps the richest nation in horses of any residing east of the Rocky Mountains. It is not uncommon for a single family to be the owner of 100 of these animals. Most middle-aged

---

as "a good easy man & lets his people do as they please" about the fort. In 1858 the pioneer Lutheran missionaries to the Crows, Braueninger and Schmidt, stayed in Bear's Head's camp. (In McDonnell's "Fort Benson and Fort Sarpy Journals," 106–15, 158–59, 176, 183, 186, 286.)

[10] The pattern of Crow horse trading was well established as early as the first decade of the nineteenth century. They obtained horses, Spanish riding gear and blankets, and horn bows from the Flatheads, Shoshones, and Nez Percés farther west in exchange for objects of European manufacture (metal knives, awls, spear and arrow heads, kettles, ornaments, and a few guns). At the Hidatsa villages they traded some of the horses and other articles received from the western tribes, together with dried meat, skin lodges, and clothing prepared by Crow women, for corn, pumpkins, tobacco, and European trade articles. (John C. Ewers, "The Indian Trade of the Upper Missouri Before Lewis and Clark: An Interpretation," Missouri Historical Society *Bulletin*, Vol. X, No. 4, pp. 432–41.)

[11] In 1811, Alexander Henry observed that the Crows were the only tribe that ventured northward to make war on the Blackfeet. (*New Light*, II, 720.) The Piegans defeated a combined force of Crows and Gros Ventres (Atsinas) in their last large-scale battle with the Crows in 1866. However, the Crows and Blackfeet continued sporadic horse-raiding expeditions against each other until 1887. (Ewers, *The Blackfeet*, 242–43, 302.)

men have from 30 to 60. An individual is said to be poor when he does not possess at least 20.[12] The Blackfeet also have plenty, and this is cause of continual war. Scarcely a week passes but large numbers are swept off by the war parties on both sides. In these depredations men are killed, which calls for revenge by the losing tribe. During a single summer or winter several hundred animals in this way change owners. A great portion of the time of each nation is occupied either in guarding their own horses or in attempts to take those of their enemies.

The Crow Indians take good care of their horses, as much at least as is practicable in their roving manner of life, and more than any other tribe in the North West territory except the Gros Ventres. They drive them often 10 or 12 miles from the camp, where young men are stationed to guard and water them. These horse guards are the younger portion of the families who own them, from the ages of 15 to 25 years, each family taking charge of its own horses and no more. When on the borders of an enemy's country or at any time when war parties are thought to be in the neighborhood, the best horses are brought home and tied to the doors of their lodges in readiness to follow any persons who might steal the rest in the night. These people live in the hourly expectation of losing all their horses, which is their only wealth, to the warriors of the surrounding nations, particularly the Sioux and Blackfeet.

While writing this, February 1856, a party of Blackfeet took off 70 horses from the camp of Crow Indians at the mouth of the Yellowstone. This they did early in the night so that they were not known to be stolen until about 10 o'clock the next day, when the guard went to look after them. As soon as the discovery was made about 100 Crows started in pursuit, each riding one fast horse and leading another. The Blackfeet had a whole night's start, but the

[12] In 1805, Larocque observed of the Crows, "He is reckoned a poor man who has not 10 horses in spring before the trade at the Missouri takes place and many have 30 or 40, everybody rides, men, women, & children." *(Journal,* 64). In 1833 the Crows were "said to possess more horses than any other tribe on the Missouri." (Maximilian, In Vol. XXII of Thwaites' *Early Western Travels,* 351.) Agent Vaughan estimated that the Crows owned an average of 20 horses per lodge in 1853. *(Annual Report* of the Commissioner of Indian Affairs, 1853, p. 355.)

horses had to break a road through deep snow, by which they lost time, while the pursuers had the advantage of a tolerable road made by their trail. For 3 days and 2 nights they kept up the chase, leaving the horses as they became tired and mounting their lead animals. At the close of the second day their reserve horses gave out and they continued on foot. Both parties during all this time had neither eaten, drunk, nor slept, and were exposed to intense cold, but the chase being one of life or death, there was no time to be lost in any way. At dark on the evening of the third day the Crows came in the vicinity of the enemies, who also being worn out with fatigue and hunger, had camped, killed a buffalo, and were cooking. They had taken the precaution to drive the horses some miles farther, and being unaware of the proximity of their pursuers, were making fine preparations to pass an agreeable night around their fire. The Crows approached the camp under cover of the darkness and woods of the Yellowstone, but were obliged to make a circuit of a few miles where they found their horses, quietly grazing, which they recaptured and drove some distance below the fires of their enemies. After accomplishing this, some of them wished to charge upon them in the night. But their leader waited the breaking of day, when, as he expected, they would separate in different directions to hunt the horses, and they could kill one without danger to themselves. The result was what he anticipated. Early in the morning two men followed the tracks of the horses to near where the Crows lay in wait for them. These they charged upon. One escaped but the other did not or could not run. He endeavored to fire his gun, but was stabbed and scalped alive, and afterwards cut up. No further attempt was made on the rest hard by. They had accomplished what they came to do— got back their horses and killed a man without losing any of their party, which is a better coup than killing several enemies with the loss of a man on their side.

Such skirmishes and chases are of daily occurrence summer and winter around both the Crow and Blackfeet camps. During a year more than 100 are killed on each side. When the parties are strong, severe battles take place and 50 to 100 are killed on each side if they are pursued and overtaken. But they often get away with the horses free of loss; particularly in the summer season when the trail cannot be followed fast, or when large war parties make a descent on small camps. Whatever losses in horses the Crows sustain, they are supplied by yearly peregrinations to the Flat Heads and Nez Percés with whom they exchange guns, blankets, etc., the produce of their robes and furs, for these animals. On their return the same scenes are enacted over again. The Blackfeet, being four times more numerous than the Crows, gain by these expeditions.[13] The latter are gradually becoming weaker in men from this and other causes. The Assiniboines supply themselves with horses by stealing from the Blackfeet, and the Sioux in their turn take them from the Assiniboines. Thus the poor animals are run from one nation to another, frequently in this way returning to their original owners several times. This, with the chase of buffalo and travel of the camp, packing meat, etc., soon wears the beasts out. The Crows value their horses from $60 to $100 each, and those of the Blackfeet can be obtained for from $20 to $60 in merchandise.

It is thought best to be somewhat lengthy and particular about these animals in this history, as it will go far to explain one of the principal causes of personal warfare existing among the tribes, which is destined to lead to their entire extinction. Without horses Indians cannot support their families by a hunter's life. They must have them or starve. Tribes who have few must furnish themselves from those who have many, and smaller nations become so reduced in number by the frequency of these expeditions as to fall an easy prey to the larger ones. This is now the case with the Crows who, 'tho brave enough, can scarcely protect what animals they have, much less go in quest of others from their enemies. They do it, however, and consequently are becoming gradually thinned.

[13] Denig probably classed the Gros Ventres (Atsinas) with the Blackfoot tribes in his comparison of Crow-Blackfeet populations. Still his proportion seems exaggerated. Vaughan included the Atsinas in his estimate of the population of the "Blackfeet Nation" in 1858, yet that figure of 1,175 lodges was nearer two and one-half times the number of the Crows. (*Annual Report* of the Commissioner of Indian Affairs, 1858, p. 432.)

SOME CHARACTERISTICS OF THE CROW INDIANS

This tribe has strongly marked national features, differing in some respects greatly from any others. Their general character is peaceable toward Whites. They are not ever very bloodthirsty toward their enemies, except in case of immediate revenge for the loss of some of their people. One excellent trait in their character is that, if possible, in battle they take the women and children prisoners, instead of dashing their brains out as the rest of the tribes do. They and their friends and brethren (the Gros Ventres) are the only nations we know who exhibit this mark of humanity.

About 12 years ago in a great battle with the Blackfeet in which the Crows killed all the men of 45 lodges of the former, they also took 150 women and children prisoners. These they did not even use harshly. The women were made to work like their own wives—'tho not abused. The children were adopted into their own families, have grown up, and are now as much Crow as those of their own producing.[14] It is also worthy of remark that the women, after a year's residence, and understanding some of the language, will not return to their people when given their liberty. This speaks volumes in favor of the Crows, proving how much better they are with strangers than with their own friends. The male children become Crow warriors, and carry the tomahawk and scalping knife against their relations, often murdering their own fathers or brothers without knowledge or remorse. The loss of a male child or a warrior is always a great misfortune with Indians. It is one less to defend the camp or to hunt. Therefore, in thus raising the children of their enemies, they in a manner supply the loss of a portion killed in war. These children are not always adopted as sons or daughters of those who capture them. This only happens when those who have taken them have recently lost by sickness some of their own children, to which the prisoner child is supposed to bear a resemblance.[15] Whether or not this step is taken, they always

[14] This doubtless was the battle between the Crows and the Small Robes Band of the Piegans in 1846, which reduced the Small Robes from a prominent band to one of minor importance among the Blackfeet. (Ewers, *The Blackfeet*, 188.)

[15] Gray-bull, one of Lowie's informants, stated that he had "raised a boy

become attached to them, who as they grow up show much affection and are instructed in the customs of war and the chase the same as others. The children knowing no other parentage except from the descriptions received from their protectors, which are always unfavorable, their feelings, of course, toward their masters are the same as though they were their own parents.

The Crows are cunning, active, and very intelligent in everything appertaining to the chase, war, or their own individual bargaining. In all other respects they are in a primitive state of ignorance. They are the most superstitious of all the tribes, and can be made to believe almost any story however improbable if the same is of a superhuman nature. Thus they ascribe powers to Whites, and to their own conjurors, far beyond those admitted by any other nation. Residing as they have and still do in the isolated regions of the Rocky Mountains, they have not had the opportunity to improve themselves in any branch of knowledge, even in the most simple things, that those who reside on the Missouri have. They seldom see any white persons in their own country except the fur traders, who are with them part of the winter and who only attract their attention to matters relating to the trade. Surrounded by hostile and powerful tribes, they have not until late years had the advantage of associating with other nations, and from that source gleaning some information concerning the world around them. They may be said to be yet in a state of nature, and but little elevated above the brute creation.

Some of their habits are of so filthy and disgusting a nature as not to admit of being published. In other respects they may be reckoned good. For instance, scarcely an incident has happened during the last 40 years in which they have killed a white man. Even the Rocky Mountain trappers, that desperate set of men who imposed upon and ill-treated them on all occasions, were suffered to trap their country of beaver without molestation. Not that they feared them, for these trappers were scattered through their dis-

because he looked like one of his own sons, who had died." (Lowie, "Social Life of the Crow Indians," Am. Museum of National History *Anthropological Papers*, Vol. IX, pt. 2, p. 219.)

trict in small parties, which could at any time be cut off without loss, but by some natural formation of their disposition, they would not kill them and seldom robbed them. This is the more singular when we reflect that inveterate war was kept up between these trappers and all other nations, in which many were killed on all sides, and which resulted in the Whites abandoning that dangerous business. While the Assiniboines, Sioux, Blackfeet, Crees, and all have murdered Whites at different times, the Crow Nation can step forward and declare themselves unpolluted by their blood.

Another thing equally strange is that such a savage nation, living without any law and but little domestic regulation of any kind, should be able to settle all their individual quarrels with each other without bloodshed, while yearly brawls and murders take place among the rest of the tribes. In the space of 12 years but one Crow Indian has been killed by his own people. The cause of this was: An Indian struck another's wife across the face with his whip, upon which the husband stabbed him on the spot. The relations of the deceased armed to kill the other. But his friends protected him till dark, when he fled to the Snake Indians, with whom he resided 12 years. Then, thinking the affair had blown over, he returned to his own people. But the old grudge was renewed, and he was obliged to leave the second time, with the intimation that should be again return he would be killed. Since that time he has not been heard from. Though this is the case, and they do not kill or strike each other, yet we must not infer therefrom that no quarrels take place. On the contrary, differences arise more frequently among them than among others who carry quarrels to extremes, because, where the penalty of offense is death, persons are more circumspect in their behavior. But the Crows settle all disputes by abuse and taking each other's horses. Thus, if an Indian elopes with another's wife, the unfortunate husband will seize upon the whole of the offender's horses. Should he have none, then he takes those of his relations. In this he has the support not only of his own relations, but of the greater part of the camp. Now an action of this kind would be death to the offender with all other nations, besides taking a good deal of his property.

When retaliation is made by taking horses, the person who has committed the offense keeps the woman, and in the course of time his relations buy back his horses from the other. Any crime or misdemeanor can be paid for among the Crows except murder. Even should this happen, we feel convinced that their fondness for horses would overrule their disposition to revenge, and that a reasonable number of these animals given to the friends of the deceased would settle the affair. Any large thefts, and all disputes concerning women, are arranged on this system.[16]

Smaller pilferings and discord are decided by heartily abusing each other. At this game both men and women are equally adept, and their language affords a fine variety of beautiful epithets, which they bestow upon each other in great profusion. Most of these expressions consist of comparing the visage and person thus abused to the most disgusting objects in nature, even to things not known in the natural world. Or they likewise cast in each other's teeth the poverty of themselves or their relatives.[17] The men are as bad as the women on these occasions, though men when angry usually commence relating their brave actions, count each coup distinctly on their fingers, calling on their antagonist to do the same and show which is the bravest man. In the course of a dispute of this kind the lie is given many times, which attracts no further notice than sending the like back with the addition of coward, thief, etc. In this way also whole bands abuse each other. The band of the Platte sometimes takes offense at the band along

---

[16] A half-century earlier Larocque noted that quarrels among the Crows generally were settled through gifts of horses or guns to the offended persons, "but there happen few quarrels, and they are generally occasioned by their wives and jealousy." (*Journal,* 58, 61.)

[17] Lowie found that songs "composed in derision of someone that had transgressed the rules of propriety, or in revenge for some personal or group affront, seem to have figured prominently in Crow society. . . . Similar punishment was meted out by jilted lovers, and by one of the three local groups, when affronted by one of the others." ("Social Life of the Crow Indians," Am. Museum of Natural History *Anthropological Papers,* Vol. IX, Pt. 2, p. 245.)

the Yellowstone. Every traveler that comes from one to the other during 1, or sometimes 2 years, brings threats, abuse, and defiance. One who did not know them would think that in case the bands met a desperate struggle would take place. Nevertheless when they meet, after all this parade of threats, they are the most peaceable people in existence. They will remain together for months on good terms. But when they separate, and have a river between them, so that no harm can be done, their war commences and terrible is the abuse shouted across the stream, accompanied by throwing stones that do not reach halfway, or shooting in the air with powder. This kind of conflict is often kept up for a day or two. Then they go different directions, swearing vengeance at their next meeting.

These people also are remarkable for never being the first to break a peace between them and other nations. They have at several periods been on friendly terms with the Assiniboines, Flatheads, Arikaras, Arapahoes, Cheyennes, Snakes, and other tribes. Whenever these transient peaces were interrupted, it was done by the others.

Having now enumerated some of their good qualities it is time we should refer to other traits not so amiable. In the first place they are beggarly and troublesome, particularly the young men, women, and children. When camped around a fort or wintering houses they fill up every place, torment all the domestic animals, and steal everything they can lay their hands on. The men are bold and impudent, particularly the warrior class. The women are noisy, thievish. Neither have the least idea of decency or decorum. The bucks make it their whole business night and day to run after the women, who, whether married or not, appear to be perfectly unaware that virtue or chastity has any existence even in the imagination. Their conduct in these matters is carried on in broad daylight without any regard to bystanders or lookers on. Indeed it would appear that they are as destitute of the ideas of decency or modesty as any part of the brute creation, for they prefer to be seen rather than to conceal any and all transactions between the sexes. No disgrace or penalty being attached to deceiving young women, contrary to the custom of other tribes, the ruining of a woman's character appears to be lightly if at all considered; it must follow that virtue is at a very low ebb among them. The consequence of this promiscuous and illicit intercourse is that disease more or less runs through the whole nation. Another effect is that a superfluous number of unmarried women are to be found, and those who are married are neglected by their husbands who run after the rest. The married women are not a whit better than the others as they usually have had more or less connection before they were taken as wives by any one man. Before marriage a woman is not thought impudent if she has but one lover; more, however, stamps her character as a courtesan. Consequently if such a thing as an honest woman can be found in this tribe it is one who has been raised under the husband's own care from a child, and taken for a wife at the age of 10 to 13 years.[18]

The old men, chiefs, and councilors are more decorous in their behavior as regards certain matters in which women are concerned. Neither are they so impudent and forward as the young men. But they make it up in begging any and everything they think likely to be had. In their camp this system of begging is charged to borrowing articles which they invariably forget to return. The stealing of property is mostly confined to the old women who are capital hands at it. Sometimes small things such as knives, ornaments, and utensils are abstracted. But in a large camp where all are compelled to leave their buffalo hides outside their lodges for want of room, several hundred of these and other skins are stolen from each other during a winter. About a fort they find good picking —tin cups, knives, spoons, articles of clothing, tools, etc., disappear

[18] In 1833, Maximilian noted, "Of the female sex, it is said of the Crows, that they, with the women of the Arikkaras, are the most dissolute of all of the tribes of the Missouri." (In Thwaite's *Early Western Travels*, XXII, 354.) Lowie found that Crow "mythology, the reminiscences of informants, and ancient songs are all surcharged with evidence of the tendency to apparently unlimited philandering." ("Notes on the Social Organization and Customs of the Mandan, Hidatsa, and Crow Indians." American Museum of Natural History *Anthropological Papers*, Vol. XXI, Pt. 1, p. 78.)

with remarkable rapidity. They are so adroitly taken even before the eyes of the owners as always to escape detection. Larger items such as guns and horses they do not steal, either from the Whites or from each other. Frauds of this kind could not be concealed and the owner would take his property. Among kindred, however, these Indians show some liberality. If a man has all horses stolen or killed, he can generally find friends to give him others, though the giver expects payment when the receiver shall have retrieved his losses, or to be paid in some other way. Situated as they are in the constant fear of enemies, and liable at any time to lose their whole stock of animals, custom has pointed out the above plan to secure to them as far as may be the means to obtain a living. However much they may like their horses, or dislike to part with them, yet each man feels he depends on his neighbor for support when they are taken off. This happens so often as to render an understanding of this kind not only desirable, but absolutely necessary to their national existence; so that what appears at first sight to be a liberal and kind action is only one of interested principle.

The men and women are troublesome enough in many things, but the greatest nuisance in creation is Crow children, boys from the ages of 9 to 14 years. These are left to do just as they please. They torment their parents and everyone else, do all kinds of mischief without either correction or reprimand. In other nations these small fry are kept out of sight where men are, but the parents of this nation place them before themselves in every crowd or assembly, or in their own families. Thus they become intolerable, and a few years after ripen into the bold, forward, impudent young men before mentioned.

The male grown portion of the Crows are decidedly prepossessing in their appearance. The warrior class is perhaps the handsomest body of Indians in North America.[19] They are all tall,

[19] George Catlin considered Crow men "really a handsome and well formed set of men as can be seen in any part of the world." He described the faces of "the greater part of the men" as "strongly marked with a bold and prominent antiangular nose, with a clear and rounded arch, and a low receding forehead." (*Letters and Notes,* Vol. I, 49, 193.) At Fort Union in the summer of 1832, Catlin painted the earliest known portraits of Crow Indians, many of which illustrate this facial profile.

straight, well formed, with bold, fierce eyes, and as usual good teeth. These also dress elegantly and expensively. A single dress often brings the value of two, three, or four horses. The men of this age are neat and clean in their persons, fond of dress and decoration, wear a profusion of ornaments and have different dresses suitable for different occasions. They wear their hair long, that is, it is separated into plaits to which other hair is attached with gum, and hangs down their backs to several feet in length in a broad flat mass which is tied at the end and spotted over with clay. A small portion in front is cut short and made to stand upright. On each side of the head hang frontlets made of beads or shells, and alongside each ear is suspended several inches of wampum. Their faces on ordinary occasions are painted red, varied with a tinge of yellow on the eyelids. In large slits through the ears are tied sea shells cut into angular shapes, which are of a changeable blue and green color. These shells find their way from the coast of California through the different nations until handed to the Crows in exchange for other property.

As we do not wish to lose sight of the order of our history and are obliged in this place to confine ourselves to general description, the different dresses worn by these people on the occasions of their various ceremonies will be described when we come to treat of their manners and customs. It is sufficient here to state that the Crow men, as far as outward appearance goes, are much the finest looking of all the tribes.

It would seem that nature on this occasion has done so much in favor of the Crow men that she entirely neglected the women. Of all the horrid looking objects in the shape of human beings these women are the most so. Bad features and worse shapes, filthy habits, dresses and persons smeared with dirt and grease, hair cut short and full of vermin, faces daubed over with their own blood in mourning for dead relations, and fingers cut off so that scarcely a whole hand is to be found among them, are the principal things that attract the attention of the observer. The young women are hard, coarse-featured, sneaky looking, with sharp, small noses, thick lips, red eyelids caused by the venereal diseases, and bare arms clothed with a coat of black dirt so ground in as to form a portion of the skin. The old hags can be compared to nothing but witches or demons. Some of them are of monstrous size, weighing 250 to 300 pounds, with naked breasts hanging halfway down to their knees. Being always in mourning for some dead relations, they are usually seen in old skin dresses, barelegged, hair cut short, and their faces smeared over with white clay and blood. Notwithstanding all this, some of them have very handsome dresses which they wear on several occasions and which will be referred to, though they pay but little attention to dress of any kind in their ordinary everyday life. It would appear singular that such handsome men would be satisfied with such ugly women, but they do not seem to have the same idea of female beauty as we have. If a woman be young and not absolutely deformed, one appears to be as desirable for them as another.[20]

About one-half the nation have a plurality of wives, the rest only one each.[21] The property of husband and wife is separate. Each has a share of horses, merchandise, and ornaments. Not being accustomed to depend much on each other's fidelity they wisely prepare for immediate separation in the event of any great domestic quarrel. When from certain causes they decide on parting, the husband takes charge of all male children unless they are too small to leave the mother; the female part go with the wife. Guns, bows, ammunition, and all implements of war and the chase belong to the man; while kettles, pans, hides, and other baggage of the like nature fall to the woman's share. The lodge is hers, and the horses and other property having been divided years before in an anticipa-

[20] The artists, Catlin and Kurz shared Denig's opinion of the appearance of Crow women. Catlin observed, "The Crow women . . . are not handsome." *(Letters and Notes,* I, 50). Kurz stated, "Women of the Crow tribe are known rather more for their industry and skilled work than for beauty of face and form." *(Journal,* 184.)

[21] Of Crow polygamy, Larocque observed, "some of them have 8 or 11 and 12 [wives] but in such cases they do not all live with him, some are young girls that are only betrusted. But by far the greatest part have only 2 or 3 wives; some have only one, and those reason upon the folly of those that take many wives." *(Journal,* 57.)

tion of this event, each has no difficulty in selecting their own. From this state of things it must follow that differences often arise as to what kind of merchandise shall be bought with the proceeds of their winter's hunt. She maneuvers to get such articles as would finally become hers, and he works for his advantage. In these differences, where considerable affection exists between the parties, the woman usually gains the point. At other times the skins are divided previous to selling and either trades for what they like best. They exhibit great fondness for their children. Whatever they cry for they must have. When sick, no expense is spared for the services of the medicine men, and in death they evince every feeling of deep-felt grief. When anyone dies the immediate relatives each cut off a joint of a finger. This is done by placing an ax or butcher knife on the joint, and striking the same with a good-sized stick. Occasionally, in a high state of excitement, they lay their finger on a block and chop it off with a knife held in the other hand. The blow often misses the joint and the finger is divided between joints, which takes a long time to heal and leaves a portion of the bone protruding which presents a very disagreeable appearance. Both men and women mutilate their hands in this manner, so that at the present day there is scarcely an entire hand among them. The men, however, reserve entire the thumb and forefinger of the left hand, and thumb and two fingers of the right, so that they can hold a gun or draw a bow. But even these fingers often want a joint or so when all the others are cut off to the stump. They never tie up these sores, but after daubing over their faces with the blood, hold a bunch of wild sage on the stump until it stops bleeding. The blood is never washed off their faces, but let dry there and wear off, and when it is no more to be seen they cut their legs to obtain it and renew the application.[22] The hair is also sacrificed

[22] Zenas Leonard witnessed self-mutilation by scarification and amputation of portions of fingers by relatives of Crow warriors killed in battle with the Blackfeet, November 21, 1834. He saw that males preserved "the first two fingers of the right hand . . . for the purpose of bending the bow and many of the aged females may be seen with the end off each of their fingers, and some have even taken off the second crop." (*Adventures,* 152.)

on these occasions, either cut short or torn away by handfuls. In this state the mourner goes about on the hills howling dismally every day or so for a year or more, clothed with an old skin, bare feet and legs, wading through snow or mud, and crying until they are so hoarse as not to be heard.

When the camp is on the move in the summer, this tribe presents a gay and lively appearance, more so perhaps than any other. On these occasions both men and women dress in their best clothes. Their numerous horses are decked out with highly ornamented saddles and bridles of their own making, scarlet collars and housings with feathers on their horse's heads and tails. The warriors wear their richly garnished shirts, fringed with human hair and ermine, leggings of the same, and headdresses of various kinds, strange, gay, and costly. Any and all kinds of bright-colored blankets, loaded with beads worked curiously and elegantly across them, with scarlet leggings, form the principal portion of the dresses of the young men or those whose feats at war have not yet entitled them to the distinguished privilege of wearing hair. These bucks are fancifully painted on the face, their hair arranged as has been described, with heavy and costly appendages of shells, beads, and wampum, to the ears and around the neck. The women have scarlet or blue cloth dresses, others white cotillions made of the dressed skins of the bighorn sheep, which are covered across the breast and back with rows of elk teeth and sea shells. These frocks are fringed along the side and round the bottom. The fringes are wrought with porcupine quills and feathers of many colors. The price of the elk teeth alone is 100 for a good horse or in money the value of $50. A frock is not complete unless it has 300 elk teeth, which, with the other shells, skin, etc., could not be bought for less than $200. When traveling, the women carry to the horn of the saddle the warrior's medicine bag, and shield. His sword, if he has one, is tied along the side and hangs down. The man takes charge of his gun and accouterments in readiness for any attack however sudden. The baggage is all packed on the horses, at which they are very expert. Kettles, pots, pans, etc., have each their sack with cords attached. These are on the sides of the animal, and on top of the saddle is either one large child fit to guide the horse, or two or three small children so enveloped and well tied as to be in no danger of falling.[23] Often the heads of children are seen popping up alongside of pup dogs or cub bears on the same horse. The lodge occupies one horse and the poles another. The meat and other provisions are put up in bales well secured. They are so expeditious in packing that after their horses are caught they are saddled, the tents struck, everything put on the horses and on the march in less than 20 minutes. The great number and good quality of their horses make a showy appearance. Both men and women are capital riders. The young men take this occasion to show off their persons and horsemanship to the women. A good deal in the way of courting is also done when traveling. The train is several miles in length, wives are separate from their husbands, daughters at some distance from their mothers, which opportunities are not lost by these young and enterprising courtiers. They ride up alongside, make love, false promises, in short use any and all means to obtain their end.

When on the march they move rapidly and when pressed for meat to eat, still more so. On these occasions they go on a fast trot, sometimes at a gallop, making from 20 to 40 miles a day. Generally, however, their encampments are from 10 to 15 miles.[24]

[23] Larocque noticed that Crow cihldren too young to ride alone were tied in the saddle when camp was moved. (*Journal*, 64). Two decades later William Gordon wrote of Crow children, "At four or five years of age they will ride alone and guide the horse." (Chardon's *Journal*, Appendix E.)

[24] Probably the best description of daily movements of any nomadic tribe of the Upper Missouri appears in Larocque's journal of his trip with the Crows from the Hidatsa villages on the Missouri to the Yellowstone River near present Billings, Montana, via the eastern bases of the Big Horn Mountains from June to September, 1805. During this journey camp was moved on forty-seven of the seventy-six days en route. Daily movements ranged from three to twenty-four miles. The median distance traveled on those days camp was moved was nine and one-half miles. Generally they followed the courses of streams. There was no mention of a dry overnight camp. On several days rain caused a late start or an early stop. Delays of a day or more were caused by inclement weather (rain), serious illness in camp, halts to hunt (although hunting parties generally were out while camp was moved),

It is often a strange and barbarous sight to see small children but a few days old tied to a piece of bark or wood and hung to the saddle bow which flies up at each jump of the horse when on the gallop, their heads exposed to hot sun or cold. This does not appear to hurt them in the least. At sunset the cavalcade stops. The spot for each lodge is cleaned away and in the space of a few minutes the lodges are set up, the horses turned out to graze, and each family has a kettle of meat on the fire.

Owing to their having good animals and plenty of them the Crows seldom suffer for want of meat as is the case with some tribes who are not so well furnished with horses. They can move camp at any time and go in quest of buffalo, should there be none in the neighborhood. They have little else to eat but meat. Their country produces a few wild cherries, plums, and service berries, together with some esculent roots. But none of these are collected in sufficient quantities to form a resource in time of need, and as they do not cultivate, they depend entirely on the chase for subsistence.

They are good buffalo hunters on horseback with the bow and arrow, seldom using the gun for hunting except on foot when the snow is too deep for horses to catch the buffalo. They are not so good on foot as the Crees and Assiniboines, who, having few horses, have more practice in this manner of hunting.[25] They can kill elk and bighorn with their shot guns but are far behind the other nations named in this respect. They do not manage their hunts as the other tribes do. They have no soldiers' lodge to regulate the

---

to dry meat and to dress hides following a concentrated hunt, and to dry bison tongues for the forthcoming late summer ceremonial, to cut ash whips, to hold a council to determine the route to be traveled after a disagreement among the leaders, and to wait in readiness while scouts reconnoitered for signs of enemies feared to be in the vicinity. They also stopped for a day when good pasture was reached to permit their horses to feed and rest after two days of hard, long marches across barren country. *(Journal.)*

[25] In 1805, Larocque found the Crows to be "excellent marks men with the bows & arrows but poor shots with the gun . . . They say no equal number of other Indians can beat them on horseback, but that on foot they are not capable to cope with those nations who have no horses." *(Journal, 65–66.)*

hunts.[26] Each man goes out with whoever chooses to follow. Sometimes nearly the whole camp turns out to one surround, and again but few. When many hunt together several hundred buffalo are killed, the meat and hides divided, and all return packing the same on their horses. There are no poor people among this nation. That is, there are none so destitute of means that they cannot go or send to the hunt and get a supply of meat. In this respect they are much better off than some of the neighboring tribes. Another remarkably good trait in their character is they do not suffer the aged and infirm to be left behind and perish as is the custom with some other nations, but this can be accounted for from the fact of their having the means to transport them while the others have not.[27] Neither is meat ever so rare with the Crows as with the Assiniboines.

BIOGRAPHY OF CHIEF ROTTEN BELLY

Some warriors have arisen among the Crows who displayed much generalship in conducting different expeditions against their enemies. Among the foremost of these can be classed Rotten Belly, who flourished about 20 years since, 'tho he is now dead. Had this man had the same opportunities of action he would undoubtedly have ranked with Tecumseh or Pontiac, but as his operations were confined to petty attacks on the hostile nations on their bor-

[26] This statement is contrary to Larocque's earlier observation. "The hunting matches are regulated by a band of Young men who have much authority causing them to encamp or flit at their pleasure tell them where there are Buffaloes & to go hunting. They prevent them from setting out after one another and make those that are first ready to wait for the others so that they may all go together and have an equal chance. Those that behave refractory to their orders are punished by a beating or their arms are broken or their tents cut to pieces." *(Journal, 60.)* Zenas Leonard also witnessed strict regulation of the buffalo hunt by Crow police in 1834. *(Adventures, 141–42.)*

[27] Larocque wrote of the Crows: "I saw more cripples and decrepid old men among them than among any other nation except the Big Bellys and the Mandans. . . . The Mandans and Big Bellys are sedentary and the Rocky Mountain Indians [Crows] have so many horses, that they can transport their sick without trouble. Whether they did it not before they had horses I do not know." *(Journal, 57.)*

ders, and as he had but a small number to command, his friends must be contented with this small tribute to his memory.

When a very young man he commenced his career of war in going out at the head of small parties and bringing home horses from the Cheyennes, Arapahoes, Banacks, Sioux, and Blackfeet. In these expeditions he was generally successful, taking large herds of horses and bringing his own party safe to camp. This is the principal aim of a leader, for if in stealing the horses he had had some of his people killed no credit would follow the feat. On many occasions, however, he was followed and overtaken by his enemies. These were the times in which he proved himself able to command. He had taken all precautionary measures, picked his men, had them well armed, the weapons in good order, and always retreated with his booty in a direction where timber was near in which to take shelter in case of attack. When escape was impossible he forted with wood and stones and gave battle. Frequent were the skirmishes he had with his foes in this way. But fortune favored him. At every sally he either brought home their scalps or horses and always without losing any of his party. At the age of 30 he was chief of the Crow Nation.

Other things aided this man on his road to the chieftainship. He had large and rich connections, was considered a prophet or medicine man, one who could obtain supernatural aid in his operations. He made no show of his medicine, no parade of sacrifices, or smokings, no songs or ceremonies, but silently and alone he prayed to the thunder for assistance. In his general conduct he was not an agreeable man, but rather of a quiet, surly disposition. He spoke but little, but that in a tone of command. His great superiority over others consisted in decision, action, and an utter disregard for the safety of his own person.

When acknowledged as the only chief of the whole nation he enacted many good laws and rules for their preservation, led the camp with judgment, choosing places where game was plentiful, and the country suitable for their animals and defense. He caused them to trade for more guns and ammunition, established regular camp sentinels night and day, and used such vigilance that during his life the hostile neighbors could make no headway either against his people or their animals. Whoever approached the camp was killed. Warriors were on the alert and well prepared.

When arrived at the sole command he left off heading small parties and carried war into their enemies' country on a large scale. The first grand battle was with about 80 lodges of the Blackfeet on Muscleshell River. Rotten Belly had his spies out watching movements of this camp for months beforehand, and having collected the whole Crow Nation maneuvered them in such a way as not to raise the suspicion of their enemies. He appeared to be marching out of their country when in reality he was encircling them. His wish was to come upon them on some plain, and take them unprepared.

When by his runners he knew that the time and situation were favorable to his views, he, by forced marches, placed his camp near them without being discovered. Under cover of the night about 400 warriors placed themselves still closer. Early in the day when their enemy's camp was on the move, scattered over a level plain of some miles in extent, he gave the word to charge. Terrible was the storm that swept over the Blackfeet. The Crows were well armed, mounted, and prepared, the others embarrassed with their women, children, and baggage. Their long and weak line of march was literally, "rubbed out" by their savage foes. Whoever endeavored to defend was killed, the women and children taken prisoners. Most of the men of the Blackfeet were in front of the traveling van. They soon rallied and returned the charge but were outnumbered. Although they fought bravely for some time they soon were obliged to leave their families and seek safety in flight. Others died defending their children. In the end, after a severe battle of a few hours, 100 and upwards of the Blackfeet lay dead on the field. Two hundred and thirty women and children were taken prisoners and more than 500 head of horses fell to the share of the Crows, besides all the lodges, camp equipment, provisions, etc. The Crows lost 22 men in this battle, besides others badly wounded.

But upon the whole it was a great victory for these wild tribes who seldom have an opportunity to do half that much. They did not scalp half their enemies, there were too many and they tired of the employment. But few men of this small camp of Blackfeet escaped. The male children taken were brought up to be Crow warriors, and the females to be the wives of their captors with the view of repairing the former losses of these people in their constant wars with neighboring tribes.

Although others besides Rotten Belly distinguished themselves on this occasion, yet he being the leader received the greater share of applause. Others counted individual coups, he the aggregate. His name was sung through all the camps for months. His lodge was painted with rude drawings of the fight, he being the principal figure. The scalps, after having been danced, were suspended from his lodge poles. His shirt, leggings, even his buffalo robe were fringed with the hair of his enemies—the last being the most distinguished mark that can be borne on the dress of a warrior, and one never used but by him who has killed as many enemies as to make a robe with their scalps.

It seldom happens in human affairs but that when the height of prosperity is reached some reverse follows. Too confident in their own powers and elated with their victory, contrary to the advice of their leader, the nation divided into several camps. They again, having once lost sight of their general and acknowledged head, divided into smaller parties, each moving in a different direction for hunting purposes. It has also been the custom of these Indians every year or two to visit other nations in and across the mountains for the purposes of trade and barter as has been mentioned. Sometimes they pushed their way as far as the Kiowas and Comanches and occasionally near the Spanish settlements of Taos and Santa Fe. In these travels they encountered some tribes with whom they were at peace but always rendered themselves liable to be cut off by larger nations considered enemies. At all events the profit ensuing from these adventures in horses, ornaments, etc., either bought of the one or stolen from the other, was sufficient inducement to make the attempt. They are a bold and active people and do not calculate much the danger when the expedition is likely to prove advantageous.

At the time above mentioned, when the Crows had separated into small parties for the purposes mentioned, a portion consisting of 30 lodges or upward placed their camp on the headwaters of the river Cheyenne beyond the first spurs of the Rocky Mountains called the Black Hills. The Cheyennes, a hostile nation from whom the river takes its name, had in a great measure abandoned that part of the country for several years before and moved on the South Fork of Platte River. Here, after remaining some time they suffered considerably from war parties of Comanches and were obliged to move back to their old district a little before the time the small body of Crows undertook their journey through it. The Cheyennes numbered at that time about 300 lodges, were rich in horses, good warriors, and perhaps the best horsemen in the world. Perceiving the approach of their enemies they lay in ambush for them, attacked them in the night, and massacred nearly the whole. Some few men escaped in the darkness to carry the sad intelligence to their people, but the rest, men, women, and children, were indiscriminately put to death. The few captives taken, whether male or female, young or old, were reserved for torture which was inflicted upon them in every possible way their savage natures could suggest.

In the course of a week or two those who fled reached some of the camps of their own people, who sent others in quest of the different portions of the nation scattered far and wide. Their principal aim now was to hunt up their chief, Rotten Belly, and request him once more to be their leader to revenge. He was then with the Flatheads, but these people travel fast and such was their haste to collect their forces that in a month's time they had all rendezvoused in their own country with their chief at their head ready to start on the war path.

The Crow camp on this occasion presented a grand and imposing appearance. They were all ordered to parade with their arms and accouterments ready for the inspection of their chief. As at these times distinctions of rank are observed, each warrior wore those decorations which indicated his standing among his people. The general command of the whole devolved upon Rotten Belly, but other chiefs also are deserving of notice, such as Long Hair, the Little White Bear, Yellow Belly, Two Face, etc., each of whom had under his immediate command a large band of followers. These minor chiefs composed the Council of Rotten Belly, all being well versed in the art of Indian Warfare besides having given proofs of their skill and bravery on many occasions under the eye of their head chief. The whole number of warriors thus assembled was about 600, or about one-fourth of the whole nation able to bear arms. They were also picked men, not young beginners but persons who had struck enemies, headed war parties, and given other evidences of their willingness and ability in the hour of danger. All these were mounted on fast-running horses with splendid trappings. Their dresses were of the most gay and costly description, their arms in the very best order, and their faces painted in the usual manner when starting on hazardous excursions. Clan after clan passed in review before the chief, whose keen eyes were directed to their arms and animals, occasionally finding some fault with one or detecting some defect in another which was directed to be remedied. The chief on parades of this description, or indeed on all public ceremonies, wore his whole insignia on different parts of his person and his horse. His war eagle bonnet reached from his head to the ground even when he was mounted on his tall and powerful war horse. His robe and dress were everywhere fringed with the scalp hair of his enemies. Where this was wanting the beholder was reminded of his rank by rude drawings explanatory of some of his bravest achievements at war. Very little noise accompanied this display of his troops. The cry of mourners for their lately killed relatives rang strange and wildly through the valley, and a gloomy, stern resolve was depicted on the faces of all the warriors. One sole idea, one mind, and one intent reigned, which was that of speedy and terrible revenge.

After all had been thoroughly examined, approved, and enlisted, the chief called the head men in council, where, in a few words, he explained to them his decision and plan of action. This was to leave the camp where it then was, take the force he had aroused and pursue the Cheyennes until he found them, even into the heart of New Mexico. He took a solemn oath, in which he was joined by the whole council, never to return until they had taken full revenge for the loss of their friends. The substance of this decision was harangued through the camp, 2 days given for preparation, and on the third the whole party above described were moving rapidly toward the country of the Cheyennes.

It is not our design to follow this party by describing each day's march. It will be sufficient to state that they proceeded with great caution, which, with a correct knowledge of the country, enabled them to proceed without discovery. When near the place where their enemies were supposed to be, most traveling was done during the night, the party resting themselves and their animals in the daytime. Scouts were thrown several miles who inspected the foreground and conveyed intelligence to the main body behind to move forward. Not a foot of land was traveled over that had not undergone the scrutiny of the discoverers for hours from the neighboring hills. Much time was wasted in this way in order to take their enemies unprepared, for after arriving at the place where the battle had been fought they found the Cheyennes had fled with their camp some days previous. The trail made by a tolerably large camp is not difficult to follow. The chief therefore could calculate with some degree of certainty how far they might be in advance and the time required to overtake them. Having with this view examined their late encampment and pointed out to his followers the different signs indicating the above intelligence, they proceeded to collect the human skulls and bones, which they judged very correctly to have once belonged to living persons of their own nation, being those that had been massacred. After crying over them, cutting themselves, and making promises to their spirits to take ample revenge, they dug large holes and interred them. This is contrary to their usual custom. Dead bodies are usually enveloped and placed in trees. But as these were but the bones and no other way of disposing of them presented itself, they used this method to secure even these poor remains from further insult by passing enemies.

A grand speech was made over these ceremonies in which the chief artfully stirred up the spirit of his followers to a pitch of revenge bordering on desperation. Their vows were renewed, arms examined and at once the march was resumed more rapidly.

In about 10 days after this occurrence they found themselves in the valley watered by the Arkansas where they saw such fresh indications of the Cheyennes being at hand as induced Rotten Belly to proceed with great caution, having his best spies out in all directions. These soon brought certain information of their enemies' camp, having approached it in the night and made a correct examination of its locality. The next night they were stationed along two creeks between which the Cheyennes had placed their lodges. The Crows were concealed in the valley of the creeks among the wood and timber and at the distance of a mile from the camp, presenting an extended line on each side of men ranged from 10 to 20 paces apart. One detachment was headed by Rotten Belly and the other by the Little White Bear. Early in the morning, or as soon as day broke, seven Crows were sent down each creek who, running between the Cheyennes' horses and their lodges, drove all the animals slowly in the direction of the main body of their people who lay in ambush. The Cheyennes perceiving but few persons taking away all their horses gave chase on foot at different distances as they could arm and run. Thus some 60 to 80 persons, the principal warriors of the camp, were led between the files who simultaneously raised the war whoop and encircled them. Of these not one escaped. There was but one rush, one discharge of arms and arrows, and the whole lay dead. Others now sallied out from the camp and were likewise cut off in detail. But few remained in the lodges. These were charged upon—some absconded but all males met with were put to death. The result of the whole was a complete victory on the part of the Crows. Upward of 200 enemies were killed, 270 women and children were taken prisoners. More than 1,000 horses, besides all the camp baggage, merchandise, and ornaments, were divided among the Crows. Their loss on this occasion was but 5 men killed and some 10 or 15 wounded. The object of the expedition having been accomplished, the party traveled back to their own people elated with victory and satisfied with revenge.[28]

The above circumstance brings up the life of the Crow chief to the year 1833, at which time the whole Crow Nation might number 800 lodges, which, averaging 8 persons to each tent would make about 6,400 souls. At this period emigration was fast flowing toward Arkansas and each year the trains of movers became more numerous over the fertile plains watered by that river. It so happened that this Crow party on their way home rejoicing came suddenly upon a caravan of emigrants, or rather the advanced guards of the Indians met with some stragglers belonging to the expedition. By the sign of waving their arms imitating the flying of a crow the Whites judged they belonged to that nation and, being aware of their friendly disposition, gave them warning not to approach the wagons as some of the Whites were then lying sick with smallpox. It was with great difficulty they were made to understand the nature of the danger attending their visit to the wagons, and either not believing the tale or not realizing the consequences they soon gathered round the emigrants bargaining for horses and trafficking for other articles. It is but justice to these people to say that on this occasion they used their utmost endeavors to prevent the Indians from receiving the infection. They tried to deal with them at a distance from the sick, but all to no purpose. Before they parted numbers had caught the pestilence. Before they reached their homes the disease commenced making its appearance and when they arrived in camp more than half the party were taken

[28] No contemporary account of this battle is known. However, nearly a century after the event Lowie collected a "quasi-historical" Crow tradition telling of a small party under Dangling-foot wiped out by the Cheyennes, of Rotten Belly's leadership of the large revenge party, of their ambush of the enemy at the junction of a river and killing of more than 100 Cheyennes, with the loss of but one Crow Indian. The lone Crow casualty, it was claimed, was the younger brother of a woman who had disobeyed Rotten Belly's warning not to kill birds and had destroyed a meadow lark en route to the battleground. *(The Crow Indians,* 230–36.) In 1876, Little Face told Lieutenant James H. Bradley of a great Crow victory on the Arkansas under Rotten Belly's leadership, emphasizing also the episode of the killing of a bird by a Crow woman, whose relative was subsequently killed in this battle. ("The Bradley Manuscript," Montana Historical Society *Contributions,* Vol. IX, 304–305.)

down by it. It is needless to dwell upon the misery, distress, and death that followed. The well-known fatality of the smallpox among savages has been often described. In this case it was the same as with the other tribes—about one in six or seven recovered. As soon as possible after the arrival of the warriors the camp broke up into small bands each taking different directions. They scattered through the mountains in the hope of running away from the pestilence. All order was lost. No one pretended to lead or advise. The sick and dead were alike left for the wolves and each family tried to save itself.

They certainly gained something by this course. At least the infection was not quite so fatal as among stationary tribes. For the rest of the fall and winter the disease continued its ravages but in the ensuing spring it had ceased. Runners were sent through their country from camp to camp and the remnant of the nation was once more assembled near the head of Big Horn River. Terrible was the mourning on this occasion. More than a thousand fingers are said to have been cut off by the relatives of the dead. Out of the 800 lodges counted the previous summer but 360 remained, even these but thinly peopled. From this time they have been slowly on the increase so as to raise about 460 lodges at the present date, 1856. Rotten Belly had escaped the infection altogether. The Little White Bear had recovered, but the ranks of his once proud force of warriors were terribly thinned.[29]

The then-existing state of the nation called aloud for someone to restore them into some order so that they might not fall an easy prey to their old and powerful enemies, the Sioux and Blackfeet. It was at this time that this chief exhibited talents and wisdom

[29] I have found no other reference to a smallpox epidemic among the Crows in the early 1830's. Neither Maximilian, who was on the Upper Missouri in 1833–34, nor Leonard, who was among the Crows in 1834–35, mentioned such an epidemic. Certainly there was smallpox on the Central Plains among the Pawnees, southeast of the Crows, in 1832. (Catlin, *Letters and Notes,* II, 24.) If the Crows contracted the disease at that period, as Denig claimed, they must have been infected by traders or other Indians, rather than by emigrants. It is known that the Crows suffered little loss during the severe smallpox epidemic on the Upper Missouri in 1837. (Chardon's *Journal,* 395.)

seldom met with among savages and deserving the highest praise. He first took a census of all men, women, and children, then counted those able to bear arms, and lastly noted how many adults, both male and female, remained unmarried. These last he counciled to select wives and husbands without loss of time, but to avoid as much as possible connection with kindred. Here the women prisoners of the Cheyennes aided considerably to reorganize families. Some of them escaped during the general confusion consequent to the prevalent disease, and that nation having previously been visited by the smallpox, but few of the prisoners had died. By unremitting exertions, forced marriages, and equal distribution of arms, horses, and other property, this chief succeeded in restoring the nation to something like order. But much remained to be accomplished before they could successfully defend themselves against their powerful and warlike neighbors. He saw that something more was to be done to retrieve their hopes. Some grand attempt must be made to acquire property, arms, ammunition, and other things necessary to their national existence.

It has always been the custom of these ignorant savages to consider white people the cause of all diseases, even of other evils in which they have no agency or object. They evince a great disposition to lay all blame on Whites, although they deny they are the cause of any good. The difference of habits and occupations, together with the superstitious awe with which all writing, pictures, and books are viewed, suggests to their disordered minds the idea of sorcery and supernatural powers, which they suppose are made subservient to bad ends. This they know would be the case with themselves had they the power to work unseen evil. Now if this be the case in ordinary events, that white people bring on distress, how much more so it must have been in the instance of the smallpox which they could distinctly trace to its origin when they encountered the emigrant train? Indians seldom reason. They act on impulse. Although the Whites referred to had used all means to prevent the pestilence from being communicated to them, yet they only recollected the cause of their present calamity and swore to take revenge on the authors of their misery. This was the prevalent idea stored up by Rotten Belly. But, as has been stated, these Indians are not murderous in their disposition, had heretofore been on the most friendly terms with Whites, and a good many of the head men and councilors were averse to doing any damage to the traders and trappers in the upper country for suffering brought upon them by strangers.

All questions agitated in Indian councils must have unanimous approval to expect a successful result. This the Crow chief well knew. He also was aware that the aforesaid idea of the cause of their misery would fail to produce the desired effect if not supported by some other. It was a long-cherished wish of this leader, and one which his whole life tended to bring about, to rob the American Fur Co.'s fort at the Blackfeet situated near the mouth of Maria River. For this he could give many cogent arguments likely to obtain universal consent. The Blackfeet were their enemies, and that fort supplied them in guns, ammunition, knives, and other implements of war. That nation also had killed many white people, and those who dealt with them as friends after losing so many of their own color deserved no better fate than the Blackfeet. It was also urged that all war parties passing by the fort to the Crows were furnished with ammunition and that most of the Crow horses stolen by their enemies were purchased at the fort on their return. Another thing was that in their present reduced state they were unable to cope with the Blackfeet. Their arms had mostly been buried with their dead owners. They had but little ammunition. Numbers of their horses had been killed, lost, strayed, and stolen during their prostration by disease. They had in fact but little property of any kind. They were scarcely able to support themselves, much less to defend against a powerful nation. All these views were advanced by the chief in full council and many other arguments added showing that a stroke of this kind, if successful, would retrieve their losses, ruin their enemies, and revenge themselves on the Whites—the primary cause of their present feeble condition. It was a popular measure and received the approval of the entire nation. But it was also firmly put forward by the other chiefs that, although they would help themselves to the property in the fort, yet they would not consent to killing the people therein. The result of their deliberations was that they would lay siege to the fort and compel the traders to evacuate, afterwards share the plunder, which at that time amounted to 15 or 20 thousand dollars of arms and other articles suitable for the purposes of hunting and war, besides large quantities of provisions, clothing, etc.

This being decided upon, the Little White Bear was ordered to go forward with a party of 30 men and examine the country while the rest of the nation prepared to move the whole camp to the fort. So certain were they of success that they made about 1,000 pack-saddles on which to carry the great booty that was to become theirs. The discovering party had left about 10 days when the main body was put in motion, which moved slowly with their tents and families through a district well stocked with buffalo, stopping a day or two occasionally to dry meat to enable them to sustain the siege. The whole amount of men able to bear arms in these 360 lodges was about 1,100 or 1,200 but as has been observed they had but few arms and were otherwise badly furnished for war.

The detachment under the Little White Bear traveled nearly the whole country of the Blackfeet without meeting any signs of their enemies who at that season were on a visit to some of the Hudson's Bay Co.'s posts on the tributaries of the Saskatchewan, but who usually returned in the later part of the summer to the Missouri.

The party also approached near the fort in the night and made observations during the day, noting the number of persons in the establishment who pursued their usual outdoor occupations. From the neighboring woods and hills they could see unperceived, what number of horses the Whites had, how they were guarded, and examine that part of the ground most favorable to place their camp outside the reach of the fort cannon. After having satisfied themselves in every particular without being discovered they started homeward to give a most favorable report to their leader. Everything seemed to encourage the expedition so far. Buffalo were numerous near the fort, therefore meat could be had to sustain the siege, and the absence of all enemies relieved their minds as to any difficulty in marching the camp thither.

The return party went on their way in high spirits. So anxious were they to reach their people and urge the expedition forward that they neglected the usual caution observed by savages when traveling through a strange and hostile country. In place of inspecting the district, as they had done in their advance, they scattered over the hills shooting at everything in the way of game and raising the buffalo in every direction. This course soon attracted the notice of a large party of Blackfeet then on their way to war against the Crows. The former had all the advantage. Knowing from the signs mentioned that strangers were near, they hid the main band and sent out scouts to reconnoiter, who in the course of the day brought intelligence of a small body of people whom they had seen. In the night the whole body of Blackfeet moved forward within sight of the campfires of their enemies. Here they halted and sent a few expert scouts to crawl near enough to hear them talk. In this they also succeeded, and returned stating their number together with the pleasant news that they were their old and inveterate enemies the Crows. The party of Blackfeet numbered about 160 and were headed by Spotted Elk, a tried and experienced warrior.

About the break of day, while most of the Crows were yet asleep and their arms scattered carelessly around, they made the attack and in a short time most of the Crows were killed or disabled. Some fought like men but several saved themselves by flight. The Little White Bear was killed together with all but four who made out to escape and reach their own camp. Great was the mourning for their loss, and terrible vows taken for revenge. The Little White Bear was a great favorite with his people. He was a pleasant, liberal Indian, and being closely related to Rotten Belly, was his great support. Besides, his popularity in no way interfered with that of the head chief but rather reflected credit upon it by his submission to his orders and aid on all expeditions. On this occasion, the leader harangued through the camp his firm determination either to leave his body in the Blackfoot Country or to take ample revenge. The capture of the fort now became an object of more interest than ever. With the stores and ammunition that could thus be furnished they would be better able to contend with the powerful enemy whose country they were then invading.

As soon as the first burst of mourning was over he again put the camp in motion and by rapid marches soon came near the trading establishment, though they used every possible precaution to conceal their approach. About the first of August 1835, they encamped in the pine mountain situated 20 miles east of the fort. Here they all assembled to deliberate for the last time and make arrangements for their proceedings before entering upon a course of action so different from their former operations.

It was at this place also they fell in with a white trapper named James Coats, whom they well knew. He had made his spring hunt in the Rocky Mountains and was now on his way to the Blackfeet fort to dispose of his beaver. This man had been several years living and trapping with the Crow Indians, spoke their language tolerably well, and had some friends among them. Fearing, however, that if left to proceed he would disclose their intentions to the gentleman in charge of the fort, they forced him to remain. It has been said that Coats was in league with them for the purpose of pillaging the establishment, and as his usual character was of that description of renegades it may have been so, 'tho as will appear his conduct does not merit this reproach.

The American Fur Co., after considerable difficulty, had succeeded in opening a trade with the Blackfoot Indians in the year 1829. This large and fierce nation, previous to that period, visited the upper part of the Missouri along Maria and Belly Rivers only in the winter season in quest of beaver skins and buffalo robes, which they carried to the Hudson's Bay Co.'s post on the Saskatchewan and traded for arms, etc., to continue their hunts. Owing to their constant encounters with the white trappers in the Rocky Mountains near the heads of the Missouri, they conceived a deadly hatred to all white men, which continues in a measure to this day. In these battles the trappers invariably came off victors when taken in a body, but were cut off in detail when separated into small parties for the purpose of hunting beaver. Upon the whole the amount of loss was on the side of the trappers, though on many occasions they had fought desperately and killed numbers of the Indians.

In the year above mentioned, however, a few venturous persons with an interpreter were sent by the company with the pipe of peace, and a request to obtain permission to build a fort for their trade, promising to sell everything necessary for Indians at a lower rate than the British traders, and save the Indians the trouble of taking their skins to a distant market. After a good deal of parley this was agreed to. The post was built and well furnished with everything the Indians needed.[30] Still, however, suspicion existed on both sides. The fort was built of logs enclosed with high and strong pickets forming a square with the houses ranging along the sides and bastions on two corners built so as to command the four sides of the picketing. These bastions were furnished with cannon of small caliber, which, with a good number of muskets, were always kept loaded in readiness for any attack from savages. From 30 to 50 men were usually stationed here during the fall and winter; most of them, however, were sent down the Missouri with the boats containing the robes and skins early in the spring leaving some 10 to 15 persons to pass the few summer months in the fort. In the month of August or September the annual supplies were received by a keel boat sent from Fort Union, hauling the same with a cordelle manned with 30 or 40 boatmen. Thus the fort received its reinforcement of men and stores before the Blackfeet returned from the English posts in the north, whither they always went in the summer.[31]

30 It was actually in the winter of 1830–31, that Kenneth McKenzie sent Jacob Berger, a Canadian, who had become well acquainted with the Blackfeet and their language in his earlier employment by the Hudson's Bay Company, to seek to establish friendly relations with the Blackfeet. He returned to Fort Union with about one hundred Piegans. They agreed to the construction of a trading post in their country, and Fort Piegan was built at the mouth of the Marias that fall. (Ewers, *The Blackfeet*, 56–57.)

31 Fort McKenzie, built as successor to Fort Piegan in 1832, was located "on the north side of the Missouri, about six miles above the mouth of the Maria, and about forty miles below the great Falls of the Missouri, on a beautiful prairie . . . about 225 feet from the river." (*Audubon and His Journals*, II, 188–95.) Prince Maximilian spent a month at this fort in the late summer of 1833, and described

It was during this interim the Crows (who knew all these things) expected to take the fort by surprise or reduce the small garrison to surrender by siege. The gentleman in charge of the post at the time they arrived in its vicinity was Mr. Alexander Culbertson, an experienced and determined man, who has since risen to be Chief Agent of the company for the whole Upper Missouri.[32] He had been a trader years before among different Indian tribes, spoke several languages fluently, and was well versed in all things regarding the business and the character and customs of the Indians. This gentleman, 'tho unaware of the hostile intent of the Crows, or even of their approach, did not neglect the usual precautions to be observed in a country surrounded by fierce and warlike tribes. He kept up a guard in the bastions both day and night and had his people mostly employed within the fort, except the few who were detailed on horse guard. They kept the animals but a few paces from the fort gates.

From the hills on the opposite side of the Missouri the advance scouts of the Crows could see and note undiscovered all that was going forward. They were not long in perceiving that the fort was well guarded and a surprise impracticable. They therefore reverted to their alternative, to lay siege. With this view some 25 or 30 active men concealed themselves during the night under the bank of the river about 100 yards from the front gate and as soon as the horses of the fort were turned out to graze rushed between them and the guards and drove them off. The men fired but missed their aim. So this source of subsistence was taken away. Very shortly after the whole camp made their appearance and pitched their lodges in three divisions commanding the three sides of the fort but at such a distance as to be out of reach of cannon. The front of the fort was left unguarded as the inhabitants, having neither boats nor horses, could not escape with any property, 'tho it gave them

both the fort and the trade there in great detail. (In Vol. XXIII of Thwaites' *Early Western Travels*.)

[32] Biographical sketches of Alexander Culbertson and his Blood Indian wife, Medicine Snake Woman, appear in *"The Fort Benton and Fort Sarpy Journals,"* (240–46.)

an opportunity of evacuating the place without danger by fording the river.

As soon as this disposition of his people was made, Rotten Belly came to the fort with a few followers and requested permission to enter, stating if that was granted he would willingly bring back the stolen horses. He spoke very friendly, said they intended no harm to the place or people, that they were on their way to find the Blackfeet, etc. The drift of this was he wished to see what force the place contained and to learn from some woman in the fort who spoke the Crow language what quantity of provisions were on hand. To all these requests and fine promises Mr. Culbertson turned a deaf ear and bade him go about his business.

On the second or third day of the siege the trapper Coats, came to the fort and told Mr. Culbertson for the first time the real purpose of the Crows, advising him by no means to admit any of them. This certainly showed well on the part of Coats, but he also was particular in his enquiries regarding the amount of provisions on hand. It is thought he was sent by the Indians to ascertain this point. If so, he failed either in getting admission or information. It happened most unfortunately that the siege commenced at a time when the fort was actually in want of everything to eat. Buffalo had been scarce the previous winter. Very little dried meat had been made by the Blackfeet and still less traded by the fort. All flour, bread, pork, etc., had been expended 2 months before, 'tho the garrison would have had no difficulty in supporting themselves were they not prevented from hunting, as buffalo were numerous within sight of the fort. As the case then stood, but a few bales of dried meat formed their only resource. However, to produce an impression on the Indians that they had an abundance, nearly half was thrown over the pickets to them at different times when they came around asking for meat.

It may appear singular that the besieged would allow their enemies to come close to the pickets and parley every day without firing upon them, but those who are acquainted with the nature of the fur trade and the habits of the Indians will not be surprised. The company intended to locate trading establishments with all the tribes and to use conciliatory measures everywhere with the object of securing the friendship of all the nations. It was not their policy to use force except on occasions of self-defense and extreme emergencies. Had Mr. Culbertson killed any of these Indians it would have proved a great obstacle to the establishment of a trading post in their country, and likewise would have cut off all hope of escape in the event of being obliged to evacuate.

Matters being brought to this issue, the Indians generally remained quiet in their camp or hunting buffalo in the vicinity, at the same time keeping up a strict watch both night and day upon the fort, having come to the conclusion that ere long it would surrender for want of provisions. The garrison on the other hand, apprehending a long siege, reduced their rations to less than one-quarter of their customary allowance. Occasionally the Crows would come alongside and a parley would take place, though nothing important was thus elicited. At the end of 2 weeks the same state of things existed, with the exception that the people in the fort had exhausted everything in the way of provisions. Even the few favorite dogs remaining were served up and dished out with a sparing hand to all. They had next to resort to the rawhides which had been used as coverings to the dried meat. These, although covered with dirt, grease, and paint, were cut up and boiled to something like the consistency of glue, and this mixture of all that was disgusting was used to sustain life for a few days longer. The hides being consumed, there remained only the cords made of skin which also were cooked and eaten, and absolute famine presented itself. Things now assumed a serious aspect. Most of the engagees were Canadians who, however hardy when well fed, are always the first to complain or revolt in trying time, notwithstanding their bragging. These urged Mr. Culbertson to abandon the place before they all starved to death. Loud were their murmurs and deep their curses upon his head for what they termed his desire to see them all die. But this gentleman, having determined on his course of action was not a man to be deterred in carrying it out, neither by the murmurs of his own people nor the persevering siege of the Indians. He knew if they could preserve their lives for a short time, the whole Blackfeet Nation would soon arrive. The season for their appearance had already passed, as also that of the arrival of their annual keel boat up. Assistance might be expected from either or both these quarters. It appeared to him wrong and cowardly to surrender at the commencement of difficulty.

However, day after day passed by bringing forth nothing but increasing hunger—old skins, shoes, and all offals were greedily devoured. Still nothing turned up to encourage them. Men began to look at each other fiercely and that pitch of distress had been reached beyond which all would become too debilitated to act in any way. At this juncture Mr. Culbertson called up all hands and gave orders to prepare to give battle to the Crows as it was his intention to sally out in the morning with all his force and cannon, proceed near them and fight as long as any remained of his now feeble command. He was led to think, and experience had taught him, that a few well-directed discharges of artillery would drive them away. It is true that by evacuating the place they would all have been gladly allowed to pass unharmed, as their lives were not what the savages sought, but their property. But Mr. Culbertson knew that by leaving the establishment his act would be misinterpreted and lead to the stigmatizing of his character. All who are acquainted with the persons in the employ of the fur companies are aware that no allowances are made for circumstances, and that there is a prevailing disposition to traduce the name of anyone, more especially if he stands in a high position. He therefore decided either to force his enemies to leave the place or to die at the head of his people. It is somewhat remarkable that this plan met with but little opposition. Hunger had made his men desperate. Even those who some time before feared death in the distance now stood boldly forward to face the reality.

The siege had now occupied nearly a month. The camp was well supplied with meat and everything betokened a determination on the part of the Indians to hold out much longer. All hands then were armed and supplied with ammunition, having been informed that the sally would be made about midday following. This was about the time most of the young and efficient warriors were either out guarding their horses at a distance or hunting in different directions. It was a sorrowful night in the fort. All felt that their chance of success was doubtful, their death little short of certainty, but their wretched famished condition threw over the whole a gloom of sullen, silent resolve.

The eventful morning arrived; steadily and quietly this determined man proceeded to carry out his views, but it wanted yet a few hours to the time. When nearly ready the sentinels from the bastions observed some unusual commotion in the camp. Horses were being caught, warriors running about half armed, others riding off in various directions. Old men harangued, the council was called, and everything denoted some new and important event. The cause of all this was explained when on looking to the northwest small blue wreaths of smoke rose up in several places which were hailed with a shout of joy by all the fort. "The Blackfoot camp, our friends, our friends," was the cry of all. Arms were put away and once more smiles were seen on the lank and haggard countenances of these poor people. The Crows sent on discovery soon returned, the whole camp began taking down their lodges, packing their horses in great haste, and before the afternoon the whole camp had moved across the river and were out of sight. That same evening some Blackfeet runners arrived and the next day 800 lodges of these people encamped at the fort bringing plenty of meat.[33]

It is not our intention to give lengthy descriptions of circum-

---

[33] This siege actually occurred in June, 1834. In a letter to Kenneth McKenzie, written from Fort Union, Sept. 17, 1834, J. Archdale Hamilton stated that the Crows compelled the defenders of the fort "to live on Cords Parfleche for 15 days." (Letter in Missouri Historical Society.) Yet the detailed account of the siege in "Extracts from Mr. Culbertson's Journal Kept at Fort Mc Kenzie, Blackfeet Indian Country in 1834," copied by Audubon at Fort Union in 1843, states that it lasted only 2 days, June 25–26, and that a party of Blood Indians brought meat to the defenders on June 30. (*Audubon and His Journals,* II, 178–80.) Bradley's two accounts of this siege, presumably based upon information he obtained from Culbertson four decades after the action, also differ in detail from Denig's version on some points. (The "Bradley Manuscript," Montana Historical Society *Contributions,* Vol. II, 181–82; Vol. III, 210–15.) Probably the bare facts of this dramatic siege had become somewhat embroidered through two decades of verbal retelling before Denig penned his version of the action in 1856.

stances of this kind or much more might be added that would interest the general reader. Strange things occur in this wild country. Singular emergencies arise which could be wrought up into romantic narrative. But we must not lose sight of the great Chief Rotten Belly, a sketch of whose life is here attempted.

The Blackfeet, as soon as they had been made aware of the conduct and number of the Crows, called a council but could not agree as to the expediency of pursuit. It was argued that although the Crows were inferior in numbers yet they were in a desperate state, greatly disappointed, and a bloody battle would be the result without much advantage to be gained. Indians usually reason in this way. They seldom risk much to gain little. They do not fight grand battles merely from a thirst for blood. Great disparity of force must exist before slaughter commences. Equality of numbers mostly prevents attack, in fact always does when not counterbalanced by the prospects of plunder or national revenge. These considerations had weight enough with chiefs and warriors of the Blackfeet to defer their operations against their enemies until a more favorable opportunity presented, when they could take them by surprise or cut them off in detail according to the usual custom of savage warfare.

The Crows, on the other hand, were glad to escape from their well-armed and numerous enemies. But having got beyond immediate danger they were halted by their chief. Rotten Belly was far from being satisfied. He had so far failed in every point he undertook to perform. His vows remained unfulfilled with the exception that should he fail he would leave his body in the country of the Blackfeet. This was yet in his power and was what he secretly resolved upon for he knew this defeat and disgrace would lead to his downfall among his people.

While deliberating how to act so as in some way to regain his position and recover in a manner the ground he had lost, chance threw in his way what perhaps he would have most desired. It happened that a war party of 20 Blackfeet had been in the country of the Crows, and not finding them was on its return to its own nation. These proceeding in a careless way were discovered by the Crows while traveling. The chief and a few warriors in advance of the camp charged upon them, killed two, and the rest took refuge in one of the small wooden forts made by war parties, everywhere to be met with in the Blackfeet district. It was urged by most of the Crows that they should leave them alone, as they had already killed two without any harm to themselves, and by attacking the fortress they would undoubtedly lose some people. All agreed to this except Rotten Belly, who would have charged alone into the fort, but was detained by his people who held the bridle of his horse. It had not escaped the notice of the Crows that, since turning their backs on the trader's fort, this chief was dressed in his most gay and costly war suit. He wore his shirt and leggings fringed with human hair, his war eagle feather bonnet, and his robe of state covered with the scalp locks of his enemies hung over his shoulders. All this display on the occasion of defeat betokened some deadly determination which his friends, both by entreaty and gentle force, attempted to prevent. After disputing with them for a short time he promised to go away along with the rest and leave their enemies for some other time when they could destroy them with less risk to themselves. His horse being set free of the grasp of his followers, he made him prance around as though in sport, then shouting aloud, "One last stroke for the Crow Nation; two Blackfeet cannot pay for the loss of The Little White Bear," he rushed at full speed upon his foes. Making his charger leap the small stockade into the midst of his enemies, he pinned one to the ground with his lance, but received a dozen arrows in his body and fell to rise no more. His people followed close behind, fell upon the Blackfeet, and cut them off to a man without further loss than that of their leader. But this was to them the greatest that could happen. In conformity with his request on several occasions, his body was wrapped in its warrior shroud and deposited on a tree in the country of the Blackfeet to be, as he said, a terror to them even after death.

The lives of most Indian chiefs bear a strong resemblance. The history of one is that of all—the same battles, victories, defeats, and deaths proceed from their unvarying wars with their enemies, and are likely to continue as long as any tribes remain. Among all these nations, where daily struggles take place for each others' lives and property, instances of individual daring arise which, among civilized men in what is called honorable warfare, would immortalize their names but which, for want of record, must soon be forgotten. The fame of any Indian chief is but short-lived. A few days of mourning is all that can be devoted to his memory. Their existence demands action, their force a leader. Their disposition is ambitious, and long before the death of their favorite chief takes place, some other candidate for his office is spoken of and approved. This often happens before the decease of a leader. Any great defeat or mismanagement on his part would transfer the power to another who had given proof of his bravery and abilities.

The loss of Rotten Belly was deeply felt and regretted by the Crows, perhaps more than that of any other man either before or since his time. Even to this day he is spoken of as *the* Chief, or the *Great Chief*.[34] Other men now took charge of different portions of the Crows who separated into several bands and resumed their old habits and hunting grounds.

OF TRADE AND WAR

The year after the above event, a fort was built at the mouth of Rose Bud River on the Yellowstone for the trade with this nation.

[34] This is the most detailed biography of the great Crow chief, Rotten Belly, that is known. It is corroborated in part and expanded in the works of other writers. Curtis was told that Rotten Belly was second chief of the tribe at the time of the first Crow treaty with the United States at the Mandan villages, August 4, 1825, although he refused to sign this treaty. (*American Indian*, IV, 48.) Maximilian witnessed the presentation of a medal to Rotten Belly by John A. Sanford, Indian subagent, at the Mandan villages, in June, 1833. He described this chief as "a fine tall man, with a pleasing countenance" who "had much influence over his people." (In Vol. XXII of Thwaites' *Early Western Travels*, 351.) Rotten Belly was well known to such prominent fur traders as Robert Campbell, and N. C. Wyeth. News of Rotten Belly's death in battle was entered in the Fort Pierre Journal, August 8, 1834. (Chardon's *Journal*, 253.) In 1876, the Crow Indian, Little Face, told Lieutenant Bradley a number of stories illustrating Rotten Belly's war record and the potent supernatural powers attributed to his medicines by his tribesmen. ("The Bradley Manuscript," Montana Historical Society *Contributions*, Vol. IX, 299–307.)

It furnished them with arms and other necessaries, and they slowly recovered from the disastrous effects of the smallpox.

Before a trading post had been permanently placed in their country the Crows carried their furs to the Arikara and Mandan forts on the Missouri and disposed of them there. At that time they hunted nothing but beaver, the skins of which were then valuable and easy of transportation. They had not as yet turned their attention to preparing buffalo robes for sale, making only a sufficiency for the use of themselves and families. When the company paid them good prices for their robes it gave them an opportunity to equip themselves better for hunting and war than heretofore and tended considerably to restrict their wandering habits. The camps remained stationary during the fall and winter months near the fort, where they employed their time in killing buffalo, dressing their hides, and purchasing such articles as they most wanted either for defense, convenience, or barter for horses with the tribes farther in the mountains.

Still war was kept up, mostly in the spring and summer, with the different nations mentioned who were considered enemies. In these conflicts the Crows generally lost. At least, they being the smaller tribe, the fall of every warrior or hunter was more severely felt. All winter parties of Blackfeet, Sioux, Assiniboines, and other hostile nations hovered round their encampments, killed stragglers, and drove off numbers of their horses. On the return of the summer months the Crows went in large numbers to revenge these coups and often bloody battles ensued with considerable loss on both sides.

FACTORS LIMITING THE INCREASE OF CROW POPULATION

No great national calamity overtook them until the year 1848, when the smallpox again made its appearance, they having received the infection from the Snake Indians with whom they were at peace; the Snakes having contracted the pestilence in their dealings with emigrants passing along the Platte Trail. It does not appear to have been nearly so destructive as the same disease at the former period mentioned, 'tho numbers of children died.[35] In 1849 the greater part of the Crow Nation was visited by an influenza of so destructive a nature as to take off about 600 persons, among whom were some of the best warriors and wise councilors.[36] Since the last date no great havoc has been wrought by epidemics, 'tho they cannot be said to be much on the increase.

Several things tend to prevent their augmentation. Setting aside the loss by war and deaths by different maladies incident to human life, the propagation of the venereal disease among them appears to be the greatest bar to their prosperity, both by its fatal nature and the inability of the tainted persons to procure wives or husbands. Infanticide is also publicly practiced by two-thirds of the married women. Unwilling to be troubled by raising their children, they either kill them in utero, or as soon as brought forth, 'tho the former manner is the most common. Abortions are produced by administering blows on the abdomen or by pressing upon it with a stick, leaning their whole weight thereon and swinging to and fro. The foetus is thus ejected at different periods of its growth varying from 3 to 7 months. As they are not aware of the danger attending the practice many women die in attempting it. It has been computed by those well acquainted with this tribe that three-fourths of all the women who die are lost in this manner. Usually the husband consents to it, or at least does not punish his wife for so doing, but of late years the voices of all or most of the men are against the crime and it is becoming more rare. The act now reflects disgrace on both the father and mother of the child and, if not done so frequently, it is at least concealed from the public.[37]

[35] Indian Agent Vaughan claimed that the Crows on the headwaters of Powder River caught the smallpox from the Shoshones, who had contracted it from California emigrants, in the fall and winter of 1851. He said this epidemic reduced Crow numbers by thirty lodges, killing some four hundred members of the tribe in a short time. (*Annual Report* of the Commissioner of Indian Affairs, 1853, p. 354.)

[36] On October 28, 1851, Kurz wrote that influenza had been "dangerously prevalent" among the Crows the previous winter, killing some 150 members of the tribe "among them some of their most prominent tribesmen." Some of the Crows believed Denig had inflicted the disease upon them in retaliation for their theft of ten horses from Fort Union. "To prevent further spread of the disease . . . the Indian brought back nine of the stolen horses." (Kurz, *Journal*, 215-16.)

This disgusting and unnatural custom is not peculiar to the Crows. It exists to a more or less extent among all nations of the Upper Missouri but not in such a degree as to affect much their natural increase.

CROW HERMAPHRODITES

Another thing worthy of note with these Crows is the number of Berdêches or hermaphrodites among them. Most civilized communities recognize but two genders, the masculine and feminine. But strange to say, these people have a neuter. This does not proceed from any natural deformity, but from the habits of the child. Occasionally a male child, when arrived at the age of 10 or 12 years or less, cannot be brought to join in any of the work or play of the boys, but on the contrary associates entirely with the girls. Now all the amusements of boys and girls are marked and distinct. The former, at a very early age, are instructed in the use of the bow, shooting at birds, guarding horses, trapping rabbits and other small game, while the latter are taught to cook, dress skins, make moccasins, work with beads and porcupine quills all articles of clothing, and other servile and feminine acquirements. Children of different sexes seldom associate either in their work or play, 'tho as has been observed instances do occur in which a boy acquires all the habits of a girl, notwithstanding every effort on the part of his parents to prevent it. The disposition appears to be natural and cannot be controlled. When arrived at the age of 12 or 14, and his habits are formed, the parents clothe him in a girl's dress and his whole life is devoted to the labors assigned to the females. He is not to be distinguished in any way from the women, 'tho is seldom much respected by either sex. The parents regret it very much but to no purpose. There used to be some five or six of these hermaphrodites among the Crows, 'tho at the present time there are but two or three. One of these has been married and pre-

[37] Denig elsewhere estimated, "It is not far from the correct number if we state that one-eighth of the children are destroyed in utero or after birth by the Crow women." (*Indian Tribes of the Upper Missouri,* 521.)

187

sents the anomaly of husband and wife in the same dress attending to the same domestic duties.[38]

THE CROW TOBACCO-PLANTING CEREMONY

Before closing our remarks on these people, some account of their superstitions appears to be demanded. The power ascribed to their priests and medicine men differ in many respects from those of other tribes. Wherever this is the case, separate descriptions and explanations have been promised in former parts of this work. Hereafter the religion of all the tribes will be minutely considered, its elements disclosed and its effects commented on; but in this place it will only meet with notice so far as to inform of some rites and ceremonies which have a great influence on their national character and government.

The term "medicine men," as now used, has no reference to those who use drugs to cure diseases, but to such as are thought by the entire population to possess superhuman powers to bring about events. Sometimes these persons are supposed to be gifted with the spirit of prophecy, or to work evil ends. This is a prevalent idea with the majority of the roving tribes and will meet with further explanation. But the Crows center *all* power in the *Tobacco*

---

[38] Sexual abnormalities among the Crows were mentioned by both earlier and later writers. In 1806, Alexander Henry wrote, "I am informed they are much addicted to unnatural lusts, and have no scruple in satisfying their desires with their mares and wild animals fresh killed." *(New Light,* I, 399). Maximilian, a quarter century later, stated, "They have many bardaches, or hermaphrodites, among them, and exceed all other tribes in unnatural practices." (In Thwaites' *Early Western Travels, XXII,* 354.) Father De Smet referred to a Crow warrior who "in consequence of a dream had put on women's clothing and subjected himself to all the labors and duties of that condition, so humiliating to an Indian." *Life, Letters, and Travels,* III, 1017.) While on the Crow reservation in 1912, S. C. Simms was informed that there were three hermaphrodites in the tribe and that "a few years ago an Indian agent endeavoured to compel these people, under threat of punishment, to wear men's clothing, but his efforts were unsuccessful." ("Crow Indian Hermaphrodites," *American Anthropologist,* new ser., Vol. V, 580–81.) Lowie reported but one surviving berdache on that reservation in 1912. ("Social Life of the Crow Indians," Am. Museum of Natural History *Anthropological Papers,* Vol. IX, Pt. 2, p. 226.)

Planters. These are their own people and exhibit no outward difference either in dress or manners from their neighbors, 'tho they are believed to have control over events, seasons, the elements, animals, and all things usually attributed to the works of an overruling Providence. In fact they have no idea of a Supreme Being, a first cause, or of a future state. Neither do the great luminaries the sun and moon appear to them objects of much veneration, 'tho they are somewhat afraid of thunder.

This nation has from time immemorial planted tobacco. They have carefully preserved the original seed discovered with the continent, which produces leaves similar to the cultivated plant in the Western States and has something of its taste and flavor. They believe that as long as they continue to preserve the seed and have in their homes some of the blossom they will preserve their national existence. They say as soon as none is found they must pass away from the face of the earth. Several other traditions also tend to the continuation of the custom of tobacco planting. Among the first is that those who fulfill the orders of their ancestors in this respect shall be endowed with supernatural powers, to bring rain, avert pestilence, control the wind, conquer disease, make the buffalo come near their camp, and increase the number of all kinds of game, that they can in fact bring about any event not dependent upon ordinary human possibility. This is confined to the few who plant the tobacco, and who, knowing the power and standing thus to be gained, are very anxious to keep up the superstition with the ceremonies attending it. Sometimes, with a view to acquiring property, one of them will sell his right or powers to some aspiring individual. In this case the candidate gives everything he has in the world—all his horses, dresses, arms, even his lodge and household utensils—to pay for the great medicine and honor to become a Tobacco Planter. On an occasion of this kind the applicant is adopted with great ceremonies into the band of Planters. His flesh is cut and burned in large and deep furrows around the breast and along his arms, leaving for a long time dangerous and disgusting wounds difficult to heal. He is also obliged to go several days without food or water. After passing through this ordeal, he is furnished with some tobacco seed, in exchange for everything that he possesses. In this way the rite is perpetuated, and never has received the least check or interruption. On the contrary, it appears to become more honorable from being more ancient and from the difficulties attendant on becoming a conductor of the ceremony.

The customary place for the planting of the tobacco is on Wind River at the base of the mountain having this name, 'tho it is not confined to this spot alone. Other places are sometimes sought more convenient for the camp when the season arrives. At an appointed spot then the whole nation are invited to meet in a certain moon, which corresponds with about the middle of the last of April. When encamped in the vicinity the women of the camp are detailed to clear off all bushes and rubbish from a space of ground about half an acre square. Even the cleaning of this place is accompanied with the beating of drums, singing, smoking at intervals. This usually occupies the first day. On the next the spot is hoed, either with iron instruments or with the shoulder blades of buffalo. The latter is the primitive utensil. This operation consumes the greater part of the second day. The third is ushered in by loud haranguing, feasting, singing by the Planters, and all married men and women, mounted on horseback, proceed in file to the neighboring trees and cut each a faggot of wood which is tied together and carried before them on the horses. The women take precedence, and it is distinctly understood that the female who brings in the first bundle of wood must be one who has had no illicit connection with any man but her husband. If she attempts to deceive, the person who is aware of, and a participator in, her guilt steps forward and cries aloud, "she is lame," or unfit for the post of honor; in which case she is forever disgraced. This has happened more than once. Indeed so rare is a virtuous woman in this nation that the above requisition has several times been nearly the cause of an entire suspension of the custom; for they would rather relinquish the whole than alter the manner in which the ceremony has been transmitted to them by their forefathers. Heretofore, however, they have succeeded in finding *one* virtuous female, or one said to be so, 'tho, as has been observed, the search has been attended with difficulty. The next important step taken in this great national solemnity is to select a man who will solemnly swear he has never slept with any of his relatives' wives more nearly akin than a brother-in-law, that tie included. This individual is found previously to their going after the wood and he brings in the second faggot. Singular as it may appear, the moral character of the males is not superior to the female part of the community, and several weeks have often been employed in the seeking and approving of a man free from the crime of incest. At one time so great was their anxiety to proceed with their custom, and so rare was the proper person that they were obliged to employ one of the gentlemen of the Fur Company to fill the office. Therefore, it may safely be conjectured that if no improvement takes place in their moral condition the rite of tobacco planting will soon be at an end. To proceed. When the two loads of wood are thus cast upon the cleared spot, all the rest follow after, one at a time laying down his burden with great solemnity, encouraged by the Planters, who are stationed round singing and drumming. Beside each of the medicine men are placed pans and bowls of cooked meat, tongues, pemmican, dried berries, and other eatables considered by them as delicacies. Those who lay down a bundle of wood go and seat themselves around these dishes and eat as much as they can. Great quantities are consumed, which have been laid up for months beforehand in anticipation of the above ceremony. When the wood is all collected, it is separated into four large piles, one of which is placed on each corner of the square patch intended for cultivation. Then these piles are all separately smoked to and invoked. Indeed, any and every movement they make during the whole performance partakes of a sacred character. The wood is then strewn equally over the surface of the place, fire put to it and burned to ashes. The whole is rehoed and threshed with willows, which serves the purpose of harrowing. Much time is employed in invocation and other ceremony over the tobacco seed, which in the end is mixed with fine earth and ashes and scattered over the garden. The place is then threshed with brush a second time for the purpose of burying the seed.

Having arrived at this point of the ceremony a grand medicine lodge next claims their attention. This is made by forming a large tent with 8 or 10 lodges connected by poles, sufficiently commodious to contain 200 or 300 persons. The interior is decked out with cloths of brilliant colors, beads, and various other ornaments. Large feasts are cooked and placed therein, and a full band of drums, rattles, bells, and whistles keep up a deafening and continual noise. Dancing goes forward after the eatables have been dispatched. These dances are conducted with strict decorum, as they, with all the rest of the ceremony, are supposed to bring about a state of happy and prosperous national affairs. Several persons on these occasions cut and scar their arms and bodies, and exert themselves in dancing without food or water for such a length of time that they are carried away in an unconscious condition from which some are with difficulty revived.

This amusement, or rather devotion, usually occupies three more days, at the end of which time they move camp and march about half a mile, the next day about a mile, the third and fourth about as much more. The idea is that they do not wish the tobacco to think they are running away from it, but are so fond of it as scarcely to have the wish to depart.

As soon as possible after the seed is sown it is desirable to have rain that the same may be washed into the earth and take root. One of the Planters then undertakes to produce rain, and by his desire merchandise and other property is collected from the band often to the amount of 2 or 3 thousand dollars. These articles are freely given to the medicine man by the rest, considering them as sacrifices to the clouds. The Tobacco Planter, after hanging up the different articles on the bushes around, commences a series of smokings and prayers to the heavens for rain. If he succeeds, the whole of the sacrifices belong to him and he acquires increase of fame. But if no rain falls, the goods are suffered to lie there, 'tho no blame is cast on the Planter, for he cunningly asserts that the time is not propitious and that some of the nation have not fulfilled their promises, etc. Occasionally he takes advantage of clouds gathering to predict rain, which would most likely fall without his aid. But they are so blind and bigoted that they actually believe in his power to produce it. One of these Planters can do anything (so they think), can make the grass grow, make buffalo plenty, and foretell any great calamity arising from disease or attacks from enemies.

When all this parade is over the camp resumes its ordinary occupations and traveling, until, about the latter end of August, it marches again to the tobacco field, when they pull the plant up and pack it into sacks. The seed is separated from the blossom and preserved; the stock and leaves are carefully stored away, only to be used on great occasions such as peacemaking with other nations, and religious rites of a national character. It is also used in extreme cases of sickness, not as a drug, but in their usual superstitious manner of smoking, believing its efficacy to consist in the article itself, rendered sacred and powerful by ceremony, and the smoke emitted through the nostrils of a Tobacco Planter.[39]

The foregoing is a rapid sketch of this principal national religious rite. There are many others of smaller note, resembling in every respect those of other tribes.

CHIEF LONG HAIR

Since the time of Rotten Belly no great man has ruled the nation. It is at present separated into smaller communities, each governed by a chief. The principal man after the chief above named was Long Hair, so called from having hair on his head 36 feet in length. Although it may appear singular that any human being should be in possession of this length of hair, yet it is nevertheless true. Encouraged by a dream, when a young man, that he would become great in proportion to the growth of his hair, he tied weight to it, which aided its growth, and every few months separated the locks

---

[39] Denig's description of the tobacco-planting ceremony contains many details lacking in accounts of this ritual based upon field investigations a half-century later, and after the Crows had settled down to sedentary reservation life. A Crow tradition, obtained by Edward S. Curtis, traced the origin of the tobacco ceremony to No Vitals, who quarreled with the Hidatsas and led the Crows westward to become their first chief. (*American Indian,* IV, 61–67.)

into small parcels which were stuck together with the gum of the pine tree. In this way none of his hair could be lost. If any fell out the gum prevented it from dropping. At the age of 50 his hair was the length mentioned, 'tho no single stalk was longer than usual among females of our own color. This cumbersome bunch of hair he rolled up into two large balls and carried them in front of his saddle while riding. When on foot, the rolls were attached to his girdle. On great festivals he mounted on horseback, unrolled his hair, and rode slowly around the camp with his scalplocks trailing some distance behind him on the ground.

Whether or not it was this peculiarity that brought him into notice we cannot say. No doubt it aided considerably, 'tho he also is spoken of as a brave man. He rose to high power, was well liked, and died a few years since.[40] At this date, 1856, the Crows have peace with the Assiniboines and some bands of Sioux with whom they occasionally reside and exchange presents.

CHIEF BIG ROBBER

At the treaty of Laramie in 1851, The Big Robber was made chief of the nation by the United States Commissioners, but since that time he has not governed his people. In place of remaining with the greater portion, he is generally found near the emigrant

[40] "The Long Hair was the first signer of the Crows' first treaty with the United States at the Mandan villages, August 4, 1825. He was head chief of the numerically superior Mountain Crows, and Rotten Belly head chief of the River Crows, after jealousy between them led to division of the tribe. ("The Bradley Manuscript," Montana Historical Society *Contributions,* Vol. IX, 312–13.) Zenas Leonard, meeting Long Hair in the fall of 1834, termed him, "the principal chief or Sachem of the nation and is quite a worthy and venerable old man of 75 or 80 years of age," who "worships nothing but his hair, which is regularly combed and carefully folded up every morning into a roll about three feet long by the principal warriors of his tribe." His tresses were "no less than nine feet eleven inches long." *(Adventures,* 140–41.) Maximilian reported that they were "ten feet long." (In Vol. XXII of Thwaites' *Early Western Travels,* 353.) While George Catlin, in 1832, claimed that the fur traders Sublette and Campbell, assured him "they had measured his hair by correct means, and found it to be ten feet and seven inches in length; closely inspecting every part of it at the same time, and satisfying themselves that it was the natural growth." *(Letters and Notes,* I, 49–50.)

trail along the Platte with a few lodges who do nothing but beg and steal, and contract diseases from passing emigrants which sweep off numbers of his people. He is now despised by the other bands. He has no command, is not respected, as much for seeking other districts as for not remaining and assisting in defending his own country.

PROSPECTS FOR INTERTRIBAL PEACE

A portion of the nation now passes the winter with the Assiniboines, with whom they make out to agree, 'though the latter steal their horses to some extent. But the Crows are solicitous for peace with all tribes except the Blackfeet, with whom they wish to be at war as long as one of them remains.

The late treaty with the Blackfeet may have the effect of annexing the Piegans and Gros Ventres of the Prairie to their list of friends, but the Blood Indians and Blackfeet will never be brought to live at peace with any of the surrounding nations.[41]

BIOGRAPHY OF WOMAN CHIEF

Perhaps the only instance known of a woman attaining the rank of chief among any of the tribes whose histories we attempt has happened among the Crows. It has ever been the custom with these wandering people to regard females in an inferior light in every way. They have no voice in council, or anything to say at assemblies formed by men for camp regulations. Even the privilege of intimate conversation with their husbands is denied them when men are present. They have their own sphere of action in their domestic department, from which they are never allowed to depart, being considered by their husbands more as a part of their property than as companions.

This being the case, they seldom accompany parties to war.

[41] Denig's hope for peace between the Crows and Piegans following the first Blackfoot Treaty with the United States at the mouth of the Judith River, October 17, 1855, was not realized. For three decades thereafter the Piegans continued to make raids upon Crow camps.

Those who do are of the lowest possible description of character, belong to the public generally, have no home or protection. Sometimes females of this stamp are taken along to make and mend shoes, dry meat, cook, etc., but they are never allowed to take part in battle. Even if they were, their inexperience in the use of weapons would soon cause their death. For such as these there is no opportunity to distinguish themselves. They must be content with the station of servant and that of the very lowest kind of drudgery.

The case we are about to relate is that of a Gros Ventre of the Prairie woman taken prisoner by the Crows when about 10 years of age. From a personal acquaintance of 12 years with this woman we can lay her true history before the reader.

Shortly after her capture the warrior to whom she belonged perceived a disposition in her to assume masculine habits and employments. As in the case of the Berdêche who, being male inclined to female pursuits, so this child, reversing the position, desired to acquire manly accomplishments. Partly to humor her, and partly for his own convenience, her foster father encouraged the inclination. She was in time placed to guard horses, furnished with bow and arrows, employing her idle time in shooting at the birds around and learning to ride fearlessly. When further advanced in years she carried a gun, learned to shoot, and when yet a young woman was equal if not superior to any of the men in hunting both on horseback and on foot.

During her whole life no change took place in her dress, being clad like the rest of the females with the exception of hunting arms and accouterments. It also happened that she was taller and stronger than most women—her pursuits no doubt tending to develop strength of nerve and muscle. Long before she had ventured on the warpath she could rival any of the young men in all their amusements and occupations, was a capital shot with the rifle, and would spend most of her time in killing deer and bighorn, which she butchered and carried home on her back when hunting on foot. At other times she joined in the surround on horse, could kill four or five buffalo at a race, cut up the animals without assistance, and bring the meat and hides home.

Although tolerably good looking she did not, it seems, strike the fancy of the young men, and her protector having been killed in battle, she assumed the charge of his lodge and family, performing the double duty of father and mother to his children.

In the course of time it happened that the Blackfeet made a charge on a few lodges of Crows encamped near the trading fort in their country—our heroine being with the lodges. The attack was sudden. Several men were killed and the rest took refuge within the fort saving most of their horses. The enemies made a stand beyond the reach of guns and by signs exhibited a desire to speak to someone in the fort. Neither Whites nor Crows could be found to venture out. But this woman, understanding their language, saddled her horse and set forth to meet them. Everyone sought to detain her, but she would not be persuaded. The fort gates were opened and she went on her dangerous errand. When arrived within hailing distance, and about half rifle shot, several Blackfeet came to meet her, rejoicing in the occasion of securing an easy prize. When within pistol shot, she called on them to stop, but they paid no attention to her words. One of the enemies then fired at her and the rest charged. She immediately shot down one with her gun, and shot arrows into two more without receiving a wound. The remaining two then rode back to the main body, who came at full speed to murder the woman. They fired showers of balls and pursued her as near to the fort as they could with safety approach. But she escaped unharmed and entered the gates amid the shouts and praises of the Whites and her own people.

This daring act stamped her character as a brave. It was sung by the rest of the camp, and in time was made known to the whole nation. About a year after, she collected a number of young men and headed her first war excursion against the Blackfeet. Fortune again favored her. She approached their camp in the night, stole 70 horses and drove them with great speed toward her home. But the enemies followed, overtook them, and a sharp skirmish ensued, which resulted in the Crows getting off with most of the animals and two Blackfeet scalps. One of the two Blackfeet the woman chieftain killed and scalped with her own hand. The other, although shot down by one of her followers, she was the first to strike and take from him his gun while he was yet alive 'tho severely wounded. It may reasonably be supposed that coups such as these aided to raise her fame as a warrior, and according to their own usages, from the fact of striking first the bodies of two enemies, she could no more be prevented from having a voice in their deliberations. Other expeditions of a still more hazardous nature were undertaken and successfully carried through by this singular and resolute woman. In every battle around their own camp or those of their enemies some gallant act distinguished her. Old men began to believe she bore a charmed life which, with her daring feats, elevated her to a point of honor and respect not often reached by male warriors, certainly never before conferred upon a female of the Crow Nation. The Indians seemed to be proud of her, sung forth her praise in songs composed by them after each of her brave deeds. When council was held and all the chiefs and warriors assembled, she took her place among the former, ranking third person in the band of 160 lodges. On stated occasions, when the ceremony of striking a post and publicly repeating daring acts was performed, she took precedence of many a brave man whose career had not been so fortunate.

In the meantime she continued her masculine course of life, hunting and war. Heretofore her attention had been but little attracted to personal gain in the way of barter. Whatever hides she brought home from the hunt were given to her friends, 'tho the meat was cured and dried by herself and the children under her charge. When horses were wanting she drew upon her enemies for a supply and had been heretofore uniformly successful. She had numbers of animals in her possession, with which she could at any time command other necessaries.

But with Indians it is the same as with civilized persons. The richer they become the more desirous they are to acquiring more. As yet no offer of marriage had been made her by anyone. Her habits did not suit their taste. Perhaps they thought she would be rather difficult to manage as a wife. Whatever the reason was, they certainly rather feared than loved her as a conjugal companion, and she continued to lead a single life. With the view of turning her hides to some account by dressing them and fitting them for trading purposes, she took to *herself a wife.* Ranking as a warrior and hunter, she could not be brought to think of female work. It was derogatory to her standing, unsuited to her taste. She therefore went through the usual formula of Indian marriage to obtain an authority over the woman thus bought. Strange country this, where males assume the dress and perform the duties of females, while women turn men and mate with their own sex!

Finding that employing hands advanced her affairs in the lodge, in a few years her establishment was further increased by taking three more wives. This plurality of women added also to her standing and dignity as a chief; for after success at war, riches either in horses or women mark the distinction of rank with all the Prairie tribes. Nothing more was now in her power to gain. She had fame, standing, honor, riches, and as much influence over the band as anyone except two or three leading chiefs. To either of their offices she could in no wise expect to succeed; for to be a leader required having strong family connection, extensive kindredship, and a popularity of a different description from that allotted to partisans. This being the case, she wisely concluded to maintain her present great name instead of interfering with the claims of others to public notice. For 20 years she conducted herself well in all things appertaining to war and a hunter's life.

In the summer of 1854 she determined to visit in a friendly way the Gros Ventres of the Prairie to which nation, it has been observed, she owed her parentage. The treaty with the Upper Missouri tribes held at Laramie in 1851 had been followed up by overtures of peace to the Blackfeet and the Gros Ventres of the Prairie. The entire body of the latter, with a portion of the former, evinced a willingness to abstain from war excursions, and sent friendly messages to the Crows and Assiniboines containing invitations to visit them. The Assiniboines did so, were well received, hospitably entertained by the Gros Ventres, and dismissed with horses as presents. This intercourse was kept up for 3 or 4 years, with entire satisfaction to both parties, although the Crows had not as yet presented themselves at the camps of their former enemies. With the view of ascertaining how far their hostile spirit had been quelled, and perhaps of gaining a goodly number of horses, this Woman Chief undertook a visit there, presuming that, as she was in fact one of their nation, could speak their language, and a general peace was desired, she could associate with them without being harmed. Many old and experienced fur traders endeavored to dissuade her from this journey, as her feats against them were too notorious to be easily overlooked. But contrary to the advice of her friends she proceeded.

When near the camp, however, she encountered a large party of the Gros Ventres of the Prairie who had been to Fort Union and were returning home. These she boldly met, spoke to, and smoked with. But on their discovering who she was, they took the advantage while traveling with her to their camp to shoot her down together with the four Crows who had so far borne her company.

This closed the earthly career of this singular woman and effectually placed a bar to any hopes of peace between the Crows and her murderers. Neither has there since appeared another of her sex who preferred the warrior's life to that of domestic duties.[42]

DANGERS ENCOUNTERED IN THE FUR TRADE WITH THE CROWS

Before closing our remarks on this people, something regarding

[42] Kurz met "the famous Absaroka amazon" at Fort Union, October 27, 1851. He observed that she "looked neither savage nor warlike. . . . She is about 45 years old; appears modest in manner and good natured rather than quick to quarrel." She gave Denig a Blackfoot scalp, which she had taken herself, which Denig presented to Kurz for his collection. (*Journal*, 213–14.) Denig included a briefer description of this woman's career in *Indian Tribes of the Upper Missouri* (pp. 433–44.) He also mentioned that an Assiniboine woman had attempted to follow the Crow woman warrior's example, only to be killed on her first war expedition. J. Willard Schultz has written a fictionalized biography of Running Eagle, a famous Piegan woman warrior of a later period. (*Running Eagle, The Warrior Girl.*) Running Eagle, who was killed by the Flatheads following her leadership of a number of successful war parties, was remembered by some of my elderly informants on the Blackfeet reservation in the early 1940's. Her career may have been inspired by that of the Crow, Woman Chief, the most famous female war leader in the history of the Upper Missouri tribes.

the trade with them might not be amiss, for the fort built in their country has been the theater of more war and bloodshed both of Whites and Indians than any other spot occupied by the fur traders. From the year before named until 1855, forts have been built in different places along the Yellowstone at distances varying from 150 to 300 miles from its conflux. The mouths of the Tongue River, Rose Bud River, Powder River, Big Horn, O'Fallon's Creek, and the Little Horn have all at times been occupied by trading posts, to which annual supplies were sent up in a mackinaw boat towed with a cordelle by 15 to 20 men, some of whom remained to bring down the peltries the ensuing spring, the others returned to the starting point, Fort Union, at the mouth of the Yellowstone.[43] This river is very difficult to navigate at any season. During the summer flood the banks fall in. The current is very swift and the whole surface of the river is covered with floating trees and driftwood. After this stage the river falls too low and the danger then is confined to the sandbars, snags, and ledges of rock reaching nearly across the stream. Through these rocks the waters run with such velocity as not to admit of a loaded boat being hauled through. It is unloaded and the merchandise transported on men's shoulders by land to where the river is less turbulent. These rapids occupy nearly 100 miles in length. For the greater part of this distance the goods are carried by the men and the empty boats dragged up the stream. The downward navigation is more dangerous still. On these rapids the boats are often broken and both men and cargoes lost. The banks of the Yellowstone, moreover, are infested by hordes of Blackfeet Indians or Sioux, both hostile to either Whites or natives. The well-timbered bottoms of the river and deep-cut coulees in the hills afford excellent lurking places for marauding parties ready to kill or rob whenever opportunity offers.

But all these difficulties are of a trifling nature when compared to the situation of the traders around their own fort. Scarcely a

[43] For the Crow trade the American Fur Company and its successors built five trading posts on the Middle Yellowstone in less than a quarter century. Fort Cass (1832), Fort Van Buren (1839), Fort Alexander (1842), Fort Sarpy (1850-55), and second Fort Sarpy (1857).

week passes but attacks are made on those whose work obliges them to go beyond the gates of the stockade. The Sioux on the one hand, and the Blackfeet on the other, constantly in search of the Crow Indians who are supposed to be near the fort, make this place the center of their operations. When the Crows are stationed in the vicinity all attacks fall upon them, and well they retaliate. But when there are no Indians those who cut wood, guard horses, or go in quest of meat by hunting feel the murderous strokes of these ruthless warriors. Each and every year from 5 to 15 persons attached to the trading establishment have been killed, since commerce has been carried on with the Crows in their own district. The Blackfeet view the fort for the Crows in the light Rotten Belly did that for them. It supplies their enemies with arms and munitions of war, besides other conveniences for hunting and existing as a nation. Also the Blackfeet never entirely forgot the attempt of the Crow chieftain to cut off their support by besieging their fort in the hopes of being able to pillage it. They have always been a fierce people, killing the trappers in the mountains, in which encounters they suffered loss which they revenge to this day on any and all white persons not connected with the trading establishment in their own region. Sometimes these, too, go before their savage dispositions.

The Crows never passed the summer in the vicinity of the fort. At that season they were with the Flatheads, Snakes, or Nez Percés bartering the merchandise obtained from the traders for horses, ornaments, etc., with those nations. Late in the autumn some of them encamped near the fort but the greater portion kept in the fastnesses of the mountains, hunting in the valleys and bringing their proceeds to the trading post the following spring. About 6 months in the year the fort was left to defend itself the best way it could with its small number of men. These were further reduced when the mackinaw boats left with the annual returns. At these times those who remained could not with safety venture to the bank of the river to get water within a few steps of the gate. Indeed some were shot standing within the entrance. Whoever went forth to procure wood or meat placed their lives in extreme jeopardy.·

Every hunter there has been killed, and the fort often reduced to a famished condition when buffalo were in great numbers within sight. The few horses kept for hunting were always stolen, and those who guarded them shot down.

The Blackfeet never do these things openly; concealed among the bushes, grass, or in gullies they lie in wait for those who go out. The fort people seldom if ever killed any enemies. As soon as a man or two were shot the Indians absconded. At the time of attacking they were hidden from view or too numerous to be engaged by the few who were the victims to their bloodthirsty natures.

After keeping up the war in this way for about 16 years neither the Crow Indians nor traders could be brought to station themselves there for any length of time and the Yellowstone has been abandoned by both.[44] Men could, however, be found to continue operations in the Crow district did the trade prove of sufficient profit to the adventure. But two-thirds of the Indians have of late years taken their robes to the traders on the Platte for disposal. In some instances a few persons have come into their country with merchandise for their trade, which they brought in wagons along the Platte road as far as Laramie's Fork, thence turning off and passing the winter near Powder River Mountain. There they build houses, deal with the Crows, and take their returns of furs and skins

[44] On his visit to the Crow country in August 1854, Indian Agent Vaughan reported, "Scarcely a day passes but the Crow country is infested with more or less parties of Blackfeet, who murder indiscriminately any one that comes within their reach. At Fort Sarpy so great is the danger that no one ventures even a few yards from his own door without company and being well armed." (*Annual Report* of the Commissioner of Indian Affairs, 1854, p. 85.) By spring of 1855, hostile pressure had become so great that the traders burned Fort Sarpy (May 19) and abandoned the Crow country, ("Fort Benton and Fort Sarpy Journals," 126–27.) Thus, at the time of Denig's writing his company had no trading post among the Crows. Vaughan was prevented from reaching the Crows in the summer of 1855 by bodies of hostile Sioux on the Lower Yellowstone. When he reestablished contact with the tribe in 1856, the Crows had received no annuities for two years. Their chiefs explained to him, "they preferred to go without the goods, rather than run the risk of passing through a country beset by their deadliest enemies, the Blackfeet and Blood Indians of the north." Vaughan persuaded 350 Crows to accompany him to Fort Union to obtain the annuities for the entire tribe. (*Annual Report* of the Commissioner of Indian Affairs, 1856, p. 81.)

to St. Louis by the same road they came. As the country now stands, it is destitute of traders. Some camps come to Fort Union for supplies, others go to the Platte posts, and many rove through the mountains, supply themselves with what they want either by barter with other tribes or by robbing any emigrants on the road to the far west.

The trade with the Crows never was very profitable. They buy only the very finest and highest priced goods which are most desired for the horse trade. Their own clothing also, of European manufacture, consists chiefly of blankets, cloths, etc., which, with English guns and brass kettles, do not bear a large advance of price when sold to them. Add to this their interminable practice of begging and stealing, and the expense and risk in taking goods up the Yellowstone and peltries down, and but little remains to compensate the trader for his time and trouble.

FUTURE PROSPECTS OF THE CROW INDIANS

Situated as they now are, the Crows cannot exist long as a nation. Without adequate supplies of arms and ammunition, warred against by the Blackfeet on one side and most bands of the Sioux on the other, straying along the Platte trail where they contracted rapid and deadly diseases, together with the unnatural customs of destroying their offspring, will soon lead to their entire extinction. Or if a few remain they will become robbers and freebooters on any and all persons passing through the solitary regions of the Rocky Mountains.[45]

[45] At the time of Denig's writing the chances for the survival of the Crow Indians seemed slim, attacked as they were on two sides by the two strongest and most aggressive military powers on the Upper Missouri, the Blackfeet and Teton Dakotas. Yet Catlin had shown a similar concern for the fate of the Crows in 1832. "They are a much smaller tribe than the Blackfeet, with whom they are always at war, and from whose great numbers they suffer prodigiously in battle; and probably will be, in a few years, entirely destroyed by them." *(Letters and Notes,* I, 42–43.) Some of my aged Piegan and Blood informants, during the early 1940's, volunteered the opinion that had the U. S. government not put an end to intertribal warfare, the Blackfeet and Sioux would have exterminated the Crows.

EDITOR'S BIBLIOGRAPHY

Anderson, Harry. "An Investigation of the Early Bands of the Saone Group of the Teton Sioux," *Journal* of the Washington Academy of Sciences, Vol. LXVI, No. 3 (1956).

Annual Report of the Commissioner of Indian Affairs, 1851–58.

Atkinson, Henry. *Expedition up the Missouri, 1825.* 19 Cong., 1 sess., *House Doc. 117.* Washington, 1826.

Audubon, Maria R., ed. *Audubon and His Journals.* 2 vols. New York, 1897.

Bradbury, John. *Travels in the Interior of America, 1809–11.* Vol. V in Thwaites' *Early Western Travels (q.v.).*

Bradley, James H. "The Bradley Manuscript," Montana Historical Society *Contributions,* Vols. II, III, VII, IX. Helena, 1896, 1900, 1917, 1923.

Bell, Charles N. "The Journal of Henry Kelsey (1691–1692)," Historical and Scientific Society of Manitoba *Transactions,* No. 4. Winnipeg, 1928.

Catlin, George. *Catalogue Descriptive and Instructive of Catlin's Indian Cartoons.* New York, 1871.

———. *Descriptive Catalog of Catlin's Indian Collection,* 1848.

———. *Letters and Notes on the Manners, Customs, and Condition of the North American Indians.* 2 vols. London, 1841.

Chardon, François A. *Chardon's Journal of Fort Clark, 1834–39.* Ed. by Annie Heloise Abel. Pierre, S. D., 1932.

Chittenden, Hiram M. *The American Fur Trade of the Far West.* 2 vols. New York, 1902.

Coues, Elliott, ed. *History of the Expedition Under the Command of Lewis and Clark.* 4 vols. New York, 1893.

Culbertson, Thaddeus. "Journal of an Expedition to the Mauvaises Terres and the Upper Missouri in 1850," ed. by John Francis McDermott, Bureau of American Ethnology *Bulletin 147*. Washington, 1952.

Curtis, Edward S. *The North American Indian*. 20 vols. Norwood, Mass., 1907–30.

Dale, H. C., ed. *The Ashley-Smith Explorations and the Discovery of a Central Route to the Pacific, 1822–1829*. Cleveland, 1918.

Denig, Edwin Thompson. "An Account of Medicine and Surgery as it exists among the Cree Indians," *Medical and Surgical Journal* (St. Louis, Mo.), Vol. XIII (1855).

————. *Indian Tribes of the Upper Missouri*. Ed. by J. N. B. Hewitt. Bureau of American Ethnology *Forty-sixth Annual Report (1928–1929)*. Washington, 1930.

————. "Of the Arickaras," ed. by John C. Ewers, Missouri Historical Society *Bulletin*, Vol. VI, No. 2 (1950).

————. "Of the Assiniboines," ed. by John C. Ewers, Missouri Historical Society *Bulletin*, Vol. VIII, No. 2 (1952).

————. "Of the Crees or Knisteneau," ed. by John C. Ewers, Missouri Historical Society *Bulletin*, Vol. VIII, No. 4 (1952).

————. "Of the Crow Nation," ed. by John C. Ewers, Bureau of American Ethnology *Anthropological Paper No. 33, Bulletin 151*. Washington, 1953.

————. "Of the Sioux," ed. by John C. Ewers, Missouri Historical Society *Bulletin*, Vol. VII, No. 2 (1951).

Denig, Robert L. *The Manoe-Denigs, a Family Chronicle*. New York, 1924.

De Smet, Pierre Jean. *Life, Letters, and Travels of Father Pierre Jean De Smet*. Ed. by H. M. Chittenden and A. T. Richardson. 4 vols. New York, 1905.

————. *Western Missions and Missionaries: A series of Letters by Rev. P. J. De Smet*. New York, 1863.

Ewers, John C. *The Blackfeet: Raiders on the Northwestern Plains*. Norman, 1958.

————. "The Horse in Blackfoot Indian Culture, with Comparative Materials from Other Western Tribes," Bureau of American Ethnology *Bulletin 159*. Washington, 1955.

————. "The Indian Trade of the Upper Missouri Before Lewis and

Clark: An Interpretation," Missouri Historical Society *Bulletin*, Vol. X, No. 4 (1954).

———. "When the Light Shone in Washington," *Montana, the Magazine of Western History*, Vol. VI, No. 4 (1956).

Ford, Capt. Lemuel. "Captain Ford's Journal of an Expedition to the Rocky Mountains," ed. by Louis Pelzer, *Mississippi Valley Historical Review*, Vol. XII (1926).

Gilmore, Melvin R. *Uses of Plants by the Indians of the Missouri River Region.* Bureau of American Ethnology *Thirty-third Annual Report (1911–1912).* Washington, 1919.

———. "Arikara Fish-traps," *Indian Notes*, Museum of the American Indian, Heye Foundation (New York), Vol. I (1924).

Hanson, Charles E., Jr. "The Northwest Gun," Nebraska State Historical Society *Publications in Anthropology, No. 2.* Lincoln, 1955.

Hayden, Ferdinand V. *Contributions to the Ethnography and Philology of the Indian Tribes of the Missouri Valley,* American Philosophical Society *Transactions,* Vol. XII, No. 2. Philadelphia, 1862.

Hendry, Anthony. *York Factory to the Blackfoot Country: The Journal of Anthony Hendry, 1754–55,* ed. by L. J. Burpee, *Proceedings and Transactions* of the Royal Society of Canada, Ser. 3, Vol. I, Sec. II (1907).

Henry, Alexander, and David Thompson. *New Light on the Early History of the Greater Northwest.* Ed. by Elliott Coues. 3 vols. New York, 1897.

Hind, Henry Youle. *Narrative of the Canadian Red River Exploring Expedition of 1857 and of the Assiniboine and Saskatchewan Expedition of 1858.* 2 vols. London, 1860.

Hodge, Frederick Webb, ed. *Handbook of American Indians North of Mexico.* Bureau of American Ethnology *Bulletin No. 30.* 2 vols. Washington, 1912.

Hyde, George E. *Red Cloud's Folk: A History of the Oglala Sioux Indians.* Norman, 1937.

Isham, James. *James Isham's Observations on Hudsons Bay, 1743.* Ed. by E. E. Rich. Champlain Society Publication, Hudson's Bay Company, Ser. 12. Toronto, 1949.

Kane, Paul. *Wanderings of an Artist Among the Indians of North America.* Toronto, 1925.

Keating, William H. *Narrative of an Expedition to the Source of the St. Peter's River, Lake Winnepeck, Lake of the Woods, . . . Performed in the Year 1823 Under the Command of Stephen H. Long, Major.* 2 vols. Philadelphia, 1824.

Kurz, Rudolph F. *Journal of Rudolph Friedrich Kurz: An Account of His Experiences Among Fur Traders and American Indians on the Mississippi and Missouri Rivers During the Years 1846 to 1852.* Ed. by J. N. B. Hewitt. Bureau of American Ethnology *Bulletin 115.* Washington, 1937.

Larocque, François. *Journal of Larocque from the Assiniboine to the Yellowstone 1805.* Canadian Archives *Publication No. 3.* Ottawa, 1910.

Larpenteur, Charles. *Forty Years a Fur Trader on the Upper Missouri: The Personal Narrative of Charles Larpenteur.* Ed. by Elliott Coues. 2 vols. New York, 1898.

La Vérendrye, Pierre G. V. *Journals and Letters of Pierre Gaultier de Varennes de la Vérendrye and His Sons.* Ed. by L. J. Burpee. Toronto, 1927.

Leech, Maria, ed. *Standard Dictionary of Folklore, Mythology, and Legend.* New York, 1920.

Leonard, Zenas. *Adventures of Zenas Leonard, Fur Trader.* Ed. by John C. Ewers. Norman, 1959.

Lewis, Meriwether, and William Clark. *Original Journals of the Lewis and Clark Expedition, 1804–1806.* Ed. by Reuben Gold Thwaites. 8 vols. New York, 1904–1905.

Lowie, Robert H. "The Assiniboine," American Museum of Natural History *Anthropological Papers,* Vol. IV, Part 1 (1909).

———. *The Crow Indians.* New York, 1935.

———. "The Material Culture of the Crow Indians," American Museum of Natural History *Anthropological Papers,* Vol. XXI, Part 3 (1922).

———. "Notes on the Social Organization and Customs of the Mandan, Hidatsa, and Crow Indians," American Museum of Natural History *Anthropological Papers,* Vol. XXI, Part 1 (1917).

———. "Social Life of the Crow Indians," American Museum of Natural History *Anthropological Papers,* Vol. IX, Part 2 (1912).

———. "The Tobacco Society of the Crow Indians," American Museum of Natural History *Anthropological Papers,* Vol. XXV, Part 2 (1919).

McDermott, John Francis. "Peter Rindisbacher: Frontier Reporter," *The Art Quarterly,* Spring, 1949.

McDonnell, Anne, ed. "The Fort Benton Journal, 1854–1856, and the Fort Sarpy Journal, 1855–1856," Montana Historical Society *Contributions,* Vol. X (1940).

McKenney, Thomas, and James Hall. *History of the Indian Tribes of North America.* 3 vols. Philadelphia, 1868.

Mandelbaum, David G. "The Plains Cree," American Museum of Natural History *Anthropological Papers,* Vol. XXXVII, Part 2 (1940).

Matthews, Washington. *Ethnography and Philology of the Hidatsa Indians.* U. S. Geological and Geographical Survey *Miscellaneous Publication No. 7.* Washington, 1877.

Maximilian, Alexander Philipp, prince of Wied-Neuwied. *Travels in the Interior of North America.* Vols. XXII–XXIV in Thwaites' *Early Western Travels (q.v.).*

Morgan, Lewis Henry. *Lewis Henry Morgan: The Indian Journals, 1859–62.* Ed. by Leslie A. White. Ann Arbor, 1959.

Mulloy, William. "The Hagen Site, a Prehistoric Village on the Lower Yellowstone," University of Montana *Publications in Social Science, No. 1.* Missoula, 1942.

Nasatir, A. P. "John Evans, Explorer and Surveyor," *Missouri Historical Review,* Vol. XXV (1931).

Parkman, Francis. *The Oregon Trail: Sketches of Prairie and Rocky Mountain Life.* Boston, 1883.

Raynolds, W. F. *Report on Exploration of the Yellowstone River.* Washington, 1868.

Report of Explorations and Surveys to Ascertain the Most Practical Route for a Railroad from the Mississippi River to the Pacific Ocean, 1853–55. 12 vols. Washington, 1860.

Rodnick, David. *The Fort Belknap Assiniboine of Montana.* Philadelphia, 1938.

Royce, Charles C. *Indian Land Cessions in the United States.* Bureau of American Ethnology *Eighteenth Annual Report (1896–97).* Washington, 1899.

Schoolcraft, Henry Rowe. *Historical and Statistical Information Respecting the History, Condition, and Prospects of the Indian Tribes of the United States.* 6 vols. Philadelphia, 1851–57.

Schultz, J. Willard. *Running Eagle, the Warrior Girl.* Boston, 1919.

Simms, S. C. "Crow Indian Hermaphrodites," *American Anthropologist,* New Ser., Vol. V (1903).

———. "Cultivation of the 'Medicine Tobacco' by the Crows," *American Anthropologist,* New Ser., Vol. VI (1904).

Skinner, Allanson. "Notes on the Plains Cree," *American Anthropologist,* New Ser., Vol. XVI (1914).

———. "Political Organization, Cults, and Ceremonies of the Plains-Ojibway and Plains-Cree Indians," American Museum of Natural History *Anthropological Papers,* Vol. XI, Part 6 (1914).

Squier, E. G., and E. H. Davis. "Ancient Monuments of the Mississippi Valley," *Smithsonian Contributions to Knowledge,* Vol. I. Washington, 1848.

Stirling, Matthew W. "Arikara Glassworking," *Journal* of the Washington Academy of Sciences, Vol. XXXVII, No. 8 (1947).

Strong, William Duncan. *From History to Prehistory in the Northern Great Plains,* Smithsonian *Miscellaneous Collections,* Vol. C (1940).

Tabeau, Pierre-Antoine. *Tabeau's Narrative of Loisel's Expedition to the Upper Missouri.* Ed. by Annie Heloise Abel. Norman, 1939.

Thompson, David. *David Thompson's Narrative of His Explorations in Western America, 1784–1812.* Ed. by J. B. Tyrrell. Champlain Society Publication No. 12. Toronto, 1916.

Thwaites, Reuben Gold, ed. *Jesuit Relations and Allied Documents: Travels and Explorations of the Jesuit Missionaries in New France, 1610–1791.* 73 vols. Cleveland, 1896–1901.

———. *Early Western Travels, 1784–1897.* 32 vols. Cleveland, 1904–1907.

Trudeau, Jean Baptiste. "Journal of Jean Baptiste Trudeau Among the Arikara Indians in 1795," ed. by Mrs. H. T. Beauregard, Missouri Historical Society *Collections,* Vol. IV (1912).

———. "Trudeau's Description of the Upper Missouri," ed. by Annie Heloise Abel, *Mississippi Valley Historical Review,* Vol. VIII, Nos. 1–2 (1921).

Vickers, Chris. "Denig of Fort Union," *North Dakota History,* Vol. XV, No. 2 (1948).

Warren, G. K. *Explorations in the Dacota Country in the Year 1855.* Washington, 1856.

Will, George. "Archaeology of the Missouri Valley," American Museum of Natural History *Anthropological Papers,* Vol. XX, Part 6 (1924).

Will, George F., and George E. Hyde. *Corn Among the Indians Of the Upper Missouri*. St. Louis, 1917.

Wintemberg, W. J. "Representations of the Thunderbird in Indian Art," Ontario *Archaeological Reports*, Vol. XXXVI. Toronto, 1928.

Wissler, Clark. "The Material Culture of the Blackfoot Indians," American Museum of Natural History *Anthropological Papers*, Vol. V, Part 1 (1910).

———. "Population Changes Among the Northern Plains Indians," Yale University *Publications in Anthropology*, No. 1. New Haven, 1932.

INDEX

Abortion, Indian practice of: 186–87

American Fur Company: xiv, xv, xxxiii, xxxv, 26, 32, 46

Arikara Indians: relationship to Pawnees, 41; history of, 41–42; territory of, 42; hostility to whites, 42–43, 60; trade with whites, 43, 46; population, 43, 59–60; earth lodges, 43–44; agriculture, 44–46; trade with Sioux, 47, 55; warfare with Sioux, 47, 55–56; buffalo hunting expeditions, 48; poverty in horses, 48; fishing, 48–49; skill as swimmers, 49; eating of drowned buffalo, 49–50; cookery, 50; pottery, 51; utensils, 51; bead-making, 51; bullboats, 52; incest among, 53; uncleanliness, 53–54; battle with Ashley, 54–55; Colonel Leavenworth's campaign against, 55–57; diseases among, 57–58; character of, 60–63

Ashley, General William, battle with Arikaras: 54–55

Assiniboine Indians: territory of, 63–67; health of, 67; wild plant foods of, 68; population, 68, 79; history of, 68–69; utensils, 69; trade with whites, 69–70, 82; character of, 70–71, 88–89, 94,95, 98; smallpox among, 71–73; warfare with Gros Ventres, 75–77, 91, 93; warfare with Arikaras, 78, 93; warfare with Mandans, 78; hunting bands of, 78–82; warfare with Sioux, 81, 94; warfare with Blackfeet, 82, 91–94; warfare with Crows, 89; peace with Crows, 89–90; warfare with Hidatsas, 90–91; peace with Hidatsas, 91; peace with Gros Ventres, 92; poverty in horses, 94, 96; hunting methods, 95–96; poverty, 96–97

Audubon, John James, aided by Denig: xv–xvi

Baird, Professor Spencer F.: xxxiv, xxxv

Bear's Head, Crow chief: 143–44

Big Robber, Crow chief: 143, 194–95